EDUCATION IN EUROPE

Numbers I–6 to I–9 and II–11 and II–12 are published by George G. Harrap & Co. Ltd. Earlier numbers were published by the Council of Europe, and are on sale at its sales agents listed at the end of this book.

Each volume is published in English and in French. The French edition of the present work is entitled *L'Enseignement des sciences économiques au niveau universitaire*

COUNCIL FOR CULTURAL
CO-OPERATION OF THE
COUNCIL OF EUROPE

EDUCATION IN EUROPE
Section 1 – Higher Education and Research – No. 7

The Teaching of Economics at University Level

by

J. F. H. ROPER
Lecturer in Economics at the University of Manchester

GEORGE G. HARRAP & CO. LTD
London . Toronto . Wellington . Sydney

First published in Great Britain 1970
by GEORGE G. HARRAP & CO. LTD
182–184 High Holborn, London, W.C.1

© *Council of Europe* 1970

SBN 245 59754 9

Composed in 'Monotype' Times and printed by
W. & J. Mackay & Co. Ltd, Chatham, Kent
Made in Great Britain

Foreword

The series of publications *Education in Europe* was launched by the Council for Cultural Co-operation of the Council of Europe in 1963 in order to make known the comparative studies and surveys produced under its twenty-nation programme of educational co-operation.

The Council of Europe was established by ten nations on May 5th, 1949, since when its membership has progressively increased to eighteen. Its aim is "to achieve a greater unity between its members for the purpose of safeguarding and realizing the ideals and principles which are their common heritage and facilitating their economic and social progress". This aim is pursued by discussion of questions of common concern and by agreements and common action in economic, social, cultural, scientific, legal, and administrative matters.

The Council for Cultural Co-operation was set up by the Committee of Ministers of the Council of Europe on January 1st, 1962, to draw up proposals for the cultural policy of the Council of Europe, to co-ordinate and give effect to the overall cultural programme of the organization, and to allocate the resources of the Cultural Fund. It is assisted by three permanent committees of senior officials: for higher education and research (this committee also includes representatives of universities), for general and technical education, and for out-of-school education. All the member Governments of the Council of Europe, together with Finland, Spain and the Holy See, which have acceded to the European Cultural Convention, are represented on these bodies.

Between 1963 and 1967 some 25 titles have been published in English and French versions under the responsibility of the Council of Europe. Lists of these titles and of the Council's sales agents are given at the beginning and end of this book. In addition a number of reports of a more technical nature on educational and cultural problems have been produced in a separate series from 1965 onward.

The Council of Europe ceded the world rights relating to the series *Education in Europe* as from January 1st, 1968, to George G.

Harrap & Co., Ltd, London, for the English edition and to Armand Colin, Paris, for the French edition. Henceforth these publishers will be responsible throughout the world for the production, sale, and distribution of all studies published in the series, which is divided into four sections:

    I. Higher Education and Research (education at university level).

    II. General and Technical Education (primary and secondary —including technical, commercial, and vocational— education).

    III. Out-of-school Education and Youth (youth activities; adult education; physical education, sport, and outdoor pursuits).

    IV. General (subjects other than those included in the three sections mentioned above).

The more technical reports will continue to be published in Strasbourg.

The opinions expressed in all these studies are not to be regarded as reflecting the policy of individual Governments or of the Committee of Ministers of the Council of Europe.

Preface

This volume, which deals with the teaching of economics at university level, follows those on chemistry, general biology, physics, and geography that have already appeared in the series "Education in Europe". Studies dealing with botany, mathematics, history, and education are in preparation. These studies have been commissioned in connection with the inquiry into university teaching curricula organized by the Committee for Higher Education and Research of the Council for Cultural Co-operation.

At a preparatory stage, Mr Roper's report was discussed at a meeting of university teachers of economics, nominated by national academic authorities, which was held in Strasbourg in May 1967. While the report is solely the responsibility of the author, the participants in that meeting drafted a number of recommendations on the basis of the report (see Appendix 3), and also helped to check the information given in the Country Studies set out in Part II. The material in this report was collected in 1965 and 1966 and although it was in part revised to include developments up to the summer of 1967, it does not cover subsequent developments.

Contents

APPENDICES *Page*

PART I

Comparative Analysis

CHAPTER 1

Introduction

Economists have frequently attempted to provide definitions of the subject-matter of economics; they have been more reluctant to define the qualities required of the economist. One of the few attempts—and still perhaps the most successful—is that of Keynes in his biographical essay on Alfred Marshall.

> The study of economics does not seem to require any specialised gifts of an unusually high order. Is it not, intellectually regarded, a very easy subject compared with the higher branches of philosophy and pure science? Yet good, or even competent, economists are the rarest of birds. An easy subject, at which very few excel! The paradox finds its explanation, perhaps, in that the master-economist must possess a rare *combination* of gifts. He must reach a high standard in several different directions and must combine talents not often found together. He must be mathematician, historian, statesman, philosopher—in some degree. He must understand symbols and speak in words. He must contemplate the particular in terms of the general, and touch abstract and concrete in the same flight of thought. He must study the present in the light of the past for the purposes of the future. No part of man's nature or his institutions must lie entirely outside his regard. He must be purposeful and disinterested in a simultaneous mood; as aloof and incorruptible as an artist, yet sometimes as near the earth as a politician.[1]

In attempting a study of the higher education in economics in European countries it is not only necessary to ask again what is an economist, but also to ask how an economist should be made. While Keynes' definition may be satisfactory, it does not of itself provide a recipe as to how an economist should be trained. It is perhaps open to debate whether university teaching of economics is, or can be, the same thing as the training of economists. While most would accept the definition of a medical doctor or a graduate engineer, or even in most cases a lawyer, as one who had completed university courses in the subject—followed where appropriate by practical training—

---

[1] John Maynard Keynes, *Essays in Biography*, London, 1933. From the essay, "Alfred Marshall", pages 170–171.

many would be reluctant to class a man as an economist because his first degree had included courses in economics, even in those relatively rare cases where the majority of courses taken were in economics.

The range of qualities required of the economist is reflected in the way in which the teaching of economics has developed within the structure of higher education in patterns that vary considerably from country to country. Some of the differences that exist today as to what is considered the appropriate higher education for prospective economists are a result of the historical background. In the majority of European countries, Austria, Belgium, Denmark, France, Germany, Greece, Italy, the Netherlands, Norway, Spain, Sweden, and Switzerland, the teaching of economics in universities has been associated traditionally with the teaching of law, and particularly public law. In a sense, a study of economics was considered part of the training of a civil servant, and therefore was naturally linked to law, the other subject required by civil servants.

In most of these countries there has been a second stream of influence from institutions initially outside the universities, but more recently brought fully into the system of higher education—the higher colleges of economics and commerce. In some cases these have remained autonomous institutions, as in the Scandinavian countries (with the exception of Iceland), Greece, the Netherlands, Austria, and Switzerland, continuing to provide higher education primarily for prospective businessmen but including a large proportion of general economics within their syllabus of instruction. In other cases they have become separate commercial faculties of the universities, as in Italy and Spain, providing teaching in economics in their courses in addition to the courses in economics given in the law faculties. The third possibility, a merging of the two streams of influence, has occurred in many of the German universities, where public economics (*Volkswirtschaftslehre*) and business economics (*Betriebswirtschaftslehre*) are now taught in the same faculties.

The third historical source has probably had most influence in the development of economics teaching in the United Kingdom, Ireland, and to some extent Malta and the Holy See. Here the development of economics and the other social sciences has been associated with work in social philosophy and history. Law has had very little to do with the development of economics teaching in universities, and while there has been a great deal of variation between the approach of different universities, business or commercial economics has until recently played a relatively minor rôle. This third—philosophical or social science—approach is by no means restricted to the countries cited; it has had some influence in a number of other countries—for example, in the chairs of economics in a number of countries' faculties of philosophy. It is also an approach which is having an increasing influence in the new universities being created in a number of European countries.

These three approaches—to which has been very recently added a fourth, in the growing interest of applied mathematicians and operations researchers in the problems of economics—have led to different emphases in teaching in different institutions, and in particular between the university faculties and specialist schools. There is still in some countries a continuing difference between the political economy of the universities and the business economics of the specialized institutions. This may well influence their approach to the same topics, public finance, for example, being taught in the university from the point of view of the tax-gathering Ministry of Finance and in the School of Economics from the point of view of the tax-paying businessman. Although it is easy to exaggerate such differences, the visitor still finds some relics of them.

A further difference is that between the professional training of economists and the academic study of economics. This is a formal distinction which it is not always easy to define, but again in moving from country to country and institution to institution one finds that the weight given to each of these aspects of higher education varies.

Both of these differences are related to the question which is central to the whole of this study as to what is the purpose of the first degree in economics. This is a question which is not peculiar to economics, but is closely linked to the varying attitudes towards the function of higher education. These attitudes vary as much within countries as between countries, and would certainly appear to have changed over a period of time. In these circumstances it is probably dangerous to attach national labels to different attitudes, particularly as one finds a great deal of agreement between countries as to desirable trends in higher education in economics. The difficulties of moving from the unsatisfactory situation of the present to the ideal of the future is discussed in more detail in Chapter 10, but, as will be seen, at present there is a remarkable diversity in the nature of the education received by a graduate in economics in different countries.

It would be foolish in this introductory chapter to attempt a single definition of the purpose of higher education in economics, but probably all who teach economics would agree with the words of Alfred Marshall's inaugural lecture that our task is to show our students that economics is "not a body of concrete truth but an engine for the discovery of concrete truth".[1] We are not only attempting to equip our students with a factual knowledge of the economy, but endeavouring to equip them with the engines of analysis which will enable them to understand the workings of the economy. This study is intended to illustrate the varying ways in which this is done.

In approaching the task of surveying European higher education in economics it has been necessary to define what is meant by higher education, and in particular higher education in economics. As has already been shown, these definitional problems probably present more difficulties in the case of economics than in almost any other discipline.

There are probably more specialized institutions outside the universities, but providing higher education of university level, in the field of economics than in any other. In general this study has included all those that are regarded by the national authorities as being of university status, and this is discussed further, and a list provided in Chapter 2. This criterion has been modified in certain cases by the application of a second principle which would include in higher education any institution which produces its own future teachers or teachers for institutions of comparable status. These attempts at definition have inevitably created anomalies, and in addition to the specialized institutions covered there are in a number of European countries other institutions providing higher education in commerce not recognized by their national authorities as being of university status. In some of these institutions the teaching of economics may in fact be at least the equal of that in some institutions covered in this study.

Within the universities and other institutions selected the study has examined undergraduate or first-degree courses in economics. This has not been defined to exclude business economics, but the emphasis has been primarily on general economics. It has, however, in general excluded specialist degrees in agricultural economics, business administration, or public administration, although in some countries these are closely linked to degrees in economics. By concentrating on first degrees in economics, it has excluded that teaching

---

[1] Alfred Marshall, *The Present Position of Economics*, 1885.

of the subject which provides subsidiary subjects for those specializing in other disciplines, such as law, engineering, or the other social sciences. It has, on the other hand, included in Chapter 4 a discussion of the other subjects which are normally studied as part of an economics degree. Again the choice of first degrees has in general excluded discussion of diplomas and higher degrees. A first degree has been defined as that qualification which first-year students normally aim for, thus mentioning only in passing certain interim degrees which exist in a limited number of countries.

The countries covered are those that participate in the work of the Committee for Higher Education and Research of the Council of Europe. In the case of two of them which were not visited in the preparation of this report, Finland (which has observer status) and Iceland, the information given is not as full as would be desirable.

This study has been prepared during the two years 1965 and 1966 on the basis of information obtained during a series of visits to some fifty faculties and specialized institutions in which economics is taught. A list of institutions and the dates of visits is given in Appendix 1. This was supplemented, and in most cases preceded, by the collection of documentary information from as many as possible of the teaching institutions within the study area. Most of the visits were inevitably brief, and it was possible to make fruitful use of the limited time available only through the extremely helpful co-operation of the teaching staff in the institutions visited. Similar co-operation was also obtained from the national authorities responsible for higher education in many of the countries concerned.

A formal questionnaire was not used for obtaining information, largely because the wide variety of higher education makes it very difficult to produce a form of questionnaire that would be appropriate to all institutions. None the less for the series of visits undertaken during 1966 an *aide-mémoire* (reproduced as Appendix 2) was prepared which was sent to institutions to be visited prior to the visit. It listed certain areas of inquiry which it was hoped to discuss and outlined the purpose of the study. This proved helpful, and in some cases individual universities prepared written notes on the points covered. As the report was being written in the second half of 1966 certain gaps were discovered in the information which had been collected, and these were for the most part dealt with by further correspondence with university teachers met during the series of visits.

A third source of information was the existing literature on this subject. (A selected bibliography appears in Appendix 4.) In comparison with the considerable literature on the university teaching of economics that exists in the United States—much of it published under the auspices of the American Economic Association—there is relatively little published in most European countries on this subject.

This report falls into two sections; the first section attempts a comparative analysis under various headings. Separate chapters are devoted to various groups of topics, and these are illustrated where appropriate by statistical information covering either all the institutions surveyed or a representative sample. There are great difficulties in obtaining satisfactory statistical data, and considerable reservations must be placed on the value of precise comparisons between the figures cited.

Chapter 2 examines the varying place of economics within the structure of higher education in different countries, and the way in which students are admitted to the study of the subject. In Chapter 3 the varying length and structure of university degrees in economics are compared, and in Chapter 4 variations in the time given to different subjects in first degrees in economics are examined. Chapter 5 deals with the methods used for teaching, and Chapter 6 with the ways in which the academic work of students is controlled and assessed, through both examinations and other means. In Chapter 7 the duties and responsibilities of the university teacher of economics are discussed. The question of the adequacy of university infrastructure has been much discussed, and in Chapter 8 we look at this in general, and in particular at the provision of libraries and computers—both tools for study and research in economics.

As this study has been undertaken at the request of the Council of Europe, it was felt appropriate to include some discussion of inter-European aspects of the teaching of economics. Accordingly, Chapter 9 looks at the existing flows of students, teachers, and knowledge between European countries. Finally, in Chapter 10 an examination is made of current trends in the teaching of economics, the changes that have been made in the structure of courses in the recent past, the reforms that are in the course of being implemented, and the suggestions for change that are now being discussed. The first part of the report ends with some conclusions.

The second part of the report is made up of a series of country studies discussing particular aspects of the teaching of economics in each of the countries covered. It is not possible within the chapters of the comparative analysis to deal with all the variation that exists within individual countries. As will be seen, in certain countries there is a considerable uniformity in the pattern of higher education, but in others there is a large degree of variation between institutions, and here it has been necessary to try to show this in the country studies.

It is hoped that these country studies will complement the comparative analysis of the first part of the report and provide a fuller picture of the present state of higher education in economics in individual countries. It was impossible to cover in them all institutions of every country, and inevitably the emphasis has been mainly on those institutions actually visited.

CHAPTER 2

The Place of Economics in Higher Education

The place of economics in the university varies considerably from country to country, and even within countries. In all there are in the European countries studied in this survey over 140 universities where economics can be studied as a first-degree subject. As is shown in Table 2.1, the number per country ranges from only one university in Iceland and Malta to forty-five in the United Kingdom.

Only rarely does economics have a faculty of its own;[1] normally it is paired with law or commerce, or is contained in a general social-science faculty of some kind. In some countries the faculty structure is the same at all universities, as in France, Italy, and Spain, but in most it is not. Table 2.1 shows the main faculties in which economics is taught in the various countries, and gives some idea of the range. It is linked with law in Austria, Denmark, France, and Greece, and frequently also in Germany, where the faculty is often one of law and political science. The countries where a combination with the other social sciences is most common are Spain, Sweden, and the United Kingdom. However, in the United Kingdom the most recently created universities have on the whole deliberately avoided a rigid faculty structure. The combination with commerce is chiefly found in Italy and Iceland.

OTHER INSTITUTIONS OF UNIVERSITY STATUS

In addition to the universities, there are in a number of countries important specialized institutions of university status in which economics is taught, and in which, together with business administration, it normally makes up the bulk of study. Table 2.2 lists those

---

[1] However, in this report, faculties awarding first degrees specializing in economics will be referred to generally as economics faculties for convenience.

Table 2.1

University Faculties in which Economics is Chiefly Taught

Faculty where Economics Taught[1] — columns "Law" through "Political & Comm. Sci." fall under the sub-group "Economics and".

Country	Number of Universities	Economics	Economics and: Law	Economics and: Commerce[2]	Economics and: Social Science	Economics and: Law & Soc. Science	Economics and: Political & Soc. Sci.	Economics and: Political Science	Economics and: Political & Comm. Sci.	Law	Law & Political Science	Soc. Studies/Soc. Sciences	Commerce	Political Science	Arts/Letters/Philosophy, etc.	Other
Austria	3				2		1									
Belgium	5		2						3							
Denmark	2		2													
Finland	5				5											
France	17		17													
Germany	17		3					3			7			1	1	2
Greece	2		1											1		
Holy See	2													2		
Iceland	1							1[4]								
Ireland	4[3]			1									3[5]			
Italy	21[6]			20						1						
Malta	1				1											
Netherlands	3[7]	3														
Norway	1							1								
Spain	4[8]					1		1					1			1
Sweden	5											5				
Switzerland	7		1		1	1				2		1			1	
Turkey	3	1													1	1
United Kingdom	45[9]	2			5			1			1	20		1	8	7
Total	**148**	**6**	**26**	**21**	**14**	**2**	**1**	**7**	**3**	**3**	**8**	**26**	**4**	**5**	**11**	**11**

Notes to Table 2.1

(1) Where economics is taught in more than one faculty the main one has been distinguished. The names given cover all combinations—*e.g.*, economics and law covers law and economics, etc. 'Faculty' has been taken to cover 'school'.

(2) Includes business administration.

(3) Three of these are in fact constituent colleges of the National University of Ireland, but they have been counted separately.

(4) Economics is also taught in the School of Business Studies at this university (Trinity College, Dublin).

(5) Economics is also taught in the faculties of arts at these universities (University College, Dublin, University College, Cork, and University College, Galway).

(6) This includes the University Institute of Economics and Commerce in Venice. Economics is also taught in the faculties of law and of political science. (See country study.)

(7) Economics is taught in other Dutch universities—Leyden, Nijmegen, and Utrecht—in the faculty of law as part of the law degree, and in courses for technology degrees at the Universities of Delft, Enschede, and Nijmegen.

(8) Economics is also taught in the faculty of law at eleven Spanish universities.

(9) Of this forty-five, thirty-four are in England, of which four are colleges of London University, five are in Wales, of which four are constituent colleges of the University of Wales, five are in Scotland, and one is in Northern Ireland.

institutions of this type that are covered in this report. In many countries there are also other institutions of higher commercial education not generally recognized as being of university standard. The distinction is inevitably somewhat arbitrary, and it must be recognized that in some of these the teaching of economics may at least be of the standard of that found in different institutions in other countries included in this survey. Nevertheless, as discussed in Chapter 1, a limit has to be drawn, and only those institutions listed in Table 2.2 are included in the present survey.

The specialized institutions included in this report almost all have a bias towards business education, but their relationship to the remainder of higher education varies. In some countries—Denmark, Finland, France, Greece, and Norway—they provide an education in economics quite distinct from that in the universities, whereas in others—the Netherlands—they provide a course similar to that available in the universities. In Austria and Sweden changes in recent years have meant that the courses previously available only in the specialized institutions are now available in some of the universities. It will be seen from Tables 2.2 and 2.3 that specialized institutions are of importance in Austria, France, Greece, the Netherlands, Switzerland, and the Scandinavian countries (except Iceland). In Germany these are of lesser importance, and are different in type from those in most of the other countries. With the exception of Mannheim, they are technical universities, comparable to the former Colleges of Advanced Technology (now universities) in the United Kingdom. Mannheim, which at the time of writing this report

Table 2.2

Other Institutions of Higher Education in Economics of University Status

Country	No. of Institutions	Institutions
Austria	2	Hochschule für Welthandel, Vienna Hochschule für Sozial-und-Wirtschafts-wissenschaften, Linz
Denmark	2	Handelshøjskolen, Copenhagen Handelhøjskolen, Aarhus
Finland	4	Helsinki School of Economics (Helsingin Kauppakorkeakoulu) Swedish School of Economics, Helsinki (Svenska Handelshögskolan) School of Economics, Åbo Academy (Handelshögskolan vi Åbo Akademi) Turku School of Economics (Turun Kauppakorkeakoulu)
France	16	Ecole des Hautes Etudes Commerciales (H.E.C.) Jouy-en-Josas, near Paris Ecole Supérieure des Sciences Economiques et Commerciales (E.S.S.E.C.), Paris Ecole de Haut Enseignement Commercial pour les Jeunes Filles (H.E.C.J.F.), Paris Ecole Supérieure de Commerce de Paris (E.S.C.P.), Paris Also 12 others in the provinces
Germany	6	Wirtschaftshochschule, Mannheim Technische Hochschule, Aachen Technische Hochschule, Darmstadt Technische Hochschule, Karlsruhe Technische Hochschule, Munich Technische Universität, Berlin
Greece	1	Athens Graduate School of Economics and Business Science (A.G.S.E.B.S.)
Netherlands	2	Netherlands School of Economics, Rotterdam Catholic School of Economics, Tilburg
Norway	1	Norges Handelshøyskole, Bergen (Norwegian School of Economics and Business Administration)

Table 2.2—continued
Other Institutions of Higher Education in Economics of University Status

Country	No. of Institutions	Institutions
Spain	4	Escuela Superior de Direccion de Empresas (I.C.A.D.E.), Madrid Escuela Superior de Administracion y Direccion de Empresas (E.S.A.D.E.), Barcelona Escuela Superior de Tecnica Empresaria, (E.S.T.E.), San Sebastian Universidad de Deusto, Bilbao
Sweden	2	Handelshögskolan, Stockholm Handelshögskolan, Gothenburg
Switzerland	1	Hochschule für Wirtschaft-und-Sozialwissen-schaften, St Gallen

was in the process of becoming a university, is a specialized institution similar to the Hochschule at St Gallen or the Schools of Economics in the Netherlands. In Spain private, religiously sponsored specialized institutions are of some importance, but unfortunately the figures available for student numbers exclude these institutions, as they cover only the public sector of education.

In some countries these specialized institutions have, as Table 2.3 shows, half or more of the total number of students of economics.

While in the past these institutions may have had a status somewhat lower than that of the universities, in that they were concerned more with vocational training than with higher education and research, this position is rapidly changing. In a number of countries they provide the centres for very distinguished research institutes, and in certain countries—notably in Sweden and France, where a *numerus clausus* is placed on entry to these schools, but not to all the faculties of the university in which economics is taught—the quality of the students may well be higher than that in the universities.

ADMISSION TO INSTITUTIONS

In no country covered by this study are students normally admitted to universities before the age of seventeen, and in most cases students are eighteen, nineteen, or even older when they enter. In most countries there is no *numerus clausus*, although a student is normally required to have a higher school-leaving certificate. In some countries the entrance qualifications for economics faculties differ from those of other faculties. In Italy students can enter a faculty of economics and commerce with a classical or scientific *Maturita* or a qualification from a technical, commercial, industrial, naval, agricultural, or land-surveying institute, whereas for the faculties of law and of political science they must have a classical or scientific *Maturita*. In fact, most students in Italian faculties of economics and commerce do not possess the qualifications required for entry to other faculties. In Switzerland students can enter economics faculties with either a normal or a commercial *Matura*, whereas for other faculties a commercial *Matura* is not acceptable. In the Netherlands students are admitted to economics faculties with leaving qualifications from either the traditional gymnasium or the grammar school (*hogere burgerschool*); the latter diplomas are, however, not accepted in all other university faculties (only in the scientific, social science, and law faculties). The vast majority of Dutch students of economics are in fact drawn from these modern grammar schools.

There is little agreement as to the most effective way of selecting students for admission to university courses in economics. In the absence in most countries of secondary-school teaching in economics there is no specific information as to a student's potentiality in the subject. In some countries—particularly Norway—a strong correlation has been discovered between success at secondary school in mathematics and at university in economics. In other countries no relation of this sort has been observed, and general secondary-school performance has been taken as the best predictor.

Where there are limits on numbers admission is regulated by one of three methods. It can be by a national university-entrance examination, as in Greece, Turkey, and Spain; by an entrance examination for the particular institutions—for example, the French non-university institutions such as H.E.C. or the Norwegian School of Economics and Business Administration; or by a selection among those with the minimum entrance requirements—for example, in Finland and in the United Kingdom (except Oxford and Cambridge universities, where there are direct examinations for entry).

The quality of the student intake as compared with that of other subjects varies greatly from country to country. It also seems to vary through time. In those countries where economics has developed as a

Table 2.3

Distribution of Economics Students between Universities and Specialized Institutions

Country	Total No. of Students of Economics[1]	% in Universities	% in Specialized Institutions
Austria	12,769[2]	63 ·8	36 ·2
Belgium	4,640	100 ·0	—
Denmark	2,161	63 ·2	36 ·8
Finland	4,442	15 ·8	84 ·2
France	19,387	68 ·6	31 ·4
Germany	33,742	90 ·4	9 ·6
Greece	12,000[2]	58 ·3	41 ·7
Holy See	70	100 ·0	—
Iceland	124	100 ·0	—
Ireland	940[3]	100 ·0	—
Italy	63,090	100 ·0	—
Malta	15	100 ·0	—
Netherlands	6,784	42 ·4	57 ·6[4]
Norway	1,156	55 ·8	44 ·2
Spain	11,097[5]	100 ·0	—
Sweden	5,463	49 ·4	50 ·6
Switzerland	4,888	75 ·4	24 ·6
Turkey	6,000[6]	100 ·0	—
United Kingdom	6,500	100 ·0	—

Notes to Table 2.3

(1) An actual figure or estimate for the most recent year available.
(2) Includes all students in the law faculties of the universities.
(3) Full-time commerce students only (with the exception of Cork, for which arts students are also included).
(4) The specialized institutions in the Netherlands offer similar courses to those at the universities.
(5) Students in public institutions only.
(6) These figures are estimates covering the faculty of economics at the University of Istanbul, the faculty of political science at the University of Ankara, and the faculty of administrative sciences at the Middle East Technical University. It excludes the Academies of Economics and Commercial Science, both private and public, and students of economics at Roberts College.

subject out of the law faculties it was originally considered to be an easier alternative—the reference to German economists as *Schmalspur-Juristen* (narrow-gauge lawyers) is an example of this. However, economics faculties, particularly with the growing use of mathematics and statistics, seem in most countries to be regarded no longer as a soft option. Where entrance qualifications are more liberal for economics faculties than for others, this tends to depress the relative quality of those admitted. In Turkey, where there is a common university-entrance examination for the State universities,[1] economics is high on students' preference lists, and places are more sought after than they are for law. In the United Kingdom, where about half of the applicants in economics are accepted by the universities, the quality of the economics intake appears to be higher than the average for all university students.

NUMBERS OF STUDENTS

The total numbers of students of economics in the different countries vary both absolutely and in relation to total student numbers. Table 2.4 shows the estimated numbers of economics students and of all students, and the proportion of economics students among all students. The table also gives approximate figures for the number of students obtaining a first degree containing a major proportion of economics in the most recent year for which statistics are available. This table must be qualified in many ways, some of which are indicated in the footnotes. Many of the figures are necessarily estimates.

Any overall comparisons between the output of economics graduates and the total number of economics students with a view to estimating success rates would be unsatisfactory. Any comparison on these lines would have to take into account both the growth in numbers of students studying economics, which has occurred recently in most countries, and also the varying lengths of courses in different countries. Growth in numbers of economics students has been especially important in Italy, Norway, Spain, Sweden, and Switzerland, where particularly in the university faculties there have been large increases in numbers over recent years. The question of success rates is discussed more fully in Chapter 3, and that of growth in Chapter 10.

In column 3 of Table 2.4 the proportion of students of economics in the total student population is shown. As this appears to vary from 4 per cent to 40 per cent, some explanation is necessary for certain of the country figures. The figures for Austria and Greece are not comparable to those for other countries, since in both cases the figures are for a group of subjects including economics.

---

[1] There is also the autonomous Middle East Technical University (M.E.T.U.), which has its own entrance examination.

Table 2.4

Economics Students in Relation to All Students

Country[1]	Number of economics graduates[2]	Economics Students[3]		Total Students[3]
		Number	% of total students	
Austria	1,273[4]	12,499[4]	26 ·2	51,969
Belgium	450	4,640	13 ·3	35,000
Denmark	110	1,670	6 ·9	24,063
Finland	430	4,442	12 ·4	35,910
France	700[5]	19,387	4 ·8	403,000
Germany	2,966	33,742	13 ·5	249,355
Greece	500	12,000[4]	39 ·2	30,617
Iceland	11	124	13 ·1	950
Ireland	225	940[6]	7 ·2	12,089[7]
Italy	2,897	75,135[8]	22 ·4	334,681
Malta	—[9]	15[10]	3 ·5	433[10]
Netherlands	611	6,784	10 ·5	64,432
Norway	75	1,156[11]	5 ·4	21,265[11]
Spain	361[12]	11,097[13]	9 ·3	97,749[13]
Sweden	439	5,463	9 ·1	60,347
Switzerland	627	4,888	16 ·2	30,245
Turkey	650	6,000[14]	12 ·0	50,000[15]
United Kingdom	1,820	6,500	4 ·1	160,000

Notes to Table 2.4

(1) The Holy See has been excluded from this table. There are at the Gregorian University approximately 70 students of economics, and some 20 graduate a year.

(2) These figures refer to graduates the major part of whose degree was in economics, including business economics. They refer to the most recent year for which statistics were available, or for which estimates could be made.

(3) The figures refer to the most recent year for which statistics or estimates on a comparable basis were available. (For this reason they are not always identical with those in Table 2.3.)

(4) This figure includes all the students in the law faculties in the universities, not only the economics students.

(5) This is an estimate for the universities only, and excludes the specialized institutions.

(6) Full-time commerce students only, apart from Cork, where arts students studying economics are also included.

(7) Full-time students only. If part-time students were included the figure would be 13,059.

(8) This figure, unlike that in Table 2.3, refers to all students of economics, including those who are *fuori corso.*

(9) As the economics degree course started only in the autumn of 1966, no economics graduates had been produced at the time of preparation of this report.

(10) This figure is an understatement, as there are substantial numbers of Maltese abroad, chiefly in the United Kingdom.

(11) Both these figures are understatements, as large numbers of Norwegian students go abroad to study.

(12) These figures are an underestimate, as they include only those graduates who paid the fees necessary formally to take their degrees.
(13) These figures relate only to the public sector of education, and do not include the private universities and specialized institutions. The figures are for students of economics, and all students are not for comparable years. The percentage of economics students is, however, calculated for an earlier year for which comparable figures are available.
(14) These figures are estimates covering the faculty of economics at the University of Istanbul, the faculty of political science at the University of Ankara, and the faculty of administrative sciences at the Middle East Technical University. It excludes the Academies of Economics and Commercial Science, both private and public, and students of economics at Roberts College.
(15) This figure refers to the universities in the public sector only, and is an estimate.

Unfortunately, it is not possible to get detailed figures for economics for these countries. In France the relationship of economics to other subjects, especially law, is changing—the economics *licence* is a relatively recently established degree, and the effects of its introduction have not yet fully made themselves felt. This is even more true in Malta, where the honours degree course in economics started only in the autumn of 1966. There is the further problem with the Maltese figures that students go overseas, especially to the United Kingdom. The question of student movement[1] also arises in connection with the Norwegian and the Swiss figures. A high proportion of Norwegians go abroad to study at the first-degree level. In 1966–67 there were 3656 Norwegian students studying abroad, in addition to the 21,265 studying in Norway itself shown in Table 2.4. If the student total were taken as the total of these two figures, the students studying abroad would account for 17 per cent of all Norwegian students. Of the 3656 Norwegian students abroad, 468 were studying for a qualification in economics—some 29 per cent of all Norwegian students of economics. Switzerland is in the reverse position to Norway, in that it receives a substantial inflow of foreign students. Of the 10,019 students who registered for the first time in the academic year 1964–65, 3468, or 34·6 per cent, were foreign. In economics 40·5 per cent (734 out of a total of 1590) were from abroad. This may partly explain why the proportion of economics students in Switzerland is high in comparison with other countries.

As has been noted, the economics and commerce faculties in Italy admit students with qualifications from institutions other than the gymnasia, which may well lead to an inflation of the faculty as compared with the other faculties, which admit only students from the gymnasia. There is in Italy, as in some other countries, a large

---

[1] The question of student movement between European countries is discussed more fully in Chapter 9.

number of 'phantom' students who register but take no further part in university life.

A further factor influencing the proportion of students studying economics is the extent to which degree courses have been developed in the other social sciences. Where courses in other social-science subjects do not exist, economics degree courses may well offer the best preparation available for those who wish subsequently to study other social sciences. Countries where the extensive development of alternative social-science courses may have reduced the proportion of students studying economics are Denmark, Ireland,[1] the Netherlands, Sweden, and the United Kingdom.

Table 2.5

Average Number of Students of Economics per Institution in Different Countries

Fewer than 200 students	200–500 students	500–1000 students	1000–2000 students	More than 2000 students
Holy See	Denmark	Belgium	Germany	Austria
Iceland	Ireland	France	The Netherlands	Greece
Malta	Finland	Norway	Turkey	Italy
United Kingdom		Sweden		Spain
		Swizerland		

RELATIVE SIZE OF ECONOMICS FACULTIES AND DEPARTMENTS

Table 2.5 attempts to estimate the average size of the group of students studying economics in universities and specialized institutions. Where there is a faculty which is composed exclusively of students of economics this presents few problems, but in countries where an economics department is only part of a larger faculty there are considerable difficulties in obtaining satisfactory statistics. As

---

[1] The Irish proportion is also depressed by the fact that the total for economics students includes only those students studying commerce, whereas there are, in fact, also students studying political economy in the faculties of arts for whom figures are not (with the exception of University College, Cork) available.

two examples of this we can take Austria, where at the universities economics has until very recently been taught as a specialization within the faculty of law, and the United Kingdom, where economics tends to share a social-science faculty with a number of other departments. In both these countries elementary courses in economics will be taught to all the students, but only a proportion will continue to a degree specializing in economics. In the table the figures for the United Kingdom refer to the number of students specializing in economics, but for Austria it was impossible to obtain a breakdown of this kind, and the figure includes all students in the faculties of law. The position of the United Kingdom may also be influenced by the fact that a number of the newly created universities and the technological universities have not yet completely developed their courses, or built up student numbers to their planned capacities.

It should be noted that in a number of countries there are one or more institutions which are considerably larger than the average. This is so in the case of one institution in France, Belgium, and the Netherlands. In France the University of Paris, with over 6000 students, has over 40 per cent of all university economics students; in the Netherlands this is true of the Netherlands School of Economics at Rotterdam, with nearly 3000 students; while in Belgium the University of Louvain, also with nearly 3000 students, has over half of all the students of economics. In Germany, Italy, and the United Kingdom a small number of universities are significantly larger than the average. Three German universities—Cologne, with over 8000 students, Hamburg, and Munich, with each about 4000—have nearly half the German economics students. In Italy there are three universities (Rome, Bari, and the Sacro Cuore University in Milan) each with faculties of over 6000, which between them account for about a third of all economics students. In the United Kingdom the London School of Economics and Cambridge University have considerably larger economics faculties than other universities.

CHAPTER 3

The Structure of Degrees in Economics

THE FIRST DEGREE IN ECONOMICS

The title of the first degree and the length of the course naturally vary from country to country. There is also in some cases variation within countries, as has been discussed in Chapter 2. While in some countries there is a high degree of uniformity, in others there is considerable variation between institutions. Table 3.1 attempts to list in a summary fashion the first degrees of which economics is a major constituent, and the prescribed length of their courses. It should perhaps be stressed at this stage that the prescribed length of course is not necessarily the length of time taken to complete the course by the normal successful student—a point which will be discussed in more detail later in this chapter. As far as practicable, variations within countries are shown in Table 3.1.

It can be seen from this table that the length of first-degree courses in economics at universities is normally four years. There are shorter university degrees lasting three years in the United Kingdom, where this is the normal length of the course (though there are exceptions[1]) in Malta, in the Holy See, in the French-language universities of Switzerland,[2] and for some courses in Ireland. Degrees in Sweden can take as little as three years, but the length tends to be nearer four years. In a few countries there are university first-degree courses of a prescribed length of more than four or four and a half years. This is so in Denmark, in Germany for the *Diplom-Wirtschafts-ingenieur*, where this is taken as a first degree, and in the Netherlands, Norway, and Spain.

---

[1] In England the course at the University of Keele is four years, and in Scotland and Northern Ireland honours degree courses are of four years' duration.

[2] With these is included Fribourg, where instruction is in fact offered in both German and French, but where the structure of the course follows the Swiss-French language pattern rather than the German.

At the specialized institutions degree courses tend to be shorter than at the universities, and the most common length is three years. There are longer courses in Austria, the Netherlands, Norway, Switzerland, and Spain.

THE STRUCTURE OF THE COURSE[1]

The structure of courses ranges between two extremes: on the one hand very tight control and planning—where once the student has chosen his course he has few other decisions to make (the *table d'hôte* degree); and on the other hand very loosely planned, where the student retains almost complete freedom to organize his own course and choose the subjects he studies, and to a large extent the order in which he studies them (the *à la carte* degree). These are the extremes, and many courses fall somewhere between them. The courses at many of the specialized institutions can be taken as examples of *table d'hôte* degrees—for instance, the course at H.E.C., in France. Here once the student has been admitted to the course his programme, both in terms of what subjects he studies and when he studies a subject, is almost completely determined—there is one optional subject in the third year—and almost all successful students will complete the course in the prescribed time. The opposite extreme, the *à la carte* degree, is represented by the F.K. degree in Sweden, where students have to combine subjects in such a way as to obtain six academic points. Each subject can be studied to the one-, two-, or three-point level. A one-point course normally lasts one semester, a two-point course two semesters, and so on. There is some direction and programming, but at the moment only to the extent that lower-point courses in a subject are normally prerequisites for higher-point courses in the same subject—a student cannot, for example, take the two-point course in economics unless he has previously taken the one-point course.[2]

In countries where the syllabus is laid down centrally for all universities, as in France, Italy, and Spain, courses are subject to fairly detailed planning. In France all universities offer subjects in the same order. In Italy there are slight but not significant variations in the order in which subjects are studied, and in the main the pattern

---

[1] More detailed accounts of the structure of courses in the various countries will be found in the country studies which form the second part of this report.

[2] Reforms are under discussion in Sweden which will reduce the degree of freedom open to students of economics in the universities.

is uniform. In Spain, too, the pattern is basically uniform, with very slight variations.

Where universities are free to determine their own courses it is not always the case that courses are loosely structured. In the United Kingdom, where there is a great variety in the courses offered, programming within them is usually tight, and once the student has determined his specialization—either at entry, or after a period of a year or so, during which he normally follows a common social-science course—his course is clearly mapped out. It is rare for British students not to complete their courses in the prescribed time, usually three years. In the Netherlands or Sweden, on the other hand, the general outlines for courses are laid down centrally, but within this framework there is a considerable amount of freedom. In Sweden the *Civilekonom* has always been a fairly tightly programmed course, and in both the F.P.M. and the J.P.M. degrees at the universities subject patterns are to some extent prescribed. Official policy tends towards an increasing use of study plans and programming in the other degrees. In the Netherlands courses have a common fundamental structure, of an intermediate course leading to the *Candidaats* examination, followed by a more specialized period of study culminating in the *Doctoraal*, or final examination. The detailed structures of these courses, however, vary from institution to institution. Each institution's detailed regulations are fitted into a general, centrally determined framework, but there can be quite important differences between institutions; this is especially the case in arrangements for the preliminary examination, and for the way in which specialization is achieved in the *Doctoraal*, both points discussed more fully in the country study on the Netherlands.[1]

The timing of examinations also affects and is affected by the structure of the course. It is difficult to explain the exact nature of the relationship between the structures of examinations and courses. The precise form of examinations is discussed in Chapter 6, but it is appropriate here to make some observations on the relationship of examinations to course structure. Examinations every year in the subjects studied during that year normally accompany rigidly structured courses. Such examination systems are found in France, Italy, Spain, Greece, and Turkey. Examination systems where

---

[1] Proposals now under discussion in the Netherlands may significantly alter the structure described in this paragraph. It is anticipated that 80 per cent of students will complete their studies at the equivalent of the *Candidaats* level.

examinations can either be taken frequently, and where the student can choose within reasonable limits when he presents himself for which examinations, or where there are infrequent examinations mainly at the end of the course, both paradoxically tend to be linked with less tightly programmed courses. In Sweden, for example, at the University of Uppsala there are frequent examination (*Tentamena*) sessions, and students may present themselves for examination in a subject when they feel ready (provided they have passed any pre-requisite examinations). In German universities the traditional system of having a final examination and little previous planning of the student's course, apart from the requirement of passes in certain preliminary examinations, is to some extent changing. There is now a trend in German-language universities to the development of study plans and the formalization of the various preliminary examinations into one set of examinations—*Vorprüfung* or *Zwischenprüfung*—at the end of the second year of study. With this formalization of the examination structure is going a far greater organization, in most cases still merely advisory, but in some mandatory, of the first two years of the degree course.

SPECIALIZATION

First-degree courses vary considerably in the amount of speciali-zation they permit. The range is perhaps from courses like those at the University of Athens, where economics is only a specialization in a law degree, to the Hochschule at St Gallen, where the *Licence* specialization can be in one of a number of highly specialized directions. This may, however, not be quite a fair comparison, as the specialized institutions like St Gallen tend to offer specialized vocational courses related to the career the student is planning to follow. However, even within specialized institutions there is a contrast between those like the Gothenburg Handelshögskolan, or H.E.C. in France, or E.S.A.D.E. in Spain, which offer a basic general vocational training largely in business economics, and those like St Gallen, which offer a general grounding followed by much more detailed specialization.

University degrees tend to be less vocational. The amount of specialization they offer also varies considerably; a common pattern which, as we shall see in Chapter 11, is becoming increasingly wide-spread is for all students to do a common, basic course with the minimum of specialization, followed by a specialized course of either general or business economics. This pattern is perhaps most highly developed in the Netherlands, where the first part of the five-year degree consists of a *Candidature* of three years with little specialization. There may be some differences in the courses followed at this stage, usually between those students who intend to follow a quantitative specialization later and those who do not. After the *Candidature* specialization becomes much more intensive—students normally having a choice of general economics, business economics, and quantitative economics (specializing in either general or business economics), with in some cases other options as well. (The exact organization of the specialization is discussed in the country study on the Netherlands.) Another example of the same type of course, though a shorter one, is that offered by the London School of Economics, where after a common first year students have a choice of sixteen specializations (four of them in economics), any one of which they can decide to study for the next two years. This pattern is in fact common in British universities, for although the choice is nowhere else as wide as at L.S.E. there is a tendency for the first year or so of the course to be common for the social sciences as a whole, followed by specialization in economics or a branch of it or a combination of economics and some other subject, usually another social science.

Specialization can be achieved by different options within a common degree or by different degrees. Different degrees may have a number of courses in common, and may differ very little in overall effect from different options within the same degree. This can be seen in the *Licences* at the French-language Swiss universities, where at Geneva there are separate degrees and in other universities a choice of specializations in a single degree. Germany, where there are separate degrees for general and business economics and for those wishing to teach commercial subjects, serves as a good example of the separate-degree method. It is interesting to note, however, that in a number of German universities there are common courses for the *Diplom-Volkswirt* and the *Diplom-Kaufmann*, at least for the first two years.

The amount of choice a student has as far as his course is concerned depends on a variety of factors. Most important are the degree of specialization available to him and the stage at which he must commit himself definitely to his specialization. In the case of separate degrees and institutions offering only one degree, with no specialist options, the decision has normally to be taken before the student really starts on his course. It may be possible for the student to keep another option open during his first year of study by registering for more than one subject course. This is done in France, Belgium, and Spain. In other countries, particularly the United Kingdom, the student's choice often remains open during a common first year in the social sciences, at the end of which he can finally determine in which particular social science he wishes to specialize. Even where some of the choices in the first few years are constrained by the student's choice of his specialization for later years, if a sufficient amount of the course is common he may be able to compensate for subjects not taken if he decides later to change his choice of option. This is, for example, possible in the new degree regulations in Austria.

HIGHER DEGREES

In this brief section on higher degrees it should first be made clear that no attempt has been made to cover specialist diplomas (for example, in teaching or accountancy) or post-experience courses. The concern here is with the traditional higher degrees generally awarded on the basis of independent research, but also including the much more recently developed higher degrees with course instruction.

The countries of the survey are divided, as can be seen from Table 3.2, between those where the first degree is a doctoral one and those where the doctorate is a second, or higher, degree. In the first group are the Austrian universities of Vienna and Graz[1] and the Italian universities.[2]

It can be seen from Table 3.2 that almost all countries have a doctorate. There may also be other, less advanced degrees intermediate between the first degree and the doctorate. This is the case in the United Kingdom, where post-graduate students normally begin their studies with a master's or similar degree before embarking on their doctoral thesis. Increasingly, following the American pattern, these intermediate degrees are available on the basis of course instruction and examination as well as research. This is also true to

---

[1] At the University of Innsbruck there is a doctorate, but it involves an additional course of at least one year on top of the first degree, the *Diplom-Volkswirt*. At the Linz Hochschule and the Hochschule für Welthandel in Vienna the doctorate is a degree beyond the normal first degree. The teaching of economics in Austria is in the process of change, and intermediate degrees in economics are now being introduced (see country study).

[2] There are some specialized post-graduate diplomas in Italy, but no higher research degrees. The selection of university professors is, however, a matter involving formal competition.

some extent in Ireland. In Denmark and Finland in the specialized institutions there are degrees above the ordinary first degree, and in Denmark there is also a third-tier research degree. Not all the specialized institutions offer higher degrees—those in France and Spain do not—but most do.

Information about the proportion of students graduating in economics continuing to higher degrees is rather scanty. It appears to vary upward from about 5 per cent, and in general numbers appear to be increasing faster than the growth in the output of graduates. However, in those countries such as the Netherlands and Norway where the level of the first degree is relatively high, the proportion tends to be lower.

There is a tendency—perhaps under American influence—for post-graduate education to become more organized, especially where first-degree courses are short. It is interesting to note that in Austria, where in most cases the doctorate has been the basic degree, an institute for higher studies and scientific research in the social sciences has been established with help from the Ford Foundation. Teaching is largely by visiting American academics, and the two-year course is primarily intended for assistants at the universities. A similar development is the Institute for Economic Study and Research in Rome, which organizes two-year courses of study, described in the Italian country study. A not dissimilar, but less formal, development of organized post-graduate teaching can be seen at the Centre of Economic Research in Athens.

One of the problems that arises at this stage of university teaching is that of having an adequate staff to teach and supervise advanced students, particularly in the more specialist branches of economics. Possible solutions include specialization within one country, whereby different institutions build up staffs of specialists in different branches of the subject, and the exchange of specialist staff. An example of this type of co-operation is provided by the three Swiss universities of Zürich, Berne, and Basle. Each university specializes in a field of economics—Basle in national income and growth, Zürich in money and international trade, and Berne in economic policy. Specialist staff travel regularly between the three universities to teach graduate students. In Scandinavia annual joint graduate seminars lasting a fortnight are held, enabling advanced students from Denmark, Finland, Norway, and Sweden to discuss papers given by economists from a number of countries.

The movement of students at post-graduate level, both within

Europe and to a greater extent to the U.S.A., may indicate that in some countries there is a demand for more formal post-graduate education than is at present provided. A full discussion of this question lies, however, outside the limits of this study.

RETARDATION AND WASTAGE

The questions of retardation and wastage are related. Where there are ample opportunities for students to re-sit examinations and repeat years, wastage tends to be higher than in institutions with tightly programmed courses where it is exceptional for students not to complete the course in the prescribed length of time. Detailed information on both these questions is not easy to obtain, and much that follows is necessarily based solely on personal impressions gleaned from discussions with academic colleagues in various countries.

Retardation among successful students (that is, students who eventually obtain their degree) seems to be fairly common, and frequently to exceed six months in Austria, Denmark (university only), Germany, Greece, Italy, the Netherlands, Spain (university only), and Turkey (except M.E.T.U.). In other countries it seems to be less serious—that is, six months or less—or almost non-existent.

Information on success rates is also difficult to acquire. Comparisons of student input and output are difficult to interpret, even when statistics are available, because of the problems of growth in student numbers and retardation. Success rates tend, as one would expect, to be highest in countries and institutions where entry is selective (as in the United Kingdom, where the wastage rate is about 12 per cent, and the specialized institutions in France, Finland, and Norway). In those countries where there is no selection for entry the first year of study may serve as a selective year, and it might be more useful to look at the success rate of those starting the second year. It appears, too, that success rates are generally high where groups are very small—this will probably apply in Malta as the course develops, and is certainly true in the Holy See, where there is a success rate of about 80 per cent. Fairly few countries and institutions seem to have very high success rates—80 per cent and over—and relatively few very low—less than 50 per cent. For most countries and institutions success rates seem to range between 50 per cent and 80 per cent. There seem to be five countries where success rates are low— Belgium, France, Greece, Italy, and Spain. In both France and Spain this seems to be a problem only in the universities—the specialized institutions with their selective intake achieve higher, and even very high, success rates; H.E.C. for example, probably has one of the highest success rates of any institution covered in this survey. In the case of Belgium, France, and Spain success rates are artificially lowered by 'ghost' students who register for more courses than they ever intend seriously to attend. Probably because of this, in Belgium success rates seem to be higher for the *Licence* than for the *Candidature* (at Louvain, for example, 60–70 per cent of students succeed at the *Licence*, as opposed to 50 per cent at the *Candidature*). In Spain not only does double counting raise the figures in the first years of the course, but the practice of including in the graduate statistics only those who have actually paid the fees necessary to receive their degree lowers the output figures.

Within countries there may be significant differences in success rates between institutions—this seems, as one would expect, almost always to be true when selective and less selective or non-selective institutions are concerned. Even within countries where selection is general there can still be quite large variations—in the United Kingdom wastage rates were found by the Robbins Committee to vary by university from 3 per cent to 20 per cent for the group of subjects including economics. There may also be differences between students taking various degrees in the same country—in Germany, for example, success rates appear to be higher for students taking the *Diplom-Kaufmann* than for those studying for the *Diplom-Volkswirt*. This may perhaps be related to the rather more vocational nature of the *Diplom-Kaufmann*.

There are many aspects of the twin problems of retardation and wastage on which further information and research are needed. There is a need for both more accurate quantitative data and more qualitative research on the characteristics of students who fail to complete their courses, or take longer than is normal. Comparative studies between institutions of different types and sizes would be particularly interesting. Some quantitative research has already been done in certain institutions—for example, at the Netherlands School of Economics, at the University of Paris, and at the University of Lyons.

Another question which needs to be considered with relation to wastage is how far it is really a total loss. Partially trained people may well have considerable value in certain fields. Particularly where courses are long, there may well be a case for having a fully recognized and official point before the end of the full course at which students who feel unable to complete a full degree can terminate their studies.

Table 3.1

The First Degree in Economics

Country	Degree	Prescribed Length of Course (Years)	Notes
Austria	*Diplom-Volkswirt* (Innsbruck)	4	An additional year's course after this leads to the doctorate in economics (*Dr.rer.econ.*)
	Doctorate (Graz and Vienna)	4	
	Magister Rerum Socialarum (Linz)	4	This is being extended to other institutions (see country study).
	Diplom-Kaufmann (Hochschule für Welthandel, Vienna)	3	
Belgium	*Licence*	4–5	There is a general tendency to increase to 5 years.
	Ingénieur Commercial	4–5	Varies from university to university: Brussels 4, Louvain 5.
Denmark	*Candidatus Politices* (Copenhagen) *Candidatus Oeconomices* (Aarhus)	5–5$\frac{1}{2}$	A *Candidatus Merc.* can be obtained by a further 1$\frac{1}{2}$ years' study.
	Handelshøjskolens Afgangseksamen (Copenhagen and Aarhus Handelshøjskolen)	4 (minimum) 3	

Table 3.1—continued
The First Degree in Economics

Country	Degree	Prescribed Length of Course (Years)	Notes
Finland	*Valtiotieteen Kandidaatti* (Candidacy in Political Science)	4–5	At the University of Tampere the degree is a candidacy in social science.
	Ekonomin Tutkinto (B.Sc. (Econ.)—Schools)	3	
	Akateeminen Sinteerin Tutkinto (Academic Secretary—Schools)	3	
France	*Licence ès Sciences Economiques* (Universities)	4	
	Diplôme (specialized institutions—*e.g.,* H.E.C.)	3	
Germany	*Diplom-Volkswirt (D.V.)*	4	
	Diplom-Kaufmann (D.K.)	4	
	Diplom-Handelslehrer (D.H.)	4	Bochum and Giessen only.
	Diplom-Wirtschaftler (D.W.)	4	
	Diplom-Wirtschaftsingenieur (W.Ing.)	2–5	Available only at the Berlin Technical University and the Hochschule of Aachen, Darmstadt, and Munich. Length of course depends on whether student already has degree or not.
	Technischer-Volkswirt	$4\frac{1}{2}$ (minimum)	Available only at Karlsruhe University.
	Technische-Betriebswirtschaft	$4\frac{1}{2}$ (minimum)	Available only at Karlsruhe University.
Greece	*Licence*	4	

Country	Degree	Prescribed Length of Course (Years)	Notes
Holy See	*Licence* (Gregorian University)	3	
Iceland	*Candidatus Economicus*	$4\frac{1}{2}$	
Ireland	Bachelor of Arts (B.A.)	3 or 4	This is a 3-year degree in National University of Ireland and 4-year at Trinity College, Dublin.
	Bachelor of Commerce (B.Comm.)	3 or 4	At present 3 at University Colleges of Dublin and Galway, 4 at University College, Cork, but the Government has recommended that all honours courses become 4-year.
	Bachelor's Degree in Business Sciences (B.B.S.) (Trinity College, Dublin)	4	
Italy	*Laurea in Economia e Commercio*	4	
Malta	B.A. Honours Economics	3	
Netherlands	*Doctorandus*	4	There is also a 3-year bachelor's degree, but this is very rarely taken.
Norway	*Candidatus Oeconomiae* (Oslo)	5	
	Handelskandidat (Handelshøyskole)	$3\frac{1}{2}$	
Spain	*Licenciado en Ciencias Economicas* (universities)	5	
	Licenciado en Ciencias Empresariales (*E.S.A.D.E., I.C.A.D.E., and E.S.T.E.*)	5	

Table 3.1—continued
The First Degree in Economics

Country	Degree	Prescribed Length of Course (Years)	Notes
Sweden	*Filosofisk Ambetsexamen (F.M.)* (universities)	3–4 (minimum)	
	Filosofisk Kandidatexamen (F.K.) (universities)	3–4 (minimum)	
	Filosofisk-Samhällvetenskaplig examen (F.P.M.) (universities)	3–4 (minimum)	
	Juridisk-Samhällvetenskapligexamen (J.P.M.) (universities)	3–4 (minimum)	
	Civilekonom (Handelshögskolor, Umeå and Lund)	3 (minimum)	
Switzerland	*Licence*	3–4	The degree course is a 3-year one at the French-language universities—Geneva, Fribourg, Lausanne, and Neuchâtel—and a 4-year one at the German-language institutions—Basle, Berne, St Gallen, and Zürich.
Turkey	*Licence* (Ankara and Istanbul)	4	
	Bachelor of Science (B.S.) (M.E.T.U.)	4	
United Kingdom	Bachelor's Degree in Arts, Sciences or Social Sciences (B.A., B.Sc. (Econ.), B.Soc.Sci.)	3	At the University of Keele the course is 4 years.
	Bachelor's Degree in Commerce (B.Comm.)	3	
	Master of Arts (M.A.) (Scottish universities)	3 or 4	3 years for an Ordinary M.A. 4 years for an Honours M.A.

Table 3.2

Higher Degrees in Economics

Country	Higher Degrees	Notes
Austria	Doctorate	
Belgium	Doctorate	
Denmark	Doctorate (universities) *Licence Merc.* (Handelshøjskolen)	At the Handelshøjskolen the *Lic. Merc.* is a research degree which can be taken after the *Cand. Merc.*
Finland	*Licence* Doctorate	
France	*Diplôme d'Etudes Supérieures* (D.E.S.) Doctorate	The *D.E.S.* is a necessary prerequisite of a doctorate, and is taken only by students intending to proceed to a doctorate.
Germany	Doctorate	
Greece	Doctorate	
Holy See	Doctorate	An additional 4th year after the *Licence* course in which a thesis is written.
Iceland	Doctorate	
Ireland	Master's degree in Arts, Economic Science, and Commerce Doctorate	

Table 3.1—continued
The First Degree in Economics

Country	Higher Degrees	Notes
Italy	None	There are some specialized post-graduate diplomas.
Malta	None	Students go abroad.
Netherlands	Doctorate	
Norway	*Licence* Doctorate	Both these degrees are offered by the Handelshøyskole and the University, but no-one has in fact ever taken the University *Licence*.
Spain	Doctorate (universities)	
Sweden	*Licence* Doctorate	
Switzerland	Doctorate	
Turkey	Doctorate	The Doctorate can be obtained in the State universities. There are no advanced degrees in economics at M.E.T.U., but many students continue their studies overseas.
United Kingdom	Master's Degree in Arts, Sciences or Commerce Bachelor's Degree in Philosophy (B.Phil.) Bachelor's Degree in Literature (B.Litt.) Doctorate	Many of the master's degrees and the B.Phil. are course degrees (see U.K. country study). The misleadingly named B.Litt. is a research degree of a lower standard than the doctorate at Oxford University.

CHAPTER 4

The Content of Degrees in Economics

In this chapter an examination is attempted of the composition of degree courses in economics in the institutions of higher education covered by this survey. It should first perhaps be pointed out that the present allocation of time between different fields in any particular institution is by no means necessarily that which economists in the institution concerned would prefer. It is the result of a historical process in which various groups of university teachers—of whom economists have been only one—have sought to maintain and improve the positions of their subjects. As it is always easier to add a subject than to drop one, this has often led to overcrowded programmes of instruction. This may have been partially mitigated by the development of options allowing the student to choose between economics and business economics,[1] but such specialization frequently does not affect other subjects in which students are still expected to spend the same proportion of their time. The balance shifts only within the economics subjects, not between them and other subjects.

This problem of overcrowding of curricula is a problem perhaps peculiar to subjects like economies, which have developed relatively recently, and in a sense serve as a bridge between various other academic subjects. The mixed ancestry and present nature of the subject link it particularly closely with business administration (which is, indeed, in many ways only a specialized branch of applied economics), law, philosophy, and mathematics. The development of the subject has meant that these other disciplines are frequently an integral, and sometimes a dominating, part of the faculties in which economics is taught.

---

[1] Business economics is not perhaps the best name for that group of subjects which go to make up the subject known in German as *Betriebswirtschafts-lehre* and in Swedish as *Företagsekonomi*. Business administration or business studies might be more appropriate terms, as not all the subjects are strictly economic. In this report business economics has been the name eventually adopted, but with a full consciousness of its limitations.

In Table 4.1 and Fig. 4.1 an attempt has been made to analyse the degree courses of a number of representative institutions by subjects, and the discussion that follows will refer exclusively to those institutions. It should first be stressed that this is an analysis of instruction time. Instruction is measurable, and data on it is readily available, whereas this is not true of the actual distribution of students' time. It should be borne in mind, however, that not all instruction offered is actually taken by students, even in compulsory subjects. In Table 4.1 two figures are shown where there are options, the smaller figure relating to the instruction offered to all students and the larger to that available to those students taking options in this subject group. It should also be remembered that the relationship between time under instruction and private-study time varies from subject to subject as well as varying with the type of instruction, and whether the subject is being studied for examination purposes or not. It is not possible, therefore, to assume from Table 4.1 that these figures accurately reflect the overall allocation of students' study time in the various institutions, though with the cautions given above they can be regarded as the nearest approximation to such an allocation readily available.

In Table 4.1 eight groups of subjects are distinguished—economics, business economics, law, other social sciences, accountancy and commercial techniques, mathematics and statistics, foreign languages, and other subjects. In general subjects at particular institutions have been allocated to a group on the basis of the title of the course and any further information that may have been available on its substance. Titles by themselves can be misleading, especially in those countries where courses are centrally determined and the only means of change is by including different material under a given title. This process can be seen in Italian universities, for instance, and the differences shown in Table 4.1 between the universities of Urbino and Parma illustrate this. The same titles can mean very different things at different institutions: public finance particularly is a course that can be taught in very many different ways, and in some cases is a subject more akin to law than economics. Material may have to be fitted into a course, and thus find a home under some quite un-expected title—at the University of Istanbul, for example, econometrics and input-output analysis have been taught in the course on the history of economic thought. Where reliance has had to be placed solely on titles there may well have been some misallocation of subjects, but it is hoped that this has been minimized by personal visits and the collection of reading-lists. In a number of cases consideration of the content of the particular course has led to its being divided between two or more categories.

In addition to these general qualifications about the table, it is necessary to indicate in rather more detail the material covered by the various subject groups and to consider briefly their relationships to economics.

Economics itself covers the main branches of the subject, but excludes mathematical economics, econometrics, economic history and geography, and business economics taught from a business and practical standpoint. This last distinction has not always been an easy one to make, and has sometimes had to be arbitrary, though every effort has been made to take into account the actual substance of the particular course. Courses on the economy of particular countries (usually that in which the institution is situated) have been included under economics, although they might have been better included in economic geography in some cases.

Business economics covers both the empirical parts of the economics of the firm and some courses on subjects allied to business management, such as personnel and industrial relations. Those subjects which while linked with business administration are of a purely technical nature, such as book-keeping and techniques of international commerce, are not included in this group, but in that of accountancy and commercial techniques.

Law covers all legal subjects, including economic and commercial law. Other social sciences include economic history and geography, demography, sociology, government, political science, and social psychology. Mathematics and statistics cover all aspects of these subjects and also mathematical economics and operations research, but not book-keeping and accountancy. Actuarial mathematics has, however, been included in the mathematical group.

Accountancy and commercial techniques include all aspects of accountancy and book-keeping, as well as narrowly technical parts of business administration. Foreign languages cover all modern languages other than that of instruction. The other subjects group covers any subjects which are not more appropriately placed in other fields. It includes, for example, science subjects, philosophy, psychology, classical languages, political history, and the study of the language of instruction.

These groups are of themselves arbitrary, and others would certainly have classified subjects in different ways. In particular, the exclusion of mathematical economics and econometrics from the economics category and the divisions between business economics and accountancy and commercial techniques involved very difficult decisions.

The relationship of these various subject groups to economics is complex, and not all subjects in a group necessarily have the same relationship to the parent subject. The business economics and accountancy and the commercial techniques groups are both vocational subject groups closely linked to economics. Other social sciences may be contextual subjects for economics—that is, providing a wider understanding of the society in which economic relations occur—and in certain cases are also vocational and connected with business economics (for example, industrial psychology). Mathematics and statistics and foreign languages are largely tool subjects for economics, although econometrics is a higher specialized branch of the main subject and operations research a sophisticated vocational tool. Law, although it could perhaps have been included with the other social sciences, has been treated separately, as it still makes up a large part of many economics courses. Whether the relationships between law and economics are more traditional than real will no doubt long remain a disputed question. Certain aspects of commercial and fiscal law clearly have an important value for economists, but degrees which include more than 15 per cent of their instruction in law seem to be maintaining a tradition of a joint degree in law and economics, or in some cases a law degree slightly modified to include economics.

The most important fields from the point of view of this study are economics, business economics, and mathematics and statistics. The proportion these three subjects bear to the total instruction is some indication of the importance of economics in the degree course. For this reason Table 4.1 is supplemented by Fig. 4.1 in which this proportion is shown diagramatically. In Fig. 4.1 it can be seen that a distinction is made between the common core of these three subject groups taken by all students, and the further element which may be available as one of a number of options. In some cases this option can be in either one group or in one of the other two; this has, as far as possible, been taken into account in the diagram in Fig. 4.1, so that the overall maximum for the three groups is shown.

The proportion of the course devoted to the economics group varies quite widely—in one case, the French H.E.C. *Diplôme* course, it is under 10 per cent (7·1 per cent) and in two, the University of

Oslo's course for the degree of *Candidatus Oeconomiae* and the M.E.T.U. Bachelor of Science (economics option), it is more than 50 per cent. The percentage in the other degree courses ranges between these figures; it is naturally higher in general economics degrees or options than in those specializing in business economics. In the general economics degrees a figure of 40 per cent seems typical. Within some degrees options in the economics field are available, and if one assumes these were taken it would be possible for a course to contain 50 per cent or more of economics at the Universities of Copenhagen (*Candidatus Politices*) and Iceland (*Candidatus Economicus*), at the Swedish universities (the F.K. degree), and at the University of Hull. On the other hand, the proportion tends to be lower in the vocationally oriented courses in the specialized institutions.

Business economics plays in general a less important part in economics degree courses. It is predominant only in some specialized institutions, and in some of the business economics degrees or options. A number of universities have degrees that can contain no business economics at all. Most specialized institutions have a compulsory proportion of business economics of less than 30 per cent. Those that have more are the *Handelshøjskolen Copenhagen* (H.A.), the H.E.C. (*Diplôme*), the German *Diplom-Kaufmann*, the Netherlands School of Economics (*Doctorandus* degree, business economics option), and the University of Groningen (*Doctorandus* degree, economics option and quantitative business economics option). In addition to this there are a number of institutions where the compulsory and the optional proportion in the business economics group can exceed 30 per cent.

The proportion of instruction in the law group is normally less than 20 per cent. There are a number of courses that include no law—for example, at the University of Oslo and normally at the United Kingdom universities. Law is of greatest importance in the degree courses at the two Greek universities—at the University of Athens it accounts for 72 per cent of the course and at the University of Salonika for 30 per cent. At the Athens Graduate School of Economics and Business Studies the proportion, though considerably lower than at the Greek universities, is still higher than average—19·6 per cent in the economics option and 24·8 per cent in the business economics option of the *Licence*. Other courses with a high legal compulsory content—more than 15 per cent—are the *Diplom-Volkswirt* at the University of Innsbruck, the French university

DISTRIBUTION OF SUBJECTS IN ECONOMICS COURSES

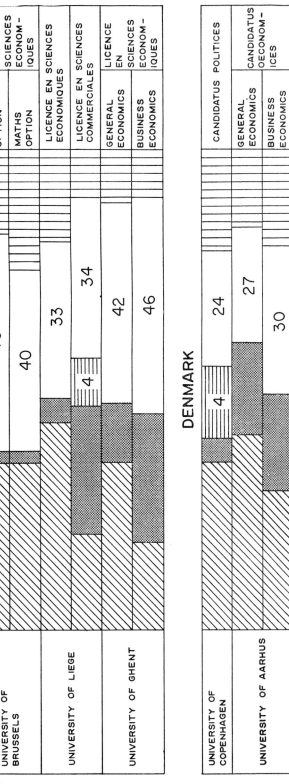

FRANCE

UNIVERSITIES— GENERAL PATTERN	7	LICENCE ES SCIENCES ECONOMIQUES / 39
H.E.C.	51	DIPLOME
INSTITUT COMMERCIAL DE NANCY	66	DIPLOME

GERMANY

UNIVERSITIES— GENERAL PATTERN	7	DIPLOM-VOLKSWIRT / 37
	4 / 33	DIPLOM-KAUFMANN

GREECE

UNIVERSITY OF ATHENS	74	LICENCE ECONOMICS
UNIVERSITY OF SALONIKA	62	LICENCE
ATHENS GRADUATE SCHOOL OF ECONOMICS AND BUSINESS STUDIES	50	ECONOMICS / LICENCE
	61	BUSINESS ECONOMICS

Legend:

ECONOMICS   BUSINESS ECONOMICS   OPTIONAL   OTHER   MATHS and STATISTICS

TYPE OF OPTION   PERCENTAGE OF OTHER

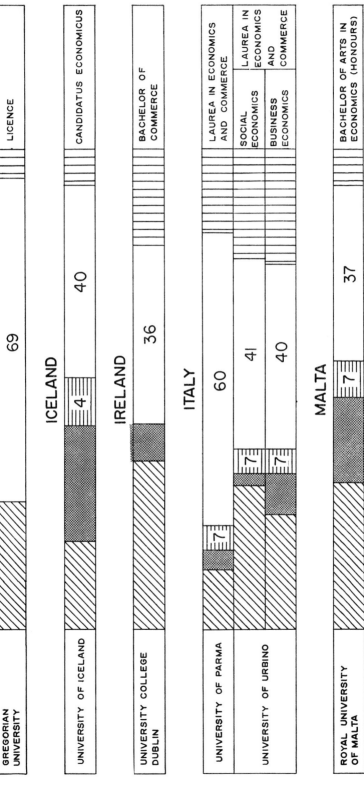

NETHERLANDS

SCHOOL OF ECONOMICS, ROTTERDAM

	BUSINESS ECONOMICS	DOCTOR-ANDUS
QUANTITATIVE (GEN.ECON.)	22	29
QUANTITATIVE (BUS.ECON.)	21	

UNIVERSITY OF GRONINGEN

ECONOMICS	5	12
QUANTITATIVE (GEN.ECON.)	10	DOCTOR-ANDUS
QUANTITATIVE (BUS.ECON.)	10	

NORWAY

| UNIVERSITY OF OSLO | CANDIDATUS OECONOMIAE | 5 | 7 |
| NORWEGIAN SCHOOL OF ECON. and BUS. ADMIN. | HANDELS-KANDIDAT | 3 | 31 |

SPAIN

UNIVERSITY OF BARCELONA	GENERAL ECONOMICS — LICENCE IN ECONOMICS	41
	BUSINESS ECONOMICS	46
E.S.A.D.E., BARCELONA	E.S.A.D.E. DIPLOMA	55

ECONOMICS   BUSINESS ECONOMICS   OPTIONAL   OTHER   MATHS and STATISTICS

TYPE OF   PERCENTAGE

SWEDEN

UNIVERSITIES — GENERAL PATTERN	F.M.	F.P.M.			
		2	4	7	67	14

HANDELSHÖGSKOLAN STOCKHOLM	CIVILEKONOM
	4	37

SWITZERLAND

UNIVERSITY OF BERN	GENERAL ECONOMICS	27
	BUSINESS ECONOMICS LICENCE	1	31

UNIVERSITY OF GENEVA	LICENCE IN ECONOMICS	3	31
	LICENCE IN ECONOMICS and COMMERCE	57
	LICENCE IN ECONOMICS SPECIALIZING IN MATHEMATICS	27

UNIVERSITY OF LAUSANNE	GENERAL ECONOMICS LICENCE	32
	BUSINESS ECONOMICS	32

HOCHSCHULE ST. GALLEN	ECONOMIC POLICY	49
	BANKING	44

TÜRKEY

UNIVERSITY OF ISTANBUL	LICENCE		
M.E.T.U.		ECONOMICS	BACHELOR OF SCIENCE
		STATISTICS	

UNIVERSITY OF ISTANBUL — 41

M.E.T.U. — ECONOMICS 27 — 33 STATISTICS

UNITED KINGDOM

UNIVERSITY OF HULL	B.A. IN ECONOMICS
UNIVERSITY OF LEEDS	ACCOUNTANCY / BACHELOR OF COMMERCE / B.A. IN ECONOMICS
UNIVERSITY OF MANCHESTER	B.A. IN ECONOMICS / B.A. IN ECONOMICS and SOCIAL STATISTICS
UNIVERSITY OF OXFORD	B.A. IN PHILOSOPHY, POLITICS, and ECONOMICS

UNIVERSITY OF HULL — 3 — 27

UNIVERSITY OF LEEDS — 3 — 3 — 37 — 16 — 3

UNIVERSITY OF MANCHESTER — 3 — 3 — 29 — 36

UNIVERSITY OF OXFORD — 1 — 3 — 46

ECONOMICS   BUSINESS ECONOMICS   OPTIONAL   OTHER   MATHS. and STATISTICS

TYPE OF OPTION

PERCENTAGE OF OTHER

TYPES OF OPTION

1. ECONOMICS
2. BUSINESS ECONOMICS
3. MATHS. and STATISTICS
4. ECONOMICS OR BUSINESS ECONOMICS
5. ECONOMICS OR MATHS and STATISTICS
6. BUSINESS ECONOMICS OR MATHS and STATISTICS
7. ECONOMICS OR BUSINESS ECONOMICS OR MATHS and STATISTICS

Licence, the *Diplôme* course at the Institut Commercial de Nancy, the German *Diplom-Volkswirt*, the business economics option of the *Lizenz* at the University of Berne, the University of Geneva *Licence* in economics and commerce, the *Licence* at the University of Lausanne, and that at the Hochschule St Gallen.

The proportion in other social sciences is frequently less than 10 per cent, and almost always less than 20 per cent. Only very rarely does the compulsory percentage of time allocated in this group of subjects exceed this, although courses in which this occurs are found at the Gregorian University, the University of Geneva (*Licence* in economics and *Licence* in economics specializing in mathematics), and the University of Manchester. Other courses would join these if the optional element were also taken into account.

It is not often that the proportion of the courses in accountancy and commercial techniques exceeds 10 per cent, though it is sometimes a little higher. Figures of over 20 per cent are found at the University of Iceland and in the Leeds University Bachelor of Commerce courses. Quite a number of universities have no instruction in this group of subjects.

The range for the proportion of the course in mathematics is far greater than in some of the other groups, as can be seen from both Table 4.1 and Fig. 4.1. It is naturally very much higher in degrees and options specializing in mathematical economics—for example, at the Netherlands School of Economics, the University of Geneva, and Manchester University. In a very few courses there is no compulsory work in mathematics and statistics at all—the University of Athens and the University of Oxford. As mathematics and statistics are tool subjects for economics it is important not only that they should be taught in economics degrees, but also that the teaching should be integrated into the general teaching of economics. Where mathematics and statistics are taught by people from outside the economics faculty and not much used by those teaching within the faculty, the instruction given may remain isolated and relatively useless in the students' minds. This problem is understood to occur in certain French and Italian universities, but it is a frequent complaint of mathematical economists and econometricians that their colleagues are not sufficiently numerate. Institutions formally offering little or no instruction in this group may in their economics teaching treat the subject in a reasonably mathematical way. This is, for example, the case in the Swedish *Handelshögskolor*. Degrees or options specializing in the quantitative aspects of economics, though they exist, are still far from common, and have not yet appeared in many countries. As separate specializations they are most developed in the Netherlands and certain United Kingdom universities, where mathematics and statistics are well integrated into economics teaching, and where the quantitative options most institutions offer provide advanced training in econometrics. The course at the University of Oslo also provides a very rigorous education in mathematical economics.

Language instruction is not often provided as a normal part of the course in universities. There are a few exceptions—the Italian universities, the University of Ghent, the University of Salonika, the University of Iceland, and the Turkish universities. Where there is no formal course there may be language requirements, either formal for examinations or informal in the inclusion of foreign-language books on reading-lists. (This point is discussed more fully in chapters 5 and 9.) On the other hand, in the specialized institutions language instruction is far more usually a compulsory part of the course. It may indeed be quite important—it is $21 \cdot 3$ per cent at the Institut Commercial de Nancy. At other specialized institutions (except those in the Netherlands, which are in this, as in most other things, far closer to the universities than to the other specialized institutions) language instruction tends to be about 10 per cent, or rather less, of the course.

The other subjects group very rarely exceeds 10 per cent. At many specialized institutions it covers some instruction in subjects of a scientific or technological nature related to the vocational aspects of the course. At the Gregorian University of the Holy See, where the category is of considerable importance, it covers religious and philosophical subjects relevant to the specialized group of students with whom this university is dealing. In Spanish universities too this field covers instruction in religion, and also political education. It is of more importance where degrees can be made up of subjects quite outside economics—the main example of this is the Swedish F.K. degrees, but it is also true of some United Kingdom degrees, of which the Oxford degree in philosophy, politics, and economics serves as an example.

The composite picture—to which there are many exceptions, as Table 4.1, Fig. 4.1, and the individual country studies make clear—is that economics and business economics between them normally account for a good half of the course time, with other subject groups each accounting for under 10 per cent, with the exception of law, which often accounts for rather over 10 per cent.

It is extremely difficult to discuss the optimal subject distribution for an economics degree course. The background of the students, the length of the course, and the purpose of the degree are only some of the many germane factors. There is also the difficulty of distinguishing temporary developments in economics from long-term trends. Especially where courses are rigidly determined and regulations difficult to alter, changes to keep up with what later turn out to be short-lived fashions may be highly detrimental to the course. The balance achieved is the result of various pressures in each institution or country in those cases where such decisions are made centrally. One can only hope that the short-term equilibrium position achieved is not too far from the long-term optimal position.

Nevertheless, if one were to attempt to lay down certain norms it would seem to be generally accepted that at least in the latter stages of a degree course the majority of courses in an economics degree should be from the economics group of subjects. It would also be important to ensure that the other subjects included in the course are relevant to economics, and are taught in such a way as to bring out this relationship. Such subjects would normally include an introduction to the mathematical and statistical techniques relevant to economics and subjects providing some understanding of the social and institutional framework in which the economy operates.

Notes to Table 4.1

(1) These figures for the new master's degree were kindly supplied by Professor Bouffier. The categories of business economics and of accountancy and commercial techniques have been combined in this case.

(2) Throughout this table where ranges are given the lower figures—in this case 14.1—indicate the proportion of their course that all students devote to this subject group and the upper the maximum proportion of instruction time that can be devoted to this subject group.

(3) In French universities the ranges given allow for the fourth-year optional subject which can be divided between a number of subject groups.

(4) This figure relates to that part of the *travaux practiques* which it is not possible to distribute satisfactorily between the various fields—that is, all sessions in the first year and one session in each of the second and third year.

(5) These figures refer only to the common, compulsory part of the course. In addition, students do optional subjects in two years of the course. This is discussed more fully in the country study on the Holy See.

(6) These percentages are calculated on the basis of the subjects stipulated in the course, not on the basis of the actual timetable which is still in process of being evolved, as the course started only in the autumn of 1966.

(7) These are all calculated simply on the basis of the subjects studied.

(8) The remainder of the F.K. can be in any subject—this could include those in the groups distinguished in the table, but since the range is so wide it has all been credited to the 'other subjects' group.

(9) These percentages are calculated on a subject basis. The degree is included as an example of a British combined honours degree.

Table 4.1

The Percentage Distribution of Instruction Time between Different Subject Groups in Representative Courses

Country	Institution and Degree	Economics	Business Economics	Law	Other Social Sciences	Accountancy & Commercial Techniques	Mathematics & Statistics	Foreign Languages	Other Subjects
Austria	Hochschule für Welthandel Vienna:								
	Mag.Rer.Soc. Economics	33·8	14·8(1)	22·5	6·3	—(1)	7·0	15·5	
	Mag.Rer.Soc. Business economics	14·1–(2) 15·5	32·4–(1) 33·1	16·9	6·3	—(1)	7·0	21·1– 23·2	
Belgium	University of Brussels:								
	Licence en Sciences Economiques (non-maths option)	36·0	2·1– 3·4	11·7	17·2– 20·0	1·6	17·2– 18·6	—	10·3
	Licence en Sciences Economiques (maths option)	34·4– 35·8	2·1 3·4	10·3	15·8	0·9	23·4– 24·5	—	10·3
	University of Liège:								
	Licence en Sciences Economiques	43·7– 48·0	4·3– 8·6	9·3	10·4	2·9	18·6– 22·9	—	6·5
	Licence en Economie Commerciale	19·1– 28·9	27·4– 37·2	9·8– 19·6	7·7	12·0	9·8	—	4·4
	University of Ghent:								
	Licence en Sciences Economiques (general economics option)	36·0– 39·6	11·5	8·4– 12·0	8·7– 12·3	1·8	10·8	9·6	9·6
	Licence en Sciences Economiques (business economics option)	17·8– 21·2	26·8	10·9– 14·3	9·5– 12·9	4·0	9·2	9·2	9·2

Table 4.1—continued
The Percentage Distribution of Instruction Time between Different Subject Groups in Representative Courses

Country	Institution and Degree	Economics	Business Economics	Law	Other Social Sciences	Accountancy & Commercial Techniques	Mathematics & Statistics	Foreign Languages	Other Subjects
Denmark	University of Copenhagen: *Candidatus Politices*	36·2– 50·0	4·6– 18·4	12·6	4·6	2·3	21·3	—	4·6
	University of Aarhus: *Candidatus Oeconomices* (general economics option)	41·3	16·1	10·3	7·7	3·9	15·5	—	5·2
	Candidatus Oeconomices (business economics option)	28·6	21·4	10·4	7·8	6·5	20·1	—	5·2
	Handelshøjskolen, Copenhagen: *Handelshøjskolens Afgangseksamen (H.A.)*	22·8	39·0	8·1	—	0·0– 5·7	14·6– 21·1	6·5	3·2
Finland	Comparable information not available—see country study	—		—	—	—	—	—	—
France	General pattern: *Licence ès Sciences Economiques*[3]	38·8– 47·0	0·0– 8·2	16·3– 18·4	14·3– 18·4	2·0	14·3– 22·5	—	6·1[4]
	H.E.C.: *Diplôme*	7·1	34·5– 36·2	14·2– 15·9	6·2– 7·9	12·4	7·1	10·6	6·2
	Institut Commercial de Nancy: *Diplôme*	15·0	11·8	19·7	3·1	15·7	7·1	21·3	6·3

Country	Institution and Degree	Economics	Business Economics	Law	Other Social Sciences	Accountancy & Commercial Techniques	Mathematics & Statistics	Foreign Languages	Other Subjects
Germany	General pattern: *Diplom-Volkswirt*	34·5– 39·8	15·2– 20·5	23·2– 28·5	9·9– 15·2	4·0	7·9– 13·2	– 0·0	– 0·0
	Diplom-Kaufmann	18·9– 26·9	37·0– 45·0	14·9– 22·9	2·9– 10·9	14·9	3·4	8·0	8·0
Greece	University of Athens: *Licence* (economics options in 4th year)	26·2		72·8	1·0				
	University of Salonika: *Licence*	25·4	3·9	39·0	11·9	3·9	8·5	7·6	0·8
	Athens Graduate School of Economics & Business Studies: *Licence* (economics option)	29·9	5·6	19·6	6·5	7·5	15·0	11·2	4·7
	Licence (business economics option)	17·4	9·2	24·8	2·8	14·7	12·8	11·0	7·3
Holy See	Gregorian University: *Licence*[5]	25·7		10·7	33·6		5·7		24·3
Iceland	University of Iceland: *Candidatus Economicus*	18·9– 27·1	24·3– 26·4	4·1	0·0– 8·1	22·3	6·8	8·1	5·4

Table 4.1—continued
The Percentage Distribution of Instruction Time between Different Subject Groups in Representative Courses

Country	Institution and Degree	Economics	Business Economics	Law	Other Social Sciences	Accountancy & Commercial Techniques	Mathematics & Statistics	Foreign Languages	Other Subjects
Ireland	University College, Dublin: Bachelor of Commerce	36·1	8·3	5·6	5·6	16·7	19·4	0·0–8·3	0·0–8·3
Italy	University of Parma: *Laurea* in economics and commerce	12·4–17·4	4·1–9·1	14·0–19·0	9·9	19·0–24·0	18·2–23·2	14·9	2·5
	University of Urbino: *Laurea* in economics and commerce (social economics option)	30·1–35·6	1·8–7·3	12·8–18·3	7·3–12·8	5·5	21·9–27·4	11·0–16·5	4·1
	(business economics option)	23·6–28·9	8·4–13·7	12·9–18·2	7·1–12·4	5·3	22·7–28·0	10·7–16·0	4·0
Malta	Royal University of Malta: Bachelor of Arts in economics (honours)[6]	31·7–40·0	16·7–25·0	0·0–8·3	15·0–36·7	—	6·7–21·7	0·0–6·7	0·0–30·0
Netherlands	Netherlands School of Economics, Rotterdam: *Doctorandus* (general economics option)	39·5	20·3	7·2	12·0	9·0	12·0	—	—
	(business economics option)	22·5	36·7	5·9	11·8	11·3	11·8	—	—

Country	Institution and Degree	Economics	Business Economics	Law	Other Social Sciences	Accountancy & Commercial Techniques	Mathematics & Statistics	Foreign Languages	Other Subjects
Netherlands —continued	Netherlands School of Economics, Rotterdam:								
	(quantitative general economics option)	26·8	15·6	0·0–5·6	6·7–11·2	8·4	35·8	—	—
	(quantitative business economics option)	18·8	24·3	0·0–5·5	6·6–11·1	8·3	35·4	—	—
	University of Groningen: *Doctorandus*								
	(economics option)	25·0–35·4	32·2	3·5–13·9	6·1–16·5	2·6	20·2–30·6	—	—
	(quantitative general economics option)	24·0	18·4	1·7	5·8	2·5	47·6	—	—
	(quantitative business economics option)	12·0	30·7	1·7	5·8	2·5	47·3	—	—
Norway	University of Oslo: *Candidatus Oeconomiae*	52·8–60·2	8·3	—	7·4	—	24·1–31·5	—	—
	Norwegian School of Economics and Business Administration: *Handelskandidat*	19·2–21·2	26·9–30·8	0·0–15·4	0·0–30·8	11·5	7·7–23·1	0·0–30·8	—

Table 4.1—continued
The Percentage Distribution of Instruction Time between Different Subject Groups in Representative Courses

Country	Institution and Degree	Economics	Business Economics	Law	Other Social Sciences	Accountancy & Commercial Techniques	Mathematics & Statistics	Foreign Languages	Other Subjects
Spain	University of Barcelona: *Licence* in economics (general economics option)	38·8	5·6	13·9	13·0	5·6	14·8	—	8·3
	(business economics option)	30·6	8·3	13·9	13·0	11·1	14·8	—	8·3
	E.S.A.D.E., Barcelona: *Carrera de Ciencias Empresariales*	14·5	16·2	9·0	7·8	12·6	14·7	10·9	14·3
Sweden	General pattern: F.M.[7]	16·7–33·3	—	—	16·7–50·0	—	—	—	16·7–50·0
	F.K.[7]	16·7–50·0	—	—	—	—	—	—	50·0–[8]
	F.P.M.[7]	28·6–42·9	7·1–42·9	—	0·0–42·9	—	14·3–42·9	—	83·3
	Handelshögskolan, Stockholm: *Civilekonom*	24·8–34·3	22·3–31·8	6·7	6·7	12·4–21·9	6·2	11·4	—
Switzerland	University of Berne: *Lizenz* (general economics option)	43·1	23·5	14·4–20·9	1·3–7·8	2·6	6·5	—	0·7
	(business economics option)	30·3–35·5	27·0	25·0	1·3–7·9	2·6	6·6	—	0·7

Country	Institution and Degree	Economics	Business Economics	Law	Other Social Sciences	Accountancy & Commercial Techniques	Mathematics & Statistics	Foreign Languages	Other Subjects
Switzerland —continued	University of Geneva: *Licence* in economics	22·4	13·8	3·4	27·6	—	25·9		0·0
	Licence in economics and commerce	15·0	18·0	20·3—	15·0	18·0	32·8	—	3·4
	Licence in economics (specializing in mathematics)	19·6	8·2	4·1	20·6	2·1	45·4	—	0·0
	University of Lausanne : *Licence* (general economics option)	41·2	21·2	21·2	4·7	5·9	5·9	—	—
	(business economics option)	34·1	28·2	21·2	4·7	5·9	5·9	—	—
	Hochschule St Gallen : *Lizenz* (economic policy option)	25·7	18·8	18·8	11·5	—	6·3	9·9	8·9
	(banking option)	24·6	24·6	19·4	4·2	1·6	7·3	9·4	8·9
Turkey	University of Istanbul : *Licence*	39·7	12·5	14·1	12·5	10·3	6·5	4·4	—

Table 4.1—continued
The Percentage Distribution of Instruction Time between Different Subject Groups in Representative Courses

Country	Institution and Degree	Economics	Business Economics	Law	Other Social Sciences	Accountancy & Commercial Techniques	Mathematics & Statistics	Foreign Languages	Other Subjects
Turkey —continued	M.E.T.U.: Bachelor of Science (economics option)	50·8–65·1	0·0–9·5	0·0–4·8	4·8–19·0	0·0–4·8	22·2–36·5	7·9–12·7	4·8
	(statistics option)	35·9–40·6	—	0·0–4·7	4·7–15·6	0·0–4·7	31·3–40·6	7·8–12·5	0·0–4·7
United Kingdom	University of Hull: B.A. in economics	38·2–51·2	26·0	0·0–6·5	13·7–20·2	—	9·1–15·6	—	—
	University of Leeds: B.Comm. (accountancy specialization)	34·0	9·4	11·3	0·0–7·5	34·0–41·5	3·8–11·3	—	—
	B.A. in economics	44·9	10·2	—	8·2–32·7	—	4·2–28·7	—	0·0–24·5
	University of Manchester: B.A. (Econ.) (economics specialization)	40·3	—	—	26·9–41·7	0·0–14·8	9·0–23·8	—	—
	B.A. (Econ.) (economics and social statistics specialization)	27·0	—	—	28·6–34·9	0·0–6·3	38·1–44·4	—	—
	University of Oxford: B.A. in philosophy, politics, and economics[9]	26·9–46·3	—	—	19·4–39·0	—	0·0–7·4	0·0–7·4	26·9–46·3

CHAPTER 5

Methods of University Teaching

Teaching in higher education can be given in a wide variety of ways, ranging from the formal lecture attended by several hundred students to the informal tutorial class for as few as six students, and sometimes fewer (one, in certain United Kingdom universities). There is, however, a basic distinction between formal lecture instruction and less formal group instruction. In the latter students can and, indeed, are expected to participate, whereas in the formal lecture their rôle is just to listen to the lecturer, and absorb the information he gives. In a sense the distinction can be seen as one between student-centred and subject-centred instruction. Group instruction is more concerned with evoking a positive response from the student, and ensuring that he actively benefits from the educational process, while lecture instruction offers information to students on a 'take it or leave it' basis. Although this distinction can be made, the character both of lectures, and to a greater extent of group instruction, depends on the numbers of students involved. Lectures may be sufficiently small to enable students to participate at least to the extent of asking questions, and the lecturer to gauge accurately the response of his audience—even of each member in it—and to regulate his teaching accordingly. Group instruction, on the other hand, can be for such a large group that it is in essence little different from a lecture and denies the individual student the chance of any real participation.

The relationship between lecture and group instruction is a complex one, and indeed can vary significantly from institution to institution. It may be useful to outline some alternative forms the relationship may take. Group teaching may reinforce the lecture by reiterating points and dealing with any difficulties students have in understanding the material presented in the lecture. Alternatively group instruction may extend the lecture by building on what students have already learnt, or parallel the lecture course, teaching the students the same material but in a different and less formal way, and in some cases giving the student the opportunity to do written work related to the lecture series. It is, however, also possible for group instruction to be independent of any lecture course. In the extreme case (the University of Oxford, for example) it may be the dominant element in instruction supplemented or enlivened by a few lectures. In some cases lecture classes can replace formal lectures (as is the trend in the Swedish universities). Group instruction can be concerned with the discussion of the current research work of students or staff, as in the traditional German seminar. It is also used to train students in the application of techniques, in mathematics or statistics, for example, or to give them the opportunity for laboratory work in subjects where the formal lecture might be irrelevant. Group instruction can also be used to provide an orientation to the university, and in particular to working methods in higher education, or can enable students to undertake joint research projects.

As well as this wide variety of functions group instruction can take many different forms, including seminars, lecture-classes (that is, lectures where students can ask and may be asked questions), practical classes where exercises are done and discussed, and tutorial-classes where written work done by students is discussed. In Table 5.1 an attempt is made to give some idea of the total amount of instruction at various representative institutions[1] and its distribution between lectures and group instruction. Group instruction, for the purposes of the table, includes all non-lecture instruction. Table 5.1 has been based on the information that was available from university documents, supplemented where necessary by estimates. It inevitably relates to instruction *offered*—by no means all students attend all the instruction available to them.

It would be unwise to assume any high degree of correlation between the number of hours of instruction and the level reached by students in different courses. The range in total hours of instruction from rather less than 1000 to over 3000 hours is a result of a number of factors. Apart from the difference in the number of years of the course and the length in the academic year there is considerable variation in the number of hours per week for which instruction is given, which range from ten to thirty. In general there are more hours

---

[1] The table does not include any institutions in Finland, as the necessary information was not available. It also does not necessarily include all economics degree courses or all options in a degree course at the selected institutions, as the aim is to attempt to show representative courses. Further information will be found in the individual country studies.

of instruction in the vocational degrees in business economics in the specialized institutions.

Figures for average amounts of weekly instruction over the course as a whole can cloak very wide differences between average amounts for different years of the course. There is in the majority of institutions—but by no means all—a tendency for the number of hours of instruction per week to decrease as the course progresses and students do an increasing amount of work on their own. More information on this can be found in the individual country studies.

Low average weekly hours of instruction—fifteen hours a week or less—are mainly found in the United Kingdom and other institutions modelled on the British or American tradition (the University of Malta and the Middle East Technical University), and in Sweden. In Austrian universities, too, the average weekly instruction is comparatively low, although here group instruction seems to be given to larger groups than in the United Kingdom. In most of these countries there is a relatively high proportion of instruction in small tutorial classes, and students are expected to carry out a considerable amount of work on their own.

It would appear that the two countries with very high weekly hours of instruction—Greece and Italy, both with more than twenty-five hours a week—rely extensively on lectures as the main means of instruction. They are both countries where the proportion of students attending lectures is reported to be low, and where some university teachers of economics have expressed dissatisfaction with the crowded curriculum.

A number of other questions are raised by the figures for average amounts of instruction. First, as has already been mentioned, the figures represent only instruction offered, and attendance is by no means always obligatory for the student, so the average student may receive amounts of weekly instruction falling far below the average weekly figures shown in Table 5.1. This would, for example, certainly be true in Turkey (except for M.E.T.U.), Greece, Italy, Spain, and France. Another important question is that of the relationship between instruction and the individual work done by the student. The lecture can serve to guide the student in his own study by outlining the subject and indicating the nature of the literature and the type of further study needed. The following sentence from the study plan of the law and economics faculty of the University of Zürich[1] can

---

[1] *Studienpläne der Rechts- und Staatswissenschaftlichen*, Fakultät der Universität Zürich, June 9th, 1956, p. 11.

well illustrate this commonly held attitude: "Die Vorlesungen
können den Studierenden lediglich einen Überblick über die mannig-
fachen wirtschaftlichen Erscheinungen und Probleme geben und sie
zu eigenem Arbeiten anregen." However, where books are in short
supply, either for financial reasons or because of the small specialist
literature in the national language, lectures may be the only effective
way in which a student could gain the necessary knowledge. This may
also be the case where teaching has to be compressed into a brief
period of time. An extreme example of this is the fourth year of the
degree course at the University of Athens, where so much economics
has to be covered in a year that there is insufficient time for students
to read as ideally they should.

The danger of the formal lecture is that students may use it as a
substitute for their own work, and rely too much on merely learning
what the professor has said. The same danger exists in the reliance
not on the lecture, but on what is sometimes in effect the printed
lecture—the professor's textbook or privately produced notes of the
lecture. The dangers of this over-reliance on a single source are
vividly put by the Dean of the faculty of law and economics in Paris:[1]

> Malgré les illusions, l'utilisation d'un seul instrument de
> travail, fût-ce le cours du professeur, n'est ni le meilleur ni le plus
> rapide des moyens de formation. La lecture . . . d'un chapitre ou
> d'un article traitant d'une question . . . d'économie vue au cours
> ou la replaçant dans son cadre historique, sociologique, idéo-
> logique, permet de mieux comprendre, donc de mieux apprendre
> et est amie de la mémoire: être l'homme d'un seul cours ou d'un
> seul livre, c'est ne se servir que d'un œil et renoncer à la vision
> en relief. Au surplus, les études de droit et d'économie sont
> les mêmes en première année de l'enseignement supérieur—
> lequel exclut la récitation, même exacte.

Group instruction normally demands a more immediate response
from the student, though, as has been previously mentioned, this may
not be the case if the group is a very large one. He is more involved in
active work himself during the class, and may well have to prepare
work for the next meeting. In different subjects the amount of work
he needs to do himself will vary: much of the work for the 'technique'
type of subject—e.g., statistics—may be done in the actual class,
whereas if the student has to produce a paper this will clearly need

---

[1] *Guides Officiels de la Faculté de Droit et des Sciences Economiques de Paris:
Licence en Droit, Licence ès Sciences Economiques, Première Année Commune*,
Paris, 1966, pp. iv–v.

more of his time outside the class. (The written work expected of students is discussed more fully in Chapter 6.)

In group instruction the size of the group, as we have already indicated, has a great effect on the type of instruction that can be given and the demands it makes on the individual student. The smaller the group the more chance there is for the teacher to assess each student's capabilities. This is clearly much easier in a group of ten or twenty than it is in a group of fifty. In such a large group it may be possible to note only the extremes—the five to ten best students and the five to ten worst, as is done, for example, at the University of Munich in the recently instituted classes (*Pflichtübungen*). Table 5.1 shows (where information is available) the size of the groups for instruction. Unfortunately, this information is far from complete: even where it is known there are frequently important differences between subjects in the course, and even more commonly between different years. For optional subjects numbers for group instruction in any particular subject can become small even in a university with a large number of students. At some institutions the total number in each year is small —for example, the University of Malta, the University of Iceland, and the Facultés Universitaires at Namur (Belgium)—so that even if group instruction embraced all the students in a particular year of their studies, the group would be small. Where the total group in a course is small, either in a small institution or for a specialist subject in the later part of a degree course, lectures too can become less formal, and in effect correspond much more closely to lecture classes. This could not be shown in Table 5.1.

A form of self-instruction which is not shown in Table 5.1 is the more or less formal group of students (say, 6–12) meeting regularly for discussion. These are encouraged at most Scandinavian institutions. The *Kollokvier* at the Norwegian School of Economics and Business Administration are a good example of this. They are mentioned as an important method of study in the general information which the School publishes in English.[1] The French universities' use of optional classes is similar, but here the groups are definitely led by more advanced students. These *moniteurs* are fourth-year or doctoral students. The French Ministry of Education sets as a norm ten *moniteurs* for 300 students.

While considering these supplementary types of instruction it may also be appropriate to mention the education broadcasts put

---

[1] *Norges Handelshøyskole, General Information* (Bergen, 1965), p. 11.

out for the Paris area by Radio-Faculté de Droit. These are designed primarily for those who for some reason or other cannot come to the university, but are also followed by students registered at the university who use them to supplement the normal instruction, or even as a substitute for actual attendance at lectures. These broadcasts give only a first-year course and do not provide it as fully as the course available at the universities—one hour of radio instruction being equivalent to four and a half hours of university instruction. This one hour is divided into two halves—one for the lecture (which would take three hours a week at the university) and one for the practical work (*travaux dirigés*). Students' work can be corrected, if sent in.

Part-time degrees are also offered at some institutions for those who cannot attend the normal course. The instruction for these is usually in the evening, and degrees normally take longer than their full-time equivalents—for example, at the Queen's University, Belfast, a pass degree in economics has a prescribed length of three years if done full-time, and five if taken part-time. Evening courses may also not offer the full range of choice available to the full-time students. They do, however, enable students to combine a job with study for a degree. Where comparable arrangements are not made students may register for the full-time degree, but have a job at the same time—this is quite common in Italy, Greece, Spain, and Turkey. Countries where these part-time evening degrees are available include Denmark (the Handelshøjskolen), Ireland (University College, Dublin), Italy (the Sacro Cuore University in Milan), the Netherlands (the Netherlands School of Economics), Spain, and the United Kingdom (the London School of Economics, the universities of Belfast and Manchester, among others).

As well as these official kinds of first-degree instruction there is also in some countries purely private supplementary instruction. This is most usual where there is great pressure on university resources, or a high failure rate at examinations. Such instruction is offered privately in a more or less organized way by people who have been, or in some cases still are, connected with universities. In a number of countries university staff are specifically prohibited from teaching privately in this way—this is the case in both Italy and Spain. In Greece these private teachers are even forbidden to enter the Athens Graduate School of Economics and Business Administration. Such instruction has different names and is done on different scales in various countries. Those where it is most common are Austria, France (almost exclusively in Paris), Germany, Greece, Italy, and

Spain. In some cases students may even rely on this type of instruction rather than attend lectures.

An idea of the proportions such instruction may reach in severely overcrowded faculties can be seen from Cologne, where private teachers rent, and fill, cinemas in the mornings for their teaching. In Paris private teaching is advertised in the papers—for example, an advertisement in a Paris paper for private institutions offering concentrated five-week courses for the first and second examinations for the economics *Licence*. Such institutions claim that success needs a method, and go on to enumerate what they offer. Advertisements like this commonly play on the students' fear of failure, and may indeed specifically point out how high failure rates are.

A further important aspect of higher education closely connected with the methods of instruction is the place of textbooks. The part textbooks play in a first-degree course in economics is closely linked not only to the form of teaching used, but also to the type of individual work expected of students, the ability of students to read in languages other than their own, and the availability of books and journals from libraries. Certain textbooks reoccur frequently in reading-lists—particularly Samuelson, Lipsey, and Stonier and Hague. Johnston's text on econometrics is also extremely widely used where this subject is taught. As well as these staple textbooks for introductory courses, it is remarkable how far over a wide range of topics the same books appear on reading-lists for more advanced courses.

Where the formal lecture course is of dominant importance, as in Italy, Greece, Spain, and Turkey, the textbook of the professor who gives the lectures tends to have a dominant importance in students' minds, especially as they prepare for their examinations. In France the use of *polycopiés* (printed or duplicated sets of lecture notes) is a similar phenomenon. In certain countries the reading-lists given in the official programmes of courses would seem to rely largely (and frequently exclusively) on the textbooks written by the professor giving the course. While one appreciates the opportunity thereby given to the students to digest at leisure the ideas propounded in lectures, it would be unfortunate if inadequate university salaries were to lead to misuse of this monopoly power.

Certain textbooks may be specifically set for examinations—as in Sweden, for example, where there is normally a small list of 're-quired' books, followed by a longer list of recommended readings.

While it is possible in universities where there are less than say thirty students in a particular course to refer them directly to mono-graphic and journal literature on a particular topic, this becomes virtually impossible when classes go beyond this size. In addition, the level of instruction up to the first-degree level in the majority of European countries is such that it is increasingly being covered by textbooks, either locally produced or of transatlantic origin. The practice of references to original sources is, however, aided by the production, both commercially and privately at individual univer-sities, of collections of articles which gather together important journal articles in an accessible and convenient form. In those universities where an extended essay or dissertation is part of the degree requirements, this normally involves the students making considerable use of monographic and journal literature.

The range of languages read by students at any particular institu-tion very much affects the textbooks used. Literature, particularly in English, is fairly generally recommended in European countries, particularly for the more advanced first-degree students. Its use is not unexpectedly most widespread in smaller countries whose languages are little known outside their borders: the Scandinavian countries and the Netherlands are important examples of this. Indeed, profes-sional economists in these countries increasingly publish their own work in English, in order to ensure a wider audience. In most other countries it is possible for first-degree students to obtain their degree while doing very little or no reading in languages other than their own. Where formal language instruction is not provided, students may well be expected or encouraged to acquire a reading knowledge of at least one other language, usually English. There is a certain amount of translation of major textbooks, but translation by itself can not normally make available in a country more than a tiny proportion of foreign-language publications. Although no detailed study of the extent of translation of textbooks and monographs was made, it was particularly striking to see how much of the Anglo-Saxon literature was available in Spanish translation. Much of this is published in Latin America, for use there. The extent to which students can and do read books in other European languages has important connections with the possibilities of increased contact and movement between European universities. This point will be further developed in Chapter 9.

Table 5.1

Instruction in the First Degree Course

Country	Institution	Degree	Length of Course (Years)	Weeks in Teaching Year	Average weekly Instruction			Total Hours of Instruction[1]	% Total Instruction in Group	Size of Group (where available)
					Lecture Hours	Group Hours	Total Hours			
Austria[2]	University of Innsbruck	Diplom-Volkswirt	4	30	11·5	3·3	14·8	1770	22·0	50–70
	University of Vienna	Dr. rer. pol.	4	32	12·0	3·0	15·0	960	20·0	40–100
	Hochschule für Welthandel	Diplom-Kaufmann	3	30	15·0	7·3	22·3	2010	32·7	
Belgium	University of Brussels	Licence en Sciences Commerciales et Financiales	4	30	18·6	5·0	23·6	2835	21·2	
	University of Louvain	Licence en Sciences Economiques	5	30	17·0	3·6	20·6	2460	17·9	30 or less
Denmark	University of Aarhus	Candidatus Oeconomices (business economics specialization)	4	32	16·5	2·8	19·3	2464	14·3	
	University of Copenhagen	Candidatus Politices	5½	32	17·0	0·4	17·4	2784	2·3	Whole set
	Handelshøjskolen Copenhagen	Handelshøjskolens Afgangseksamen	3	33	20·3	0·3[3]	20·6	2087	3·9[3]	15 or less
France	All universities	Licence ès Sciences Economiques	4	26	15·3	3·0	18·3	1911	16·3	Varies with university
Germany	Both these show the general pattern, not that of any particular university	Diplom-Kaufmann	4	26	16·5	5·4	21·9	2275	24·6	
		Diplom-Volkswirt	4	26	15·1	3·8	18·9	1963	19·9	

Table 5.1—continued

Instruction in the First Degree Course

Country	Institution	Degree	Length of Course (Years)	Weeks in Teaching Year	Average weekly Instruction			Total Hours of Instruction[1]	% Total Instruction in Group	Size of Group (where available)
					Lecture Hours	Group Hours	Total Hours			
Greece	University of Athens	*Licence* (economics option)	4	27	18·0	7·8	25·8	2781	30·0	100–200
	University of Salonika	*Licence*	4	33	24·0	5·5	29·5	3894	18·6	
Holy See	Gregorian University	*Licence*	3	30	24·0	1·0	25·0	2340	3·8	Total set only 25
Iceland	University of Iceland	*Candidatus Economicus*	4	30	n.a.	n.a.	18·5	2240	n.a.	Total set small about 40
Ireland	National University	B.A. (economics) and B.Comm.	3	25	12·0	2·0	14·0	1050	14·3	
Italy	University of Parma	*Laurea* in economics and commerce	4	21	18·7	11·5	30·2	2541	38·0	30–150
	University of Urbino	*Laurea* in economics and commerce (business specialization)	4	21	16·5	11·6	28·1	2362	41·3	
Malta	Royal University of Malta	Bachelor of Arts (B.A.), Honours in economics	3	30	11·0	2·0	13·0	1170	18·3	1–3

78

Country	Institution	Degree	Length of Course (Years)	Weeks in Teaching Year	Average weekl— Instruction			Total Hours of Instruction[1]	% Total Instruction in Group	Size of Group (where available)
					Lecture Hours	Group Hours	Total Hours			
Netherlands	Free University of Amsterdam	*Doctorandus* (business economics specialization)	5	26	15·2	1·8	17·0	1768	10·3	15
	Netherlands School of Economics	*Doctorandus* 1. General economics specialization	5	28	11·4	5·1	16·5	2310	30·9	
		2. Quantitative (general economics specialization)	5	28	12·3	5·3	17·6	2464	30·0	
Norway	University of Oslo	*Candidatus Oeconomiae*	5	27	9·3[4]	2·7[4]	12·0[4]	1620	22·2	
	Norwegian School of Economics and Business Administration	*Handels-Kandidat*	3½	28	13·5	5·0	18·5	1477	26·9	12–20
Spain	University of Barcelona	*Licence*	5	28	18·2	3·4	21·6	3024	15·7	20–150
Sweden	University of Stockholm	*Filosofisk-Sämhall-vetenskapligexamen (F.P.M.)*	3	28	7–11	3–4	10–15	850	30·0	
	University of Uppsala	*Filosofisk-Kandidatexamen (F.K.)*	3	28	7·5	5·0	12·5	750	40·0	
	Handelshögskolan, Stockholm	*Civilekonom*	3	30	5·8	5·8	11·6	1050	50·0	

Table 5.1—continued

Instruction in the First Degree Course

Country	Institution	Degree	Length of Course (Years)	Weeks in Teaching Year	Lecture Hours	Group Hours	Total Hours	Total Hours of Instruction[1]	% Total Instruction in Group	Size of Group (where available)
Switzerland	University of Geneva	*Licence ès Sciences Economiques*	3	30	11·3	8·0	19·3	1737	41·5	
	University of Zürich	*Lizenz* (economics specialization)	4	30	16·0	3·0	19·0	2277	15·8	
	Hochschule St Gallen	*Lizenz* (economic policy specialization)	4	29	16·7	7·1	23·9	2770	29·8	
Turkey	University of Istanbul	*Licence*	4	30	21·0	2·0	23·0	2760	8·7	Small
	Middle East Technical University (M.E.T.U.)	Bachelor of Science (economics specialization)	4	28	14·0	1·8	15·8	1764	12·0	
United Kingdom	Queen's University, Belfast	Bachelor of Science (economics) pass degree	3	25	n.a.	n.a.	9·3	750	n.a.	5–12
	University of Bristol	Bachelor of Science in social sciences (honours in economics)	3	25	9·3	3·7	13·0	975	28·2	
	University of Manchester	Bachelor of Arts (honours in economics)	3	22	7·0	4·3	11·3	759	38·0	5–30
	University of Newcastle	Bachelor of Arts (honours in economics and accountancy)	3	25	11·0	2·5	13·5	1012	18·5	

(1) Figures in this column have been rounded to the nearest whole number, where necessary.
(2) These figures referred to the degrees which are being superseded. For further details of the new master's degree see country study.
(3) This almost certainly underestimates the seminar element.

CHAPTER 6

Examination Systems and Other Controls

Any higher education system will have some methods of assessing students and deciding which have successfully completed their studies. This chapter will attempt to outline the various controls used in higher education in economics. The principal method is the examination, which can be either oral or written or both, but there are a number of other controls, including attendance requirements, written work, and practical training.

EXAMINATIONS

In general the tradition in Continental universities has been for examinations to be oral. Such oral examining puts a considerable strain on academic staff if there are a large number of students, and to alleviate this problem written preliminary examinations are frequently used as a means of determining which students are ready to take the oral examination. In the British Isles oral examinations have not been as important, and where they are used are normally only for borderline cases. In most countries, however, oral examinations still play a very important part, and in some countries a dominant one. Written examinations vary in length, and may be anything from three to six hours; oral examinations also vary in length, but where time is specified it tends to be about fifteen minutes.

The frequency of examinations also varies: in some institutions they take place at the end of each year, and cover all or almost all the subjects studied in the year. This is usual in Belgium, France, Greece, Italy, Ireland, the Holy See, Spain, in the French-language universities of Switzerland, and in some British universities. Where there are yearly examinations they normally control the students' passage to the next year. Students have in general to pass in all or almost all subjects if they are to proceed to the next year's work, although at some institutions failures in one or more subjects may be carried forward to the next year. An alternative pattern is to have two sets of examinations; this is the case in Belgium, Denmark, Iceland, Malta, the Netherlands, Norway, the German-language Swiss universities, and many of the British universities. The first set are taken at the end of the introductory part of the course, which may be common to a number of specializations, and the final examinations at the end of the degree course. This can be very clearly seen in the Dutch institutions, where there is a very definite division between the *Candidaats* course and the *Doctoraal* course. It is also the pattern that has been adopted in one of the newest European institutions covered by this survey—the Hochschule at Linz—and will be extended generally in Austria.

In some cases these two parts of the course may be used in conjunction with annual examinations. This is the case in Belgium, where there is the division between the *Candidature* and the *Licence*, but examinations take place in all years.

In certain countries there are few examinations until the final set. This was traditionally the case in Germany, where only a few preliminary examinations had to be passed in such subjects as bookkeeping before the final examinations were taken. This is, however, changing, as there is a general tendency to introduce an intermediate examination, or *Vorprüfung*.

In Finland and Sweden there are no formal final examinations. Students at the universities have to accumulate a set number of academic points—six or seven—and when they have acquired these they are entitled to their degree. Examination sessions are frequent, and consist normally of preliminary, written examinations, followed by oral examinations. Each student progresses at his own pace, presenting himself for examination when he feels adequately prepared. Each student has a record-book in which his examination performance is noted. An examination must be passed for each academic point, and a half, one, two, and three points represent successive levels of difficulty. It is sometimes possible to proceed straight to the examination for two points in a subject, thereby by-passing the one-point examination. Half-point courses and examinations are taken only in subsidiary subjects.

Institutions vary in the provisions which they make for examinations to be retaken in case of failure. The general practice is to allow students at least one resitting. A common pattern where examinations are held in June or July is for them to be repeated at the end of the long summer vacation. After the first chance to retake examinations students may be able to resit again. In some institutions, however, this is not permitted—for example, in German, Swiss, and British universities a third attempt is allowed only in exceptional cases. In those cases where further chances to retake failed examinations are permitted these are often dependent on repeating the year's courses, and there may be restrictions on the number of times this may be done; for instance, at the Athens Graduate School the first-year course may not be repeated more than twice. Limits may also be placed on the number of times a student may attempt an examination —in French universities, for example, a candidate is allowed up to four failures, but after that cannot re-register. At the University of Ankara in the faculty of law there is an interesting disincentive against repeated failures: the examination fee is doubled for the second attempt, quadrupled for the third attempt, and so on.

Related to the question of success in examinations is the extent to which a student can compensate for a poor performance, or even a failure in one subject, by a better or excellent performance in another. In institutions where there are individual examinations in each subject separated in time, as in Sweden, such compensation is clearly impossible. Other systems that specify that a student must pass a certain stated number of subject examinations also tend to rule out compensation, either implicitly or explicitly. Systems which have sets of examinations which are given an overall or average mark are the most likely to allow compensation, though this is not necessarily always the case. It may depend on the extent to which these sets of examinations are marked as a unity; if papers are marked individually by separate university teachers who do not co-ordinate their activities such compensation is clearly less likely than if the papers, once marked, are all discussed by a committee. Compensation in general is not, however, a subject on which information is easy to collect, as it is frequently an informal rather than a formal process.

In most countries examination results, and particularly the final degree result where such an overall result exists, are classified. In general four grades seem common: this is, for instance, the case in Belgium, Germany, Italy, Turkey, and the United Kingdom. In some countries numerical marks are used, as in Denmark, France, and the French-language universities of Switzerland, Iceland, and Norway. In Sweden half-points denoting special merit are awarded in addition to the normal academic points—for example, a student studying economics for 2 points could be awarded $2\frac{1}{2}$ points, indicating an especially good performance. There is, however, very little information available as to the distribution of students between the various classes, and although this is perhaps not of great importance for appointments within a country, it may be of greater importance as students move between European countries to take up appointments and pursue post-graduate studies.

At some institutions the final result obtained by a student does not only depend on how he does in a particular set of examinations, but takes into account his cumulative performance, either in class-work during the course or in other examinations. At H.E.C., France, for example, a student's final assessment depends on his performance in tests and examinations throughout the course, each semester's work being allocated an individual weight. The weighted average he maintains is of prime importance. In British universities performance during the course can in principle be taken into account in assessing a student's final result, especially in borderline cases.

In most countries the university teacher who has taught a particular course has primary responsibility for examining students on its contents. In some countries there are boards of examiners or juries who attempt an overall assessment, and on some occasions these include an external examiner from another institution. This latter practice, which is general in English-language universities—the United Kingdom, Ireland, and Malta—helps to ensure comparable standards between institutions with similar courses. There would be considerable problems involved in extending this practice of external examiners on a wider basis because of the absence of boards of examiners, differences in the structure of examinations, and language problems. None the less, if solutions could be found to these problems external examiners on a European-wide basis could be one important way of developing a European academic community.

ATTENDANCE CONTROLS

In addition to examinations, students may be controlled in various other ways during the course. Attendance at certain lectures, seminars, or classes may be compulsory—as, for example, in France, where students must attend the *travaux practiques*, or at some British universities, where lecture attendance is compulsory. The German practice of requiring certificates of participation in certain seminars and classes (*Übungen*) as a prerequisite for the final examination is another way of enforcing attendance. There are some countries, however, where nothing is compulsory except examinations.

DISSERTATIONS

In many institutions a dissertation is required as part of the final examination. This naturally varies in quality and length. A dissertation—*Diplom-arbeit*—is necessary in almost all German-language universities. In Belgium students must submit a *mémoire d'étude*, which is normally of sixty pages or more. In Denmark, at the University of Aarhus, a dissertation and two seminar papers account for a third of the marks in the final Part II examination. Italian universities all require a dissertation, although even in the economics degree not all of these are on a topic in economics, as they can be in almost any of the subjects studied. At the University of Oslo a dissertation is necessary, and it usually takes a student two to four months to write it. In Spain dissertations are not required in the universities, but are at E.S.A.D.E. in Barcelona.

The length of time taken for the preparation of dissertations varies considerably. In some cases in their final form they may be ready for publication as monographs or journal articles. They may well take six months to more than a year to prepare. On the other hand, some institutions—particularly the German-language universities—have a definite time-limit, often of as little as six weeks, on the preparation of dissertations.

OTHER WRITTEN WORK

In institutions where dissertations are not required students may be expected to prepare a number of seminar papers—this is the case in Greece, Iceland, the Netherlands, in Sweden (in any subject studied for more than one academic point), in Switzerland, and at the Gregorian University of the Holy See. Some work is expected at most other institutions. This is especially the case in English-language universities, where written work is an important part of the course, and essays are normally written for tutorial groups. A recent inquiry in the United Kingdom found that 54 per cent of all social-science students (a group including students of economics) submitted written work at least once a week, and 85 per cent at least once a fortnight.

The importance written work plays in the course is related to the staff-student ratio. In universities with relatively low staff-student ratios it would often be difficult to expect written work because of the problems of marking it; for example, at the University of Istanbul, where written work is officially encouraged, severe difficulty is experienced in ensuring that it is marked. Written work tends in some countries to be more important in specialized institutions, with their smaller numbers of students, than in universities. This is, for instance, the case in Spain, and to some extent also in France. Similarly, at the Middle East Technical University, which shares some of the characteristics of the specialized institutions, more written work (five papers per student per quarter) is expected than at the Turkish State universities.

PRACTICAL EXPERIENCE

For some degrees practical industrial or commercial experience is required, in particular for those specializing in business economics. On the whole this requirement is more normal at specialized institutions than at universities. In German universities it is, however, necessary for the *Diplom-Kaufmann*; a period of six or twelve months is stipulated, its length varying with the institution. The German degree of *Diplom-Handelslehrer* requires twelve months' practical experience, and may also involve periods of teaching practice. The *Diplom-Wirtschaftsingenieur* also has a practical experience requirement of from two to twelve months, depending on the institution. In Ireland practical experience is required in connection with commerce degrees at University College, Cork (two months, one at the end of the first and one at the end of the second year), and at Trinity College, Dublin (at least a month). In Sweden the only university where practical work is recommended (though not required) is at Lund, for the *Civilekonom* course. In the United Kingdom practical work is involved in some social-science degrees at the technological universities which have recently been created from the former Colleges of Advanced Technology; at Brunel University, for example, the degree in psychology, sociology, and economics involves a 'sandwich' course for the first three years, with six months working alternating with six months at college, followed in the fourth year by a full year of study. The few universities where combined honours degrees of economics and a modern language are possible (for example, Sussex and Reading) may well entail a year abroad, but this is normally spent in academic rather than industrial work, and usually means a year at a continental European university. At the Gregorian University all students have to participate in a four-week practical project of community development for which they are well prepared, and which they analyse and discuss extensively

afterwards. The University of Louvain, in Belgium, has taken steps to include a two-month period of practical experience for its degree in business economics.

Some universities where no extended period of practical experience is required may include factory visits on which reports have normally to be written as part of the course. This is so, for example, at University College, Dublin, where such visits form part of the business administration course. At the University of Leeds one of the third-year options in the Bachelor of Commerce degree is to undertake a report on a project in a firm. Liège University includes factory visits in the course for its *Licence* in commercial economics.

At the specialized institutions a practical experience requirement is far more general, although not universal. Sometimes a number of periods of work are required; at both H.E.C. and E.S.S.E.C. in France, for example, one month's industrial work is required in the first year, another month in the second with a firm outside France, and a final period in the third year. Experience is either required during the course, as in the example just given, or may be a prerequisite for entry, as in the case of the Finnish Schools. In Norway students have normally spent sixteen to eighteen months in industry or commerce before they start their course at the Handelshøyskole. At I.C.A.D.E., in Madrid, in the sixth year of the course students work in the morning and come back to the School each afternoon to discuss their experiences. This seems a useful way of integrating a course with the real world. Factory visits are fairly usual in courses in specialized institutions, often in addition to periods of practical work.

At Tilburg students are required to work for six weeks in the Economic and Social Institute assisting with research work. Similarly, at the Netherlands School in Rotterdam work in a research institute is suggested as a possible alternative to work in an industrial firm.

Where no period of practical work is required or recommended students may very well acquire such experience as the result of financial necessity. In some countries—notably Italy—it is quite common for students to have jobs during the academic year, and in almost all countries it is normal for students to take jobs in the summer vacation. It is appropriate here to note the excellent scheme organized by A.I.E.S.E.C.[1] whereby periods of work in foreign countries are arranged for economics students. Some more detailed

---

[1] Association Internationale des Etudiants en Sciences Economiques et Commerciales.

figures on the use made of this scheme by students of the various European countries will be given in Chapter 9.

THE FUNCTION OF EXAMINATIONS

Having outlined the main kind of academic controls, it may be useful to consider in rather more detail the rôle and purpose of examinations, since these are in many ways the most important assessing element in the structure of control. Examinations, if they do nothing else, provide a stimulus to work. It is important, however, to ensure that this stimulus to work for examination purposes does not militate against true academic work. There is a danger that having to master information for mainly factual examinations will interrupt the reflection and the acquisition of the techniques of analysis so essential to the economist. Here, clearly, the frequency and type of examination must be considered, and in written examinations the type of examination question and the number of questions to be answered during the time-period. There may well be—indeed, there almost certainly is—a difference in the kind of written examination suitable in the subjects which are the tools of economics (for example, mathematics, statistics, or languages) and economics itself. In the 'tool' subjects the kind of knowledge required—the ability to use the tool adequately and accurately, the reading knowledge of a foreign language, and so on—can be measured by examinations. In such examinations, in so far as they are a test of ability rather than of memory, it may be appropriate to allow books to be consulted in written examinations. This is perhaps particularly relevant in language examinations, as in general in later life an economist reading, say, an article in a foreign-language journal will usually need the dictionary for the occasional word. The successful passing of 'tool' examinations, whether 'open book' or conventional, will, however, have little meaning unless the tool once mastered is used.

In economics itself it is more difficult to say exactly what examinations are measuring. It is not only the factual material a student has acquired, but also, and probably more importantly, the way he can use the facts he knows.

In general, examinations measure a student's progress, both for his own information and for that of the teaching staff. Fairly frequent examinations may be essential where student numbers are large and there is little personal academic contact between staff and students. Examinations may well have to serve also as a selection process where entry to university is not selective but open to all with a minimum qualification. Study of the figures for the number of students in the first and second year (taking growth of numbers into account) at a number of institutions reveals the extent to which the first year is used as a selective year.

Of all aspects of their higher education in economics, it is probably in the type of examinations used that there are the widest differences between different European countries. This is not necessarily to suggest that the quality of graduates varies because of differences in the form of examination, but rather that it is a subject on which there could usefully be further comparative research. Different national examination systems clearly vary in the amount of time and effort required from the university teacher for their administration. They also probably vary as far as the criteria they employ, implicitly, to assess the student, and almost certainly in their technical efficiency in carrying out this assessment. There is a built-in, if irrational, assumption in most universities that their own particular system is preferable, if not optimal. While one realizes that it would be impossible, even if it were desirable, to introduce a uniform system of examinations throughout Europe, it would be useful to establish what were the objectives of alternative systems and what were their respective costs and benefits (and to whom such costs and benefits accrued). Such a study would at least make apparent the variety of systems, and oblige those who are responsible for at least some of them to re-examine the principles upon which they are based.

CHAPTER 7

University Teachers of Economics

TOTAL NUMBERS

It is extremely difficult, if not impossible, to give any satisfactory estimate of total numbers of university teachers of economics in the countries covered by this survey. Statistics of the number of teachers of economics, as distinct from all those who teach students of economics (who may include teachers of law, sociology, mathematics, etc.) are hard to obtain. There are also certain university teachers of economics who teach students specializing in subjects other than economics, and are therefore not included in this study. The numbers of the junior ranks of university teachers are particularly difficult to obtain.

Given these two important provisos, and also that the structure of university posts varies widely from country to country,[1] Table 7.1 attempts to give some indication of the numbers of university teachers in the different countries. As numbers themselves without information as to the normal weekly hours of teaching expected tell us little, the table also includes some information on this. Those staff listed as part-time are those officially recognized in the country as part-time staff. In many cases the 'full-time' members of staff will also have considerable outside commitments, but at least in principle their university work is their chief employment. In some countries there are differences between different institutions in the amount of work expected of the various grades of staff; in these cases more than one figure is given in the table. The figures in all cases refer to the most recent year for which numbers were available.

STAFF-STUDENT RATIOS

In view of the very unreliable nature of the figures for the total number of university teachers, the variations in teaching load, and the fact that in many cases the student numbers (see Chapter 2, Table

---

[1] *cf.* "Structure of University Staff", *Education in Europe*, I–3, 1966.

2.3) are also estimates, calculations of staff-student ratios for each country have not been attempted. It would in any case be somewhat misleading to prepare statistics of this sort for higher education, because unlike primary and secondary education (where there is a high degree of similarity between the nature of education in different countries, and where statistics for the number of pupils and teachers represent comparable units) in higher education one would be comparing very disparate situations. As has been seen in Chapter 2, student numbers are inflated in some countries by students who register at the university with no intention of serious study, and, as will be seen in this chapter, there are a number of problems in assessing the appropriate way of satisfactorily measuring the staff of a given institution, particularly in a subject like economics, where there are a number of part-time university teachers and full-time university teachers with substantial responsibilities outside the university. It may be possible to do this in terms of hours of staff-time, but figures for this are not available on a comparable basis.

It is worth noting, however, that in a few countries norms are officially laid down for staff-student ratios. In France the Ministry of Education has a standard of six professors, four *maîtres assistants* and *chargés de cours*, and ten *moniteurs* for every 300 students, but in practice these norms are not yet realized. In Sweden there is a rule whereby the number of teachers authorized by the State expands automatically with the number of students on the basis of class size. The number of staff required is worked out from the student numbers, given a set size of class. In the Netherlands a staff-student ratio of 1:12 is laid down by the authorities, but in this context staff is interpreted very widely to include the clerical and service staff. The development of such norms on a national basis may be useful if there is a high degree of homogeneity between institutions. Until there is a considerably greater similarity of higher education between countries it would be foolish to try to suggest any international norms. It is in any case difficult to know how one would interpret any divergence from an international norm. A higher than average staff-student ratio could imply either a higher quality of education or a less efficient use of resources. The ratio between the number of teachers of economics and the number of students of economics would also, in any case, vary according to the share of economics within the students' programme of instruction. As has been seen in Chapter 4, this varies considerably between countries, and in some cases within countries.

UNIVERSITY WORK

Table 7.1 gives an idea of the amount of formal teaching expected of university staff in different countries. On the whole, professors are expected to spend from three to seven hours on lectures and seminars, with rather more being expected of other full-time staff. In many countries part-time staff are of considerable importance. They tend to be used more in the specialized institutions, since in so far as these retain a vocational character it is particularly valuable for students to be taught, at least in part, by those who are actually working in industry and commerce.

The type of teaching expected from university staff also varies by grade. In many countries lecture teaching is primarily given by professors, while junior teachers assist with less formal instruction and individual study guidance.

An important part of the university teacher's work is examining. The extent of this varies, as does the nature of the work, depending on the frequency and type, written or oral, of the examinations and the number of students. Where oral examinations are important they may take up a considerable amount of a professor's time. At the Amsterdam Free University, for example, a professor can expect to have about seventy hours of oral examining a year, while in Switzerland a professor probably spends some twenty-five hours a semester conducting oral examinations. In Italy oral examinations also take a great deal of time, often more for a professor than his actual teaching commitments. Where written examinations are used, junior teachers tend to do a larger share of the marking. Where dissertations are required, as in Belgium, Italy, and Germany, non-professorial staff often do most of the supervision of them.

As well as teaching and examining, there is also research. The rôle of this in a university teacher's life varies from country to country. In many countries research is done in institutes within the department or otherwise attached to the university. In some cases research facilities and assistance are available only through these institutes, and are not provided by the faculty. These institutes may provide an efficient place for team research to be done or they may merely provide the professor with staff and an office, primarily as a base for his private consultancy. However, they are in principle likely to be better for research than is the older tradition of a scholar working alone in libraries, with perhaps an assistant or two available.

The amount of assistance available, both for research and for administrative work, varies very much. Where universities have traditionally been teaching rather than research institutions, as, for example, in Spain or Switzerland, professors may well not even have their own offices or individual secretaries. In the United Kingdom, on the other hand, professors invariably have their own offices and secretaries, while the other members of staff have offices (the more junior may have to share) and some access (though the extent of this varies) to secretarial services. In many countries there are difficulties in getting adequate clerical and research facilities because of the salaries paid. In Greece, for example, it is extremely difficult to get research assistants because the pay is considerably less than that earned elsewhere.

NON-UNIVERSITY WORK

It is fairly usual for at least the more senior university teachers to have considerable non-university commitments which may be paid or unpaid. Professors act as consultants to Governments and private firms in many countries. Outside work is perhaps most extensive in Greece, Italy, and Spain, where much of the work is private, but in the Scandinavian countries, the Netherlands, and the U.K., for instance, senior university staff often have outside commitments, frequently as Government advisers. Outside research institutes also take up the time of university staff. In a few countries—notably Austria and Italy—professors tend to give courses at more than one institution. Indeed, the University of Urbino has an ingenious two-week pattern of instruction which enables the fullest use to be made of commuting professors, who in their free week may teach at other universities or do consultancy work in Rome.

In very few universities are staff prohibited from undertaking outside work, though the university's permission may have to be gained before it is undertaken. At the Middle East Technical University there is in principle no outside work, but salaries are considerably higher than in the Turkish State Universities to compensate for this. Similar provisions providing additional payments for those university teachers who agree not to undertake outside work exist in certain other universities.

RECRUITMENT

There are two general problems which affect recruitment in many countries—the comparative shortages of trained economists and the competitive demand for them from industry and government. In many countries economics is a growing subject, and increasing student numbers make more staff necessary, but it is becoming increasingly difficult to find good staff, especially when rewards may not be commensurate with those obtainable in non-academic life.

In countries where university professorships are usually combined with extensive consultancy it may be particularly difficult to recruit staff in provincial universities; in Spain, for example, there are difficulties in getting professors in Barcelona and Bilbao, although it is easy in Madrid. In both France and Italy there is a strong tendency for professors to live in the principal cities and commute to lecture in the provincial universities where they hold their Chairs.

Another factor affecting recruitment is the extent to which there is a reasonably secure career structure in university teaching. In Spain it has recently been found necessary to create a new intermediate grade between that of professor and that of assistant. In Sweden, too, the full-time intermediate teaching grades have been developed. Countries vary as to whether qualification for the higher grades of university teaching, especially professorships, is formal and reached by special examinations or other competitions, as for example in France, Italy, and Germany, or whether the process is informal. The latter is the situation in the United Kingdom, where there are no specific qualifications for professorships, and, indeed, the report of the Robbins Committee on Higher Education goes as far as to say, "We hope that the notion that to hold a doctorate is an essential qualification for every applicant for a university post will never become established in this country."[1]

THE HIERARCHY

The relationship between the different grades of university teachers varies considerably from country to country. In many countries the professor has a basically autocratic relationship to other grades—this is especially the case where there is no very well-defined career structure, and where junior posts tend to be part-time, or as research assistantships dependent on an individual professor. Although obviously the professor has always a senior standing in a university, in those countries where his non-professorial colleagues have security of tenure and clearly defined responsibilities the

---

[1] *Report of the Committee on Higher Education*, London, H.M.S.O., Cmnd. 2154, 1963, p. 101.

relationship will become more one of *primus inter pares*. The relative standing of the different grades of university staff affects teaching, examining, and research. Although this is, of course, a general problem affecting all subjects, it would seem to be of particular importance in economics, where, the alternative rewards available outside the university being relatively greater, assistants may be less willing to accept a traditional subordinate rôle.

Table 7.1

Estimated Numbers of University Teachers and the Hours of Work

(The figures in brackets refer to expected minimum weekly hours of formal teaching)

Country	Estimated Numbers of Staff				Notes
	Professors	Part-time Professors	Other Staff		
			Full-time	Part-time	
Austria	31 (7)	—	70		
Belgium	53 (6)		22	2	
Denmark	29 (4–8)	16 (4)	52 (4–6)	23 +	Professors at the universities are expected to teach for 4 hours a week, but at the Schools of Economics 4–8 are expected. At the schools there are many part-time instructors —23 at Aarhus and more at Copenhagen. Students are used at the universities to help with 1st-year teaching, and there are also in the University of Copenhagen many part-time staff, mainly from Government departments.
Finland	14 (6)		21 (5–10) (or 24)	10 (2)	These figures apply only to the universities. Lecturers, of whom there are 3, are expected to teach for 5–10 hours a week and assistant lecturers to undertake educational duties for 24 hours a week, this to include such things as giving study guidance. There are in the Schools of Economics and Business Administration a further 229 teachers.

Country	Estimated Numbers of Staff				Notes
	Professors	Part-time Professors	Other Staff Full-time	Other Staff Part-time	
France	c100 (3)		c400 (3 or (7½)	c550	All these figures are estimates and cover only the universities. *Chargés-de-cours* and *maîtres de conférence* (of whom there are some 100) are expected to do 3 hours' teaching a week, while other full-time staff are expected to do 7½ hours. The part-time staff includes many *moniteurs*, usually final-year students.
Germany	226 (6–10) of which 40 vacant			81 (2)	There are also large numbers of *Lehrbeauftragten* (at least 180) and Assistants (at least 374), of whom 2–4 hours work is expected. The figures for other part-time teachers cover only *Privatdozenten* and extraordinary professors, whom it is not possible to separate.
Greece	20 (6)				There are also assistants whose exact responsibilities vary.
The Holy See			5 (4–5)		The Institute has a total staff of 11, but only 5 are economists.
Iceland	3 (1–9)			7 (2–4)	

Table 7.1—continued
Estimated Numbers of University Teachers and the Hours of Work
(The figures in brackets refer to expected minimum weekly hours of formal teaching)

Country	Professors	Part-time Professors	Other Staff Full-time	Other Staff Part-time	Notes
Ireland	5 (8–10)	2	17 (8–10)	1 (4–5)	
Italy	486 (3)		1548 (7–10)		For professors there is some double counting, as some professors teach in more than one university. Each professor is allowed 2 full-time assistants for every 40 students plus 'voluntary' assistants with whom the professor may make a private financial arrangement.
Malta	3 (7)		1 (5)	4 (2–3)	
Netherlands	35 (4–8)	21 (2–4)	21 (6)	7 (2)	
Norway	22 (4–5)		35 (5, 6.) (or 8)	33	Professors in the university are expected to teach for 4 hours a week, and those at the school for 5. *Dozents* (11 of the 35 other full-time staff) are expected to do 5 hours, *lektors* (23) 6 hours in the university and 8 hours in the school.
Spain	35 (4–5), of which 14 are vacant				There are also professors agrege (a newly created intermediate grade) and assistants; and professors of economics in the faculties of law.

Country	Estimated Numbers of Staff				Notes
	Professors	Part-time Professors	Other Staff		
			Full-time	Part-time	
Sweden	25 (4)		56		Some of the other full-time staff are *lektors*, of whom 12 hours a week instruction is expected, and some assistants who do 1000 hours a year general duties (administration and teaching). There are also part-time assistant teachers who do 6 hours a week.
Switzerland	56 (6–8)	37	147		These figures are underestimates, as they include no figures for Ankara. The grades of the M.E.T.U. staff are also unknown, so all have been included in full-time other staff. There are also assistant teachers.
Turkey	7 (4)		15 (4)		
United Kingdom	100		700 (7–8)		These figures are estimates. On average 7–8 hours teaching is expected, but less for professors, readers, and assistant lecturers.

CHAPTER 8

The Infrastructure of Higher Education

This chapter discusses various points related to the provision of physical facilities and equipment for study and research in universities. Those aspects of this provision specifically discussed will be the question of lecture-rooms, libraries, and the access to and use of computers by members of economics faculties.

LECTURE-ROOMS

The problem of lecture-room accommodation is a general one in a period of rising student numbers. It is inevitably more acute in the very large faculties—those, that is, with an annual intake of a thousand or more. In many of these there would not be enough room for all the students if they were ever all to decide to attend lectures. In a few cases this has led to the introduction of a shift system, as at the University of Paris, where first-year lectures are given in three shifts—there is a morning group, an afternoon group, and a recently introduced suburban group. The latter do not even come to the main faculty, but are taught some way away from the main university. The morning and afternoon shifts both use the main faculty lecture-rooms, but courses are given separately for each group. Pressure of numbers and the consequent demands of universities for more accommodation are also leading to consideration of the possibility of the more intensive use of the universities' capital plant. For instance, in the U.K. the possibility of introducing a four-term year is under discussion. Students and staff would continue to work the traditional three-term year, but in shifts (probably two of them), so that the university building would be used throughout the year. In Sweden similar proposals are being considered for a three-semester year.

The patterns of use of existing accommodation naturally vary not only from country to country but also from institution to institution.

At some institutions the afternoons are used for lectures, at others they are not. Saturdays also are days used for teaching at some institutions but not at others. These differences in use patterns are, however, an aspect of general university organization and are not peculiar to economics, so that a further discussion has not been included in this study.

LIBRARIES

It is possible to distinguish three aspects of the function of university libraries. They are firstly research tools for university staff and advanced students, both for their individual research and for lecture and other teaching preparation. Secondly, they are sources of books to which students have been referred by their teachers. Thirdly, they provide space in which students can study. This last aspect of their use, related as it is to the adequacy of student housing, the existence of other study rooms, and the physical size and arrangements of the library, falls into the general sphere of university accommodation. It is not discussed further here, as it is by no means peculiar to economics.

The extent to which students use the library as part of their studies depends a great deal on the type of teaching instruction, and in particular on the stress laid on textbooks (see Chapter 5). Where the course depends on relatively few textbooks, students can reasonably be expected to buy them, as libraries can never provide more than a limited number of basic textbooks. In courses where wider reading of the literature is expected, and particularly when students are required to write papers, libraries are of far greater importance. Here rising student numbers make adequate provision increasingly difficult.

An interesting idea is put forward by the dean of the faculty of law and economics in Paris when he suggests to first-year students:[1] "Si vous savez former de petits groupes coopératifs de cinq ou six membres, vous pourrez constituer, pour quelques dizaines de francs à la charge de chacun, une petite bibliothèque de base à la disposition de participants." Such co-operation doubtless occurs elsewhere, but it seems useful to make this suggestion to students in introductory guides of this character.

---

[1] *Guides Officiels de la Faculté de Droit et des Sciences Economiques de Paris: Licence en Droit et Licence ès Sciences Economiques—Première Année Commune*, Paris, 1966, p. v.

No systematic survey of general library facilities was carried out during the preparation of this study, but during the visits made to over fifty institutions some general impressions were obtained. Although many extremely fine collections of the literature of economics exist, there are some universities, particularly those in Southern Europe, where these are not generally available to students. This is frequently a problem related to the number of students and shortage of space, but it seems unfortunate that there should be universities where first-year students are forbidden general access to the university library.

As an indication of the level of various libraries as research tools, a special study was made of library holdings of selected economic journals. This survey was partly carried out while visiting the various countries and partly by subsequent postal inquiries. In all about one hundred questionnaires were issued, and replies were received covering eighty institutions. They are listed in Table 8.1. All countries were to some extent covered, except the Holy See and Iceland, from whom no returns were received. It will be seen from Table 8.1 that in some cases returns have been merged when one or more other libraries were accessible to students in addition to the library or libraries of their own institution. An example of this is Norway, where students of the University of Oslo have access to the library of the Central Bureau of Statistics. When carrying out the survey efforts were made to include all relevant libraries in the institutions themselves. No special note has therefore been made in Table 8.1 on the number of libraries included within each institution. It may be that in some universities where there are a number of subsidiary libraries in research institutes the survey may have under-represented the overall holdings.

The idea of the survey was to attempt to measure in some reasonably simple way the comparative holdings of libraries, and in particular to see to what extent institutions subscribed to journals in languages other than their own. The survey was concerned with journals rather than books, partly because it was much easier to make out a reasonably comprehensive list of leading economics journals than it would be to make up a similar and generally acceptable list of books, and partly because journals are of great importance to the university teacher and research student, if not, perhaps, to the less advanced student. The level of journal holdings can also, perhaps, be treated as being related to the general level of library holdings. A library that takes few of the journals is unlikely to have a very good book-stock. The survey did not take into account the age of holdings of the various journals at each institution; an institution that had just begun to receive a journal and another which had all the past issues of the same journal were treated equally.

The list contained altogether thirty-eight journals. For purposes of analysis these were divided into seven groups on the basis of the language in which they appeared and their country of origin. These groups, and the actual journals included in the survey, are shown in Table 8.2. One journal changed both its name and the primary language in which it was published during the course of the survey. This was the *Ekonomisk Tidskrift*, now the Swedish *Journal of Economics*. It has been left with the Scandinavian group, but its changed name may have meant that in some of the later returns it failed to be included, even though it was being received by the institution under its new name.

Table 8.2 also shows the actual number of institutions, out of a maximum of eighty, receiving each individual journal. In this, as in the next table, the nature of the sample should be borne in mind. Coverage was considerably better for some countries than for others (see Table 8.3)—thus in Finland, Malta, and Norway there was 100 per cent coverage, while in other countries coverage was less extensive. France, Germany, and Italy in particular are somewhat under-represented in the survey. However, an attempt was made to include a representative group of institutions in each country, though inevitably in some cases this was defeated by the failure of the institutions initially selected to return the questionnaire. On the whole, though, the library staffs of the various institutions were most prompt and thorough in their replies; more so, indeed, than their teaching colleagues.

Tables 8.3 shows the percentages of journals in each group held in each country. As can easily be seen, this is usually nearest 100 per cent in the journals published in the country's own language. An interesting point that emerges from the table is the extent to which English-language journals (with the exception of those from the Commonwealth and South Africa) are taken throughout Europe. The international group of journals, primarily in English, are also very widely taken in the institutions surveyed. Further study of Table 8.1 indicates the relative popularity of the individual journals within each group.

The average number of journals held was twenty-four. Countries where the average holding was above this were Belgium, Italy,

Netherlands, Norway, Sweden, and Switzerland. The Italian picture is probably over-favourable, as the institutions included were almost certainly rather above the average for the country. As far as the other countries are concerned, the picture is fair, though the Swiss average is improved by the inclusion of various international libraries in Geneva. Countries with noticeably lower averages were Austria, Greece, Ireland, and Malta. In the case of the last it should be pointed out that only very recently has a full degree course in economics been offered, and in addition there are no post-graduate students.

There is often considerable variation between institutions within the same country. In the United Kingdom, for example, the range is from as low as fifteen at the University of Durham to as high as thirty-seven at the London School of Economics. In some cases differences are presumably related to differences in function. In Spain, for example, the library of I.C.A.D.E., a specialized institution, is markedly inferior to those at the two universities included.

COMPUTERS

On the whole computers are not much used by economics faculties. There tends to be more interest in teaching students how to programme in the specialized institutions than in the universities. Computers are primarily used as a research tool; students are in general not taught how to use them.

As in general there is little interest in computers at the moment, this account will merely mention briefly some of the interesting developments in European economics faculties. In countries which are not mentioned my impression is that computers are little used, mainly because work in economics is non-quantitative or largely theoretical.

Courses on computers are almost never compulsory. There is a compulsory first-year course for all economics students at the University of Essex (U.K.) in which students are given a general introduction to computer-programming languages, and taught to programme in Algol. At the Catholic School of Economics, Tilburg (the Netherlands), a course on the working of computers is recommended for all students, but is compulsory only for students specializing in econometrics. This is also the case at the Netherlands School of Economics, Rotterdam.

Courses in computer-programming are more generally available in the Schools of Economics outside the universities (*e.g.*, in Denmark at the Copenhagen and Aarhus Schools, in Finland at Kauppakor-keakoulu, Helsinki, in Switzerland at the Hochschule St Gallen, and in Germany at the technical universities and high schools).

There are optional courses at some universities—Basle, the University of Iceland, the Middle East Technical University (Turkey), the Gregorian University (the Holy See), and the University of Keele (U.K.). At Keele, where students must take four subjects, at least one a science subject, students can take computer science to satisfy this requirement, and do a year's course leading to an examination, part of which is practical, involving actual use of the computer to solve problems.

Many universities do not yet have computers, though some which do not have one of their own have access to one; for example, the Gregorian University in the Holy See has access to an I.B.M. 1620 computer, and the University of Oslo has access to the computer in the Norwegian National Institute of Statistics. In the United Kingdom most universities already have computers, and it is Government policy that all should. In Turkey the Faculty of Economics at Istanbul has an I.B.M. 1620. E.S.A.D.E. in Barcelona had plans for a computer in its new extension.

With the growing interest in quantification in economics it would seem increasingly important that students should not merely acquire a theoretical statistical and econometric training, but also have an opportunity to practise these techniques before leaving the university. In the same way as one would not allow a dentist to qualify without having demonstrated his competence to use the techniques he has been taught at the theoretical level, so our applied economist will require to have a knowledge not only of the theory of multiple regression but also of how to put a problem using multiple regression techniques through a computer.

Table 8.1

Institutions whose Library Holdings of Periodicals were included in the Survey

Country	Institutions included	No. of Journals held (Maximum 38)
Austria	University of Vienna	23
	Hochschule für Welthandel, Vienna	16
Belgium	University of Brussels	22
	University of Ghent	25
	University of Liège	24
	University of Louvain	30
Denmark	University of Aarhus	29
	University of Copenhagen	20
	Handelshøjskolen, Copenhagen	17
	Central Library, Copenhagen	30
Finland	University of Åbo (including the holdings of the Åbo School)	26
	University of Helsinki	23
	University of Tampere	24
	University of Turku	21
	Helsinki School of Economics	29
	Swedish School of Economics, Helsinki	14
	Turku School of Economics	13
France	University of Bordeaux (including the holdings of the Institut d'Economie Régionale du Sud-Ouest, Bordeaux)	26
	University of Grenoble	21
	University of Lyons	16
	University of Paris	31
	University of Strasbourg	16
	H.E.C. (Ecole des Hautes Etudes Commerciales)	17
Germany	Free University of Berlin	26
	Technical University of Berlin	23
	University of Bonn	27
	University of Erlangen-Nürnberg	18
	University of Göttingen	24
	University of Hamburg	27
	University of Marburg	30
	University of Saarbrücken	29
	Wirtschaftshochschule, Mannheim	17

Country	Institutions included	No. of Journals held (Maximum 38)
Greece	University of Athens	20
Ireland	University College, Cork Trinity College, Dublin	9 19
Italy	Bocconi University, Milan Sacro Cuore University, Milan University of Parma University of Rome University of Turin University of Urbino (at Ancona)	32 33 22 26 25 24
Malta	Royal University	16
Netherlands	Handels-Economische Bibliotheek, Amsterdam University of Groningen Netherlands School of Economics, Rotterdam Catholic School of Economics, Tilburg	 32 27 19 31
Norway	University of Oslo (also including holdings of the Central Bureau of Statistics, Oslo) Norwegian School of Economics, Bergen	 31 19
Spain	University of Barcelona University of Madrid I.C.A.D.E., Madrid	28 30 10
Sweden	University of Gothenburg University of Lund University of Uppsala Stockholm School of Economics	17 32 26 34
Switzerland	University of Basle University of Geneva (including also the holdings of the I.L.O. and U.N. Libraries and of the Institut des Hautes Etudes Internationales) University of Zürich Hochschule St Gallen	26 36 25 23

Table 8.1—continued

Institutions whose Library Holdings of Periodicals were included in the Survey

Country	Institutions included	No. of Journals held (Maximum 38)
Turkey	University of Istanbul	27
	Middle East Technical University, Ankara	20
United Kingdom	University of Bradford	23
	University of Bristol	26
	University of Cambridge (Marshall Library)	34
	University of Durham	15
	University of Exeter	25
	University of Keele	24
	University of Lancaster	20
	University of Leeds	23
	University of London—London School of Economics	37
	University of London—Senate House Library	19
	University of Manchester	27
	University of Oxford	36
	University of Sussex	26
	University of Wales—Aberystwyth	21
	University of Wales—Cardiff	22
	University of St Andrews	14
	University of Glasgow	25
	University of Strathclyde	20
	Queen's University, Belfast	23

Table 8.2

Journals included in the Survey

Group	Journals included	No. of Libraries holding each[1]
1. English– U.S.A. (6 journals)	*American Economic Review*	78
	Economic Development and Cultural Change	49
	Journal of Political Economy	73
	Quarterly Journal of Economics	78
	Review of Economics and Statistics	73
	Southern Economic Journal	35
2. English– U.K. (7 journals)	*Bulletin of the Oxford University Institute of Statistics*	49
	Economic Journal	80
	Economica	79
	Journal of Industrial Economics	47
	Manchester School of Economic and Social Studies	58
	Oxford Economic Papers	69
	Review of Economic Studies	73
3. English– Common- wealth and S. Africa (4 journals)	*Canadian Journal of Economics and Political Science*	51
	Economic Record	39
	Indian Economic Journal	26
	South African Journal of Economics	26
4. French (4 journals)	*Economie Appliquée*	53
	Revue d'Economie Politique	61
	Revue Economique	48
	Revue Economique et Sociale	18
5. German (5 journals)	*Jahrbücher für Nationalökonomie und Statistik*	48
	Schweizerische Zeitschrift für Volkswirtschaft und Statistik	37
	Weltwirtschaftliches Archiv	64
	Zeitschrift für die gesamte Staatswissenschaft	44
	Zeitschrift für Nationalökonomie	44
6. Inter- national (5 journals)	*Econometrica*	79
	International Economic Review	48
	International Monetary Fund Staff Papers	60
	Journal of Economic Abstracts	63
	Kyklos	75

Table 8.2—continued
Journals included in the Survey

Group	Journals included	No. of Libraries holding each
7. Italian (3 journals)	*Economia Internazionale*	47
	Giornale degli Economisti e Annali di Economia	37
	Rassegna Economica	15
8. Scandinavian (4 journals)	*Economisk Tidskrift (Swedish Journal of Economics)*	31
	Nationaløkonomisk Tidsskrift	22
	Økonomi	14
	Statsøkonomisk Tidsskrift	20

Notes for Table 8.2

(1) The maximum is 80. Libraries in or accessible to one institution have been merged as far as possible.

Notes to Table 8.3

(1) This number is the number of journals in the group.
(2) The base (100 per cent) for each cell equals the number of journals in the group multiplied by the number of institutions sampled in the country. For example, in the first cell in this column it is 12 (English–U.S.A. group 6 journals x Austria 2 institutions in survey).
(3) These are not the same 4 as the 4 in the previous column as they include the Central Library, Copenhagen (accessible to students from both the University and the Handelshøyskolen of Copenhagen), and do not include the Handelshøyskolen at Aarhus.
(4) This covers 8 of the institutions in Finland, as the University of Åbo and the School of Economics attached to it were treated as one for the purposes of this part of the survey.
(5) As the Handels-Economische Bibliotheek in Amsterdam serves both the Municipal and the Free University, all 5 institutions were covered.

Table 8.3
Proportion of Journals in each Group held by the Libraries sampled in each Country

Country	Total No. of Institutions	No. of Institutions in Survey	English			French (4)	German (5)	International (5)	Italian (3)	Scandinavian (4)	Total (38)
			U.S.A. (6)[1]	U.K. (7)	Common- wealth and S. Africa (4)						
			% [2]	%	%	%	%	%	%	%	%
Austria	5	2	75	64	0	13	100	60	50	13	51
Belgium	5	4	83	82	31	88	80	85	50	0	66
Denmark	4	4[3]	75	82	25	20	65	70	17	100	63
Finland	9	7[4]	74	67	14	39	63	80	10	68	56
France	33	6	75	64	25	75	53	67	61	8	56
Germany	23	9	81	73	39	53	100	77	37	17	64
Greece	3	1	67	86	50	75	20	80	0	0	53
Ireland	4	2	42	86	37	0	25	60	0	0	37
Italy	19	6	86	81	58	87	50	83	100	17	71
Malta	1	1	50	57	25	75	0	80	67	0	42
Netherlands	5	4[5]	75	89	63	87	85	100	42	0	72
Norway	2	2	83	100	37	25	50	80	33	87	67
Spain	8	3	81	71	50	75	67	67	56	0	60
Sweden	7	4	67	71	44	56	85	80	50	100	72
Switzerland	8	4	79	79	50	100	100	75	58	19	72
Turkey	3	2	100	71	50	63	30	90	50	0	62
U.K.	45	19	91	99	64	39	28	93	30	17	64
Total	184	80	80	81	44	56	59	81	41	27	63

CHAPTER 9

European Aspects

An early statement[1] as to the purpose of the Council of Europe's studies on curricula in different subjects in European universities was "to strengthen the university community in Europe . . . drawing more closely together the content and level of university education". It therefore seems useful to consider the present extent of European co-operation in higher education in economics.

One of the more obvious forms of co-operation among countries is the long- and shorter-term movement of students and staff. The student flows can be of various kinds—long-term for a whole-degree course, for a first or higher degree, medium-term for a year or so of a course only, and short-term usually in the vacations. It is difficult in the published official statistics to differentiate the first two types of movement and to distinguish at what level, first degree or post-graduate, students move. It is also difficult to get statistics for the intra-Western European flows of economics students, as distinct from all types of students. (In this chapter the member countries of the Committee for Higher Education and Research of the Council for Cultural Co-operation will be referred to as "Western European" countries.) Information on general flows is available for certain countries from the *U.N.E.S.C.O. Yearbook of Education Statistics*, and this is shown in Table 9.1. Unfortunately it covers flows into only nine of the nineteen countries in this survey, but these include most of the larger countries. Table 9.1 shows the number of students from other Western European countries in these nine countries.

Table 9.1 illustrates the proportion which Western European foreign students bear to all foreign students. This varies considerably between the nine countries—it is highest in Austria (64 per cent) and lowest in the United Kingdom (11 per cent). Those countries that have extra-European links arising from their imperial past tend to have smaller proportions of Western European foreign students. This is the case for the United Kingdom, France, and Spain. In the

---

[1] *Information Bulletin of the Council for Cultural Co-operation of the Council of Europe*, No. 14, Summer 1964, p. 7.

cases of Belgium and the Netherlands it is much less marked. Austria and Switzerland, which use the same languages as a number of other European countries, have high proportions of students from other Western European countries among their total foreign-student populations. Ireland is in a similar position, with the additional historic link that Trinity College, Dublin, maintains with the United Kingdom.

The proportion of foreign students to all students is shown as a percentage in Table 9.1. This also indicates considerable variations between countries, being lowest in the Netherlands (1 per cent) and highest in Switzerland (28 per cent).

The table also shows the distribution in the nine countries between the different Western European nationalities. There are only two cases where one group accounts for more than half the Western European foreign students in any country—the German in Austria and the British in Ireland. However, there are ten cases where individual national groups make up more than 20 per cent of all students from other Western European countries. Five of them are German (in Austria, Spain, Switzerland, France, and the Netherlands); two of them are Greek (in Austria and Germany); one British (in Ireland); one Norwegian (in the Netherlands); and one Luxembourgeois (in Belgium). It should be stressed again that these figures relate to all students, and it may well be that the picture for economics students is not identical. This would seem particularly likely in the case of the German group in Spain, which may well be largely composed of students of Spanish language and literature.

The major outflows of students from Western European countries can be looked at in terms of absolute or relative numbers. In absolute terms the most important are Germany and Greece. However, it is probably more significant to consider these outflows in relative terms—that is, in relation to the total student population of the exporting country. Here Greece remains important, but in relative terms this is no longer true of Germany. In relative terms the outflow of students is also of considerable importance for Iceland, Malta, and Norway. Both the first two are in population terms very small countries with only one university, and their total student numbers are small. Norway is a relatively small country with a limited number of university and similar institutions, and traditionally a large proportion of its students have gone abroad. The figure has declined relatively, though not absolutely, in recent years, as provision has been increased in Norway. From two countries, Luxembourg and Cyprus, all

Table 9.1

Distribution of Western European Students in Certain Countries[1]

ω less than 0·1%

STUDENTS IN

From [2]	% Austria	% Belgium	% France	% Germany	% Ireland	% Netherlands	% Spain	% Switzerland	% United Kingdom	% Total Number
Austria	—	1·4	1·6	8·7	—	1·9	2·7	2·4	0·9	1,142
Belgium	0·2	—	5·1	1·0	0·3	18·2	2·1	2·1	1·5	637
Cyprus	0·2	0·2	—	0·3	0·4	—	—	0·1	8·7	192
Denmark	0·1	0·4	1·7	0·6	—	0·7	1·4	0·5	1·2	224
France	0·3	13·0	—	5·9	0·8	3·8	16·1	16·3	3·6	1,762
Germany	53·0	5·8	24·1	—	1·1	28·6	44·9	40·4	15·7	7,481
Greece	30·7	8·9	10·6	31·0	0·9	2·2	0·7	8·1	13·9	6,271
Iceland	ω	—	—	1·0	—	0·2	0·4	0·1	2·5	149
Ireland	ω	2·1	0·7	0·2	—	0·2	0·4	0·3	6·6	211
Italy	7·8	11·7	9·1	3·7	0·2	4·5	0·8	6·4	4·9	2,000
Luxembourg	0·2	20·6	5·5	2·9	0·1	0·5	9·6	ω	0·2	853
Malta	—	—	—	—	0·2	—	—	—	3·0	49
Netherlands	0·2	18·3	4·1	4·3	1·3	—	4·0	3·2	3·9	1,149
Norway	2·1	0·8	2·7	13·0	0·6	24·6	0·7	7·9	13·2	2,316
Spain	0·4	5·8	8·6	2·8	1·9	1·2	—	3·2	3·7	1,117
Sweden	0·6	0·5	1·1	2·5	0·1	1·2	3·3	2·0	1·1	560
Switzerland	1·4	5·0	5·1	4·4	0·2	2·9	5·1	—	3·9	998
Turkey	3·8	1·4	4·4	14·2	0·2	1·7	0·1	3·3	11·6	2,288
United Kingdom	0·7	4·4	14·6	3·5	92·6	7·6	9·0	3·6	—	2,826

STUDENTS IN

	% Austria	% Belgium	% France	% Germany	% Ireland	% Nether- lands	% Spain	% Switzer- land	% United Kingdom	% Total Number
Total Western European Foreign Students (= 100%)(3)	6,193	1,080	5,921	10,068	1,233	419	733	4,928	1,551	32,225
Western European Foreign Students as % of all Foreign Students	64·2	37·8	19·5	40·0	48·6	35·9	15·8	58·9	11·0	32·4
All Foreign Students as % of all Students(4)	20·0	8·5	7·4	6·7	16·7	1·0	4·9	28·0	9·5	—

(1) The data for this table, which covers students of all subjects, was derived from the *UNESCO Yearbook of Educational Statistics*, 1964, and the figures relate to the years 1962 or 1963. In the case of Belgium the figures were taken from the *Rapport Annuel*, 1964, of the Fondation Universitaire, Bureau de Statistiques Universitaires.

(2) This list includes all countries in the survey except the Holy See and Finland.

(3) These figures serve as a base for the percentage in the upper part of the table.

(4) The total figure for all students is not the same as that used in Chapter 2, but relates to the year available nearest to 1962–63.

students inevitably go abroad, and in one, the Holy See, all students come from outside.

Table 9.1, as has already been pointed out, refers to the intra-Western European flows of all students, not specifically to economics students. There is no particular reason to suppose that flows of economics students differ very much from the general flows. Some more detailed information is, however, available for individual countries and institutions, and this is briefly outlined below. On the whole its results bear out the general results shown in Table 9.1.

In Austria the overall percentage of foreign students in the law and economics faculties is about 14 per cent. This is a rather lower proportion than for the universities as a whole, for which the figure is about 20 per cent. It may well be the case, however, that more of the foreign students proportionally are reading the economics degree than the law degree in the faculties. At Innsbruck, for example, of the forty doctoral dissertations in economics in 1962–63, thirty-three were by foreign students. At the Hochschule für Welthandel there are fewer foreign students proportionally—about 8 per cent. The table below gives an idea of their origins:

Foreign Students at the Hochschule für Welthandel, Vienna
(Winter Semester, 1964–65)

Total Foreign Students	361
of whom Total Western European	257
of whom German	161
Italian	31
Turkish	29
Greek	15
Other Western European	21

The twenty-one students from other Western European countries were drawn from eight other countries. Similar detailed information is not available for the universities, but here again the largest single group of foreign students came from Germany.

In 1963–64 there were in Belgian universities 521 foreign students studying economic, political, and social sciences, of whom 139 (or about 27 per cent) were from Western European countries. This figure is considerably lower than the comparative proportion for all students, which was 37·8 per cent. The table below gives more detailed information on their origins:

Foreign Students of Economics, Political, and Social Sciences in Belgium
(1963–64)

Total Foreign Students	521
of whom 　　Total Western European	139
of whom from 　　Netherlands 　　Italy 　　Spain 　　Luxembourg 　　France 　　Germany 　　Greece 　　Other Western European countries	29 20 19 17 15 10 10 19

The students from "Other Western European countries" came from six different countries, so in all thirteen Western European countries had one or more students studying social sciences in Belgium.

In France detailed information was available only for Paris, by far the largest faculty of law and economics. In Paris there were 2972 foreign students in 1965–66 (about 10 per cent of the student body, a higher figure than that given in Table 9.1 for all faculties), of whom 570, or nearly 20 per cent, were from Western European countries. This last proportion is almost identical to that for all students shown in Table 9.1. The table on page 118 gives a more detailed analysis of the home countries of these students.

The 'other' group came in all from six other countries. There is some information as to the courses in which the foreign students as a whole were engaged, but not specifically for Western European students. The table on page 118 shows what courses students were studying.

In Germany there were in the winter semester 1962–63 2004 foreign students of economics, political science, and sociology, or about 6 per cent of the total students in these fields.

Foreign Students in the Paris Faculty of Law and Economics
(1965–66)

Total Foreign Students	2972
of whom Total Western European	570
of whom from Greece Germany Italy Spain Turkey Luxembourg Switzerland Belgium United Kingdom Other Western European countries	117 113 70 55 48 45 30 28 24 40

Courses of Foreign Students in the Paris Faculty of Law and Economics
(1965–66)

Course	Total	%
Capacité	551	19
Licence[1]	1,248	42
Doctorate and other higher degrees	916	31
Visiting students (*auditeurs libres*)	124	4
Certificates of various kinds	133	4
Total	2,972	100

(1) Of those on the *Licence* course, over half were studying economics.

Greece sends far more students abroad than it receives. However, at the University of Athens the law faculty admits each year about 150 students from Cyprus and from other Greek-speaking communities overseas, as compared with an intake of 750 Greek students.

Italy, too, sends out students rather than receiving them. The only faculty of economics for which detailed information is available is Turin, where there were only 8 foreign students (4 of them from

Western European countries) out of a total faculty of 2819 in 1963–64. It is probable that there would be rather more, although still few relatively, in Rome.

Norway, as already mentioned, has a considerable outflow of students. In 1967, 15 per cent of all Norwegian students were studying abroad, most of them on state grants. In 1966–67, in commercial subjects, 468 Norwegian students were studying abroad, mainly in Europe. Their distribution was as follows:

Norwegian Students abroad reading for degrees similar to the Siviløkonom

Total	468
of whom in	
Germany	203
Switzerland	98
U.K. and Ireland	50
Denmark	32
Sweden	8
Austria	7
France	7

In addition to those students of commercial subjects were also some students of general economics.

Sweden has few foreign students of economics—possibly about fifty from Western European countries in the universities and about ten in the Handelshögskolor. These come mainly from Finland, Germany, Norway, and the United Kingdom. Relatively few Swedish students go abroad to study.

Switzerland is an important receiving country for foreign students. In the faculties of Fribourg and Lausanne there are more foreign than Swiss students. The table on page 120 shows the distribution for the economics students at Fribourg, Lausanne, and the Hochschule, St Gallen. At Fribourg foreign students constituted 58 per cent of the total, at Lausanne 52 per cent, and at St Gallen 30 per cent.

Turkey has comparatively few students from other Western European countries. At the economics faculty of the University of Istanbul, for example, there were only thirty-three foreign students (twenty-one of them from Western Europe) in 1961–62. Of the twenty-one nearly half were from Cyprus, eight from the United Kingdom (these may well have been Cypriots with British nationality), two from Greece, and one from Germany. The Middle East Technical

Foreign Students of Economics at Certain Swiss Universities

	Fribourg (summer semester, 1966)	Lausanne (1965)	St Gallen (1965)
Total Foreign	289	393	363
of whom Western European	166	237	320
of whom from Germany	117	30	132
Norway	—	2	109
France	3	59	4
Greece	13	38	4
Turkey	—	38	6
Netherlands	2	14	19
Austria	3	2	20
Spain	13	8	1
Italy	10	15	6
Other Western European countries	5(3)*	31(5)*	19(5)*

* ( ) shows the number of different countries from which 'other' students came.

University does draw more of its students from abroad but, as its name suggests, these come from Middle Eastern rather than Western European countries.

The United Kingdom receives most of its overseas students from non-European countries, chiefly from the Commonwealth. In 1964–65 there were, however, 322 Western European students studying social sciences (including economics) at British universities.

It is possible in this case to distinguish students taking first degrees from those doing post-graduate degrees, and the second column shows the figures for those reading for a first degree. It can be seen that in all 171, or 53 per cent, of the students were taking first-degree courses. It is interesting to note the variations between countries in the proportions reading for the first degrees. The Norwegian students were almost all reading for first degrees, a fact which is probably generally true of Norwegian students studying abroad.

As well as these movements abroad for study there is also shorter-

Western European Students of Social Sciences in the United Kingdom
(1964–65)

	SOCIAL SCIENCES All Students	First-degree Students
Total Western European	322	171
of whom from		
Germany	63	18
Greece	49	26
Turkey	29	18
Italy	28	13
Norway	24	23
Cyprus	19	15
France	15	6
Netherlands	15	12
Ireland	14	4
Spain	12	4
Switzerland	12	9
Malta	11	9
Other Western European countries	31	14

term movement. This is even more difficult to quantify, as most of it is individual and informal. However, the figures for the exchange traineeship scheme organized by the Association Internationale des Etudiants en Sciences Economiques et Commerciales (A.I.E.S.E.C.) shown in Table 9.2 give an idea of part of this short-term movement. The A.I.E.S.E.C. scheme demands a rough balance between the number of trainees a country sends out and the number it receives, an artificial if necessary requirement which does not affect ordinary student travel. A traineeship, however, provides the definite experience of working in a foreign country. In some courses—as, for example, at H.E.C., in France—such a period may even be obligatory. At many other specialized institutions it is encouraged.

A.I.E.S.E.C. also arranges conferences and study tours. This is done mainly by the national committees, singly or jointly. For example, in the summer of 1963 the A.I.E.S.E.C. committees of Denmark, Finland, and Sweden organized a study tour of Scandinavia, and the German committee held a seminar on "The Integration of National Economies".

There is far less information readily available on staff-movement

Table 9.2

Movement of Students between Western European Countries on A.I.E.S.E.C. Exchanges 1963

Countries from which students came	Countries to which students went																	TOTAL
	Austria	Belgium	Denmark	Finland	France	Germany	Greece	Iceland	Ireland	Italy	Netherlands	Norway	Spain	Sweden	Switzerland	Turkey	United Kingdom	
Austria	—	5	1	5	16	3	0	0	0	5	1	2	6	0	3	1	4	52
Belgium	4	—	1	1	23	32	0	0	1	9	5	3	8	1	5	1	2	96
Denmark	1	1	—	1	18	22	1	0	4	3	3	0	2	0	3	1	21	81
Finland	5	1	2	—	13	59	0	0	0	3	0	0	2	0	3	1	23	112
France	20	22	18	11	—	232	4	1	2	53	23	10	65	24	19	31	21	556
Germany	3	30	26	59	206	—	4	1	3	38	24	22	38	11	7	16	20	508
Greece	0	0	1	0	3	4	—	0	0	4	0	0	1	1	0	1	1	16
Iceland	0	0	1	0	1	0	0	—	0	0	0	0	0	0	0	0	0	2
Ireland	0	1	4	0	5	4	0	0	—	4	3	1	1	1	3	1	0	28
Italy	7	3	1	2	49	34	4	0	3	—	2	0	10	3	8	10	11	147
Netherlands	2	6	3	1	20	24	0	0	3	6	—	0	4	3	0	2	12	86
Norway	1	3	1	0	10	15	0	0	2	0	1	—	1	1	0	1	17	53
Spain	10	7	2	2	10	42	1	0	1	14	4	1	—	6	5	2	5	112
Sweden	0	1	0	1	23	12	1	0	2	4	3	0	5	—	10	2	35	99
Switzerland	2	4	3	2	22	10	0	0	2	9	4	0	4	9	—	3	8	82
Turkey	1	1	1	0	32	18	0	0	1	10	2	1	2	2	3	—	7	81
United Kingdom	3	3	20	23	24	20	0	0	0	13	11	20	5	37	8	8	—	195
Total	59	88	85	108	475	531	15	2	24	175	86	60	154	99	77	81	187	2306

Source: Annual Report of A.I.E.S.E.C. International, 1963–64, p.12

than there is on student-movement. Clearly it is easier and cheaper to move one member of staff than a large number of students, and intra-European exchanges of staff on a long- or short-term basis can help with the exchange and cross-fertilization of ideas. It is a complicated question, because, quite apart from linguistic and other difficulties, it may involve the question of the recognition of degrees awarded by other countries. In countries like the United Kingdom, where appointment as a university teacher does not require any formal qualifications, this does not arise, and there are in the United Kingdom quite a number of university staff from Western Europe. In part this is the result of movement of refugees in the thirties, but it is also a continuing trend, as can be seen from a number of recent appointments in British universities.

As well as permanent appointment there is the possibility in most countries of the appointment of temporary visiting lecturers or professors. In countries where universities are rigidly controlled by law—as, for example, in Greece—there may be some difficulties in this, but it is normally possible.

In movements of staff, as in many other respects, European countries are linked quite as much, if not more, with the U.S.A. as they are with other Western European countries. Some German figures available appear to show that of the visiting economics professors in 1961–62 at least half were American.[1]

Further example of this transatlantic academic community is provided by the candidates in the 1966 elections of the American Economic Association. Of the nine men standing for office, five had at least one European degree. Four of these were in origin European —Kenneth E. Boulding (Oxford), Gerhard Colm (Freiburg), Robert Triffin (Louvain), and Franco Modigliani (Rome)—and one an American (William W. Baumol), who had taken his doctorate in London.

The survey of journals described in Chapter 8 also provides evidence of the close American and European links. American journals were among those most frequently taken by all universities in the survey. Only in the case of two countries, both small, did the proportion fall below 60 per cent.

The question of co-operation on the Western European level is clearly closely linked with language. Here again the journal survey is of interest. It shows that journals in English (with the exception of those from the Commonwealth and South Africa) are commonly

---

[1] *Stifterverband für die Deutsche Wissenschaft, Jahrbuch*, 1962, Table 86.

taken in all Western European countries. Journals in French and German are less frequently taken, but nevertheless both the groups are taken overall by more than half the sample. The journals in Italian and the English journals from the Commonwealth and South Africa come next, followed by the Scandinavian journals. Even where journals are taken they are not necessarily used, but where they are not even taken there is no chance of their being used, and thus serving to further the flow of ideas.

It is relevant at this stage to consider the language requirements of the various institutions in the different countries. This requirement may either be formal in terms of set courses or examination requirements or informal—that is, expressed in the expected use of foreign texts.

The learning of foreign languages has two functions for students—first, as an immediate tool for their studies, giving them access to foreign literature, and, secondly, for use in their subsequent careers. On the whole, in the specialized institutions, where compulsory language instruction is far more usual than in the universities, this second vocational use seems to be the dominant motive. This would also seem to be the case in the two countries, Italy and Spain, where language instruction forms a part of the university course. The advice of the dean of the Paris faculty of law and economics also stresses this vocational aspect when he writes to first-year students.[1]

> ... tout étudiant *doit* pouvoir lire, écrire et parler couramment une et, s'il se peut, deux *langues étrangères*. Il faut se souvenir que, du point de vue d'une carrière publique ou privée, il n'y a pratiquement pas de différence entre l'ignorance complète d'une langue et une connaissance ânonnante. Ce qui compte, pour un fonctionnaire, un avocat, un "cadre", c'est pouvoir, indépendamment de tout diplôme théorique, user couramment d'une langue étrangère.

In this chapter we are primarily concerned with the academic aspects of language knowledge—for the study of the economic literature of other countries, and also to enable students and staff to enjoy useful academic contact with their colleagues in other European countries. In this respect English is the most important second language. The outline guide to the *Diplom-Volkswirt* at the University of Göttingen, to take one example, stresses the need for a reading

---

[1] *Guides Officiels de la Faculté de Droit et des Sciences Economiques de Paris: Licence en Droit et Licence ès Sciences Economiques—Première Année Commune*, Paris, 1966, p. iv.

knowledge of English: "Zum volkswirtschaftlichen Studium ist die Fähigkeit zur Lektüre englischer Texte vollkommen unentbehrlich."[1] Similar statements can be found in the prospectuses of many other institutions.

In the Netherlands and the Scandinavian countries reading-lists frequently contain a predominance of references in English. In some countries part of the teaching is in English. At M.E.T.U. in Turkey virtually all teaching is in English, at the University of Louvain some advanced teaching common to both Flemish and French faculties is in English, and at the Netherlands School of Economics some lecture notes are issued in English.

In the Scandinavian countries German texts are quite often cited, though not as frequently as English. French texts are also used to some extent in non-French-language institutions—for example, in Italy and the Netherlands.

The countries where foreign languages are least used are probably the English-speaking countries (Ireland, Malta, and the United Kingdom) and France. A considerable part of English literature is available in translation or summary in French, German, and Spanish, so that in all these countries the need to read English is less pressing. The need for a reading knowledge of another language (usually English) is clearly greatest in countries whose languages are in no sense world languages.

In general the reading knowledge of a foreign language becomes more relevant as a course advances. In most countries first-year textbooks are available in the student's own language, but at more advanced stages translation and summary cannot keep pace with the advance of the subject, nor in many cases would it be economic for them to do so. Towards the end of first-degree courses even in countries using one of the major world languages a knowledge of a second language may well become imperative. In Austria, for example, a reading knowledge of English is generally considered necessary for students in the preparation of their dissertation in economics.

---

[1] *Studienplan für das Volkswirtschaftliche Studium an der Georg-August-Universität Göttingen* (1962).

CHAPTER 10

The Changing Pattern

The earlier chapters of this report have been devoted to an analysis of the present state of economics teaching in European universities. Such an analysis is inevitably static, and any examination, however cursory, of European higher education would reveal considerable movement, even if to the reformer in a university the institutional machinery often seems to slow that movement to a snail's pace. This chapter attempts to discuss the major changes that have occurred in the way economics is taught in the last decade, and the further changes that may be expected in the near future.

THE PRESSURES FOR CHANGE

There would seem to have been two principal factors for change in the post-war university situation, and while neither of these is peculiar to economics as a subject, they have both affected it acutely. These factors have been the rapid expansion in the numbers of those seeking higher education and the equally rapid expansion of the body of knowledge which students are expected to master. While it is relatively easy to quantify the former, it is more difficult to get an exact measure of the latter, although analysis of reading-lists, examination questions, or even the character of articles in the leading journals compared with those of ten or twenty years ago would give some indication of change.

Table 10.1 attempts to show the rate of growth of student numbers in the universities as a whole, and in economics in particular, over the past decade. Considerable difficulty was experienced in obtaining satisfactorily comparable figures for the whole period, and for many countries it was necessary to rely on figures up to 1963; it is hoped, however, that the table will give some indication of the rate of growth. The calculation of the annual rate of growth of students of economics was in some cases based on statistics for only a section of all students of economics—in Sweden those at the Handelshögskolor, in Greece those at the Athens School of Economics and Business

Science—as these were the only ones readily available. In other cases, as in France, it was necessary to take figures for a faculty containing more than just economics students. Here the relatively slower rate of growth of law students has masked the true rate of growth of numbers

Table 10.1

Average Growth Rate of All Students in Higher Education and Students of Economics in 1955–65[1]

		Average Growth Rate of all Students, 1955–65			
	per annum	5%—less than 7% per annum	7%—less than 9% per annum	9%—less than 11% per annum	11% and over per annum
Average Growth Rate of Students of Economics 1955–65	6%—less than 7% per annum	[Iceland] [Ireland] United Kingdom	[Austria] France [Greece]		
	7%—less than 9% per annum	Belgium	Germany Netherlands	Denmark [Turkey]	
	9%—less than 11% per annum		Italy	Sweden Switzerland	
	11% and over per annum	[Spain]			Norway

[1] The positions of those countries in brackets are based on figures for periods of less than seven years.

in economics. Although the figures in Table 10.1 must be treated with considerable caution, they show a rapid rate of growth in student numbers over the decade, and examination of the underlying data shows few signs of any relaxation of this rate of growth. On the contrary, in a number of countries the rate of growth was rising towards the end of the period. When it is recalled that a rate of growth of $7\frac{1}{4}$ per cent per annum will approximately double a quantity in ten years, and that one of just over $11\frac{1}{2}$ per cent will treble it, the impact of these rates of growth on student numbers—and thus the university structure—can be clearly seen.

Physically this increase in numbers can be seen to have affected higher education in Europe by the large numbers of new buildings, but more significant for this report has been its effect on the internal structure of the universities, and their teaching methods. Together with the expansion of knowledge referred to earlier, it has obliged institutions of higher education throughout Europe to re-examine, and in many cases to reform, the substance and the organization of their curricula. These reforms can be of one of two types, depending on the national structure of higher education; they can be either national reforms approved by the national educational authorities where these have detailed control over the institutions of higher education, or local reforms decided on and implemented by individual faculties of economics or specialized institutions. In some cases there have been both national and local reforms.

In over half the countries in the study there have been fairly substantial alterations in the structure of the teaching of economics in the last decade, and in a number of other countries changes are currently being implemented. Elsewhere they have been discussed, and in some of the countries where they have already occurred still further changes are envisaged. In certain countries, notably Italy and Greece, where many university teachers of economics feel that reform is urgently needed it is delayed by the need to get Parliamentary approval of the reform proposals.

One way in which the expansion of student numbers has been met in some countries has been by the creation of new universities. These new institutions have had freedom to develop new patterns of teaching, and in a number of countries have produced courses which appear to be significantly different from those in existing institutions. This is partly because new universities do not have the entrenched power groups which sometimes oblige existing institutions to settle for unsatisfactory compromises, and partly because new institutions need to provide some rationale apart from tradition for the structure of their degrees. Some discussion of the changes introduced by these new institutions will be found in the country studies for Austria, Germany, Turkey, and the U.K., where they would seem to have had the greatest importance.

The changes which have been or are being introduced can be grouped under four headings: changes in the overall structure of degrees, changes in the internal structure of degrees, changes in the balance of courses within the degree, and changes in teaching methods.

CHANGES IN THE OVERALL STRUCTURE OF FIRST-DEGREE COURSES

The structure of first-degree courses in economics has changed in two basic ways—by a change in the expected length of studies or by a change in the internal structure of the degree. The prescribed length of the first degree has been lengthened at a number of institutions, either to bring it into line with the actual length of studies or because of a desire to raise the level of the first degree. Instances of this include the Hochschule für Welthandel in Vienna, where the length of the *Diplom-Kaufmann* course is being increased from three to four years as part of the general reform of higher education in the social sciences in Austria. In Greece, at the Athens School of Economics and Business Science, the course was lengthened from three years to four in 1958. In Ireland the new Bachelor of Commerce degree at University College, Cork, lasts four years, compared with the three years of its predecessor, and in Switzerland the Licentiate at the Wirtschaftshochshule at St Gallen has been increased from three and a half to four years. In the United Kingdom, while the length of the first degree has been maintained at three years, an increasing number of students continue to a fourth year of studies for a post-graduate diploma or master's degree.

On the other hand, in some countries attempts have been made or considered to reduce the length of study by the introduction of an intermediate degree. This is in the process of happening in Austria, where, with the exception of the *Diplom-Volkswirt* of the University of Innsbruck, the first degree in economics in the universities has been the doctorate. There is now an intermediate master's degree. A similar change has already occurred in the German-language universities of Switzerland, where in the last decade a licentiate has been introduced as an intermediate degree before the doctorate which was formerly the first degree. Although quite a number of students continue their studies to a doctorate, the majority now terminate with a licentiate. In Denmark, where the university course lasts over five years, the possibility of introducing an intermediate qualification of the same length as the shorter H.A. of the specialized institutions—about three to four years—is being considered. Although the normal first degree in French universities is now the four-year *Licence*, it is possible on successful completion of two years' study to obtain *the Diplôme d'études économiques générales*, which may be a qualification for certain junior posts in public administration.

Although not immediately related to the first degree, the recognition in recent years of the need for organized post-graduate teaching in economics in Austria, Greece, and Italy, where until recently the first degree was effectively the only degree, is also an indication of some dissatisfaction with the present structure and length of the course.

CHANGES IN THE INTERNAL STRUCTURE OF DEGREE COURSES

The other alteration in the structure of degree courses relates to their internal organization. During the past decade there seems to have been a general tendency in those countries which previously allowed their students a great deal of freedom in the organization of their studies towards a more planned pattern of study. This would seem to result in part again from the expansion of knowledge, which has necessitated a more planned curriculum if a first degree is to provide a satisfactory introduction to economics. However, it is probably to a greater extent the result of the increase in student numbers, and possibly also the wider social background of students. Where traditionally a large proportion of university students were the children of university graduates, they may be presumed to have had some understanding of the character of university education before becoming students themselves, thus facilitating their adjustment from school to higher education. Apart from this debatable qualitative change, the sheer increase in numbers has led to greater need for organization.

In all the German-language universities covered by this survey—in the Federal Republic, in Austria, and in Switzerland—the last decade has seen the growth of *Studienpläne*. Some of these are obligatory, others merely offer guidance. However, the increasing use of intermediate examinations, usually after two years, and the introduction of a far larger proportion of obligatory courses and small-group classes is considerably modifying the traditional character of higher education in these countries. In Germany this is in the process of being extended to all universities. In both Austria and Germany the new universities of Linz and Bochum have pioneered very much more tightly organized programmes than has been common in these countries. It will be interesting to see how far this growing internal organization will affect the traditional movement of students between German-language universities.

In the Netherlands the last decade has also seen an increase in the internal organization of degrees. The *Propaedeutic*, or introductory, examination is now compulsory at the end of the first year at the majority of institutions. As is discussed on p. 214, other general reforms of the structure of Dutch degrees are being considered.

Since 1955 there have been a series of substantial reforms throughout Swedish universities, and these have particularly affected the teaching of economics in the faculties of social science. Here the amount of freedom previously allowed to students will be greatly reduced by the introduction of a certain number of fixed curricula among which a student must choose. This will mean not only a more limited range in the combinations of subjects permitted, but also a more precise timetable for the completion of a degree. A similar trend towards a restricted choice of options and a more tightly programmed course is also apparent in Finland.

Another way in which the internal structure of degrees has been changing is in the relation of business economics to general economics, and in the point at which a student must choose between them. A definite trend, both in universities and in specialized institutions, can be seen towards having a common basic course, typically lasting two years, followed by the opportunity to specialize in either general economics or business economics for a further two years of study. This change in the structure occurs in one of two ways, either by instituting a common basic programme for the first two years in those institutions where previously there were two completely separate courses or by dividing the final years of the course in those institutions which had previously had a single programme.

In this sense there is also a trend in the opposite direction. That is, in those institutions where there has previously been a very rigid structure and no opportunity for choice once the student has embarked on his course it is now possible to postpone the choice at least until the end of the first year. Alternatively, where there has previously been no possibility of specializing during the undergraduate degree there is now at least a choice between business and general economics.

In the new structure for social-science teaching in Austria the exact details of the course for the first two years vary a little according to the choice of subsequent specialization, but there is provision to enable those who wish to change their specialization after two years to do so. A similar development can be seen in the new *Diplom-Wirtschaftler* at the universities of Bochum and Giessen in Germany, where there is a common course with opportunity for specialization after two years in place of the separate *Diplom-Volkswirt* and *Diplom-Kaufmann*. At Saarbrücken, although the separate degrees are maintained, the programme for the first two years is identical, thus again postponing the point of decision between business and general economics. Again, at St Gallen in Switzerland, following the recent reforms, there is a common two-year course followed by a wide range of specializations, some in business economics and some in general economics. The pattern is not very different at the other German-language universities in Switzerland, although there the common trunk is shorter.

In Iceland there is a likelihood that the existing degree which tends to concentrate on business economics will be modified to permit an alternative specialization in general economics in the second part of the degree. If this happens it will be rather similar to the *Candidatus* degree of the University of Aarhus in Denmark, where the second part of the degree permits this specialization.

The reform of the French *Licence en Droit* in 1959, creating for the first time a *Licence ès Sciences Economiques*, also permitted a limited amount of specialization, although only in the final year. In this year all students have to take three or four courses in an optional subject in addition to the common courses. The options offered by the individual faculties vary in number and in kind, but for the majority of students there is normally a choice between an option in business and one in more general economics. (More details on this can be found in the country study.)

At the Athens Graduate School of Economics and Business Science there was no opportunity for specialization until 1958, when a fourth year permitting specialization between economics and business economics was introduced. Since 1963 this specialization has been extended back to the third year, giving a common course of two years, followed by two years of specialization. The degree of Bachelor of Science in the faculty of administrative science of the Middle East Technical University in Turkey is also, since the reform of 1964, based on a common two-year introduction followed by specialization in economics, business economics, or public administration.

Although a general reform of Italian teaching of economics awaits parliamentary approval, the faculty of economics and commerce at the University of Urbino at Ancona has found an ingenious solution to the question of specialization within a common framework. After a common first year a number of the prescribed courses in the succeeding years are taught in two ways, either with an orientation towards general economics or with an orientation towards business economics, thus enabling students to specialize. For example, the course on general and applied accountancy in the second year, which must be taken by every Italian student of economics and commerce, deals with problems of accounting of the firm for the specialists in business economics, while a course under the same title given to the specialists in general economics deals with national income and social accounting!

CHANGES IN THE COMPOSITION OF FIRST-DEGREE COURSES

The second general type of change has been in the composition of courses—the way in which a student's time in an economics degree is allocated between different subjects. Again there would seem to be certain trends which can be discerned in a number of European countries. Probably the most pronounced of these is the increasing share of time given to mathematics and statistics. While there may still be debate as to the amount of mathematical and statistical knowledge that should be made a compulsory part of a degree in economics, a cursory glance through any of the major journals will show the difficulties confronting the would-be economist who has not a minimum knowledge of the language of mathematics. To be scientifically literate it is now essential to be numerate.

In revisions to curricula of economics courses in Austria, Belgium, France, Germany, Greece, Iceland, Switzerland, Turkey, and the United Kingdom there has been a common tendency to increase the amount of mathematics and statistics. A number of countries have recently developed specialized degrees in quantitative economics, following the example of the Dutch, who with the Norwegians are probably the European leaders in these fields. In addition to this increased teaching in mathematics and statistics as separate subjects in economics degrees there has also been a growing mathematical content in courses of economics and business economics. Indeed, it is extremely important that there is a proper integration between the courses in mathematics and statistics and the teaching of economics. There have been cases when changes in the curricula have led to increases in the amount of mathematics and statistics (taught often by non-economists), but where the teaching of economics has continued to be almost entirely literary in character. This is, however, presumably largely a transitional problem.

Another change which has occurred in a number of countries,

although by no means everywhere, has been an increase in the share of time devoted to economics. This occurred in France with the reform of 1959, and will presumably occur in Austria as the new study proposals are introduced to the universities. There is a strong desire among university teachers of economics in Greece that such a change should also occur there. In the Holy See, at the Gregorian University, there is a hope that the amount of economics in the course will be increased. Although there has been no formal change in the importance of general economics (*Nationalekonomi*) in the *Civilekonom* degree at the Swedish Schools of Economics, it is considered to have increased, and the same is probably true at the Norwegian School at Bergen.

CHANGES IN TEACHING METHODS

The fourth broad type of reform consists of changes in the pattern of teaching. These have been caused partly by the impact of the increased numbers on the staff-student ratio, but also by the growing dissatisfaction as to the efficiency of traditional methods of teaching in dealing with an increasingly technical subject.

In two countries, the United Kingdom and Sweden, certain institutions have gone as far as to abandon the traditional lecture for parts of the course and to replace it with lecture-classes for groups of twenty-five to thirty students. This was found particularly useful for introductory courses to first-year students, and to some extent parallels practice in the United States. Such classes are less formal than lectures, and enable questions to be asked by both students and teacher.

With the increase in numbers the traditional structure of the seminar where the professor had the opportunity of discussing problems with his students has been distorted, and has had to be modified in a number of countries. On the other hand, there has been a growth of other forms of organization of small-group instruction. In a number of countries final-year students, or those who have just graduated and are preparing for a higher degree, are now responsible for instructing first-year students in groups of six to ten. In others the groups are autonomous, and have no external guidance. The first pattern occurs in some institutions in Denmark, Sweden, and Norway, in Germany, Switzerland, and in France. In general there is a desire to increase small-group instruction, although progress is frequently limited by staff-shortage.

The shortage of staff to cope with the growing number of students is a general problem. In theory the form of teaching based primarily on the *ex cathedra* lecture can be expanded to the limits of the physical capacity of the lecture hall, if not on occasion beyond. However, in practice there are still problems, and even if teaching presents no problem there will still be that of examining. There have, therefore, often had to be modifications, formal or informal, to the common rule that only professors could examine, or indeed undertake, certain other teaching duties. *De facto*, if not *de jure*, the majority of European universities now rely very heavily on non-professional teaching staff. This has led to attempts in a number of countries at reorganization of the hierarchy of university appointments, and to the development of a career structure in university teaching. This is not, of course, a problem peculiar to economics.

The other major change has been in the growth of post-graduate instruction. Until comparatively recently it was assumed that the student would be fully equipped on completing his first degree to continue his academic studies largely on his own. It might be useful to have a seminar for post-graduate students preparing their doctoral dissertations or other contributions to knowledge, but apart from this they worked on their own. Mention has already been made[1] of the development of new quasi-university post-graduate institutes in Austria, Greece, and Italy, but the growth of post-graduate instruction has also occurred within the university in the last decade in France, Sweden, Switzerland, and the United Kingdom. This is a recognition of the fact that a three- or four-year undergraduate degree can no longer hope to provide an adequate training for the professional economist who wishes to go on to do research.

There is little doubt that the next decade will see a continued expansion in student numbers, and there is no sign that the rate of expansion in the knowledge which it is considered that a student should master will diminish. These twin pressures will inevitably lead to further changes in the pattern of higher education.

---

[1] See Chapter 3.

CHAPTER 11

Conclusions

This final chapter contains certain general remarks, and a suggestion of one possible pattern into which the teaching of economics in Europe may be falling.

In the preparation of this report it became apparent what wide scope there was for academic economists to use the tools of economic analysis on their own institutions. While some economists have already explored certain aspects of the economics of higher education as a whole, little has so far been done to discuss the efficient use of scarce resources in the teaching of economics. No-one would deny that academic economists are considered to be a scarce resource in almost every European country, and yet little has been done to evaluate alternative ways of using their skills to obtain the highest returns. Only one economist met during the preparation of this report claimed that there was no problem, in asserting that "the job of economists is to ensure that in some areas of life such as universities we do not need to think of economic efficiency". Until we reach Nirvana economists should surely ask the same sort of awkward questions of all sorts of activity, and cannot exclude their own sphere of operations.

If this is the case it surely suggests the need for considerably extended research into our methods of teaching. We know all too little about the optimal size of group for different kinds of teaching. How satisfactory is the basis on which we determine the allocation of a student's time between different forms of instruction and between different subjects of study? What are the relative costs and relative benefits of different examination systems? It may be difficult for us to decide on the allocation of resources between alternative ends in higher education if there is only limited discussion of the ends themselves. Can we attempt to define these ends, let alone quantify them?

Perhaps the economist has been wise to avoid the problems that confront him so close at hand, but in view of the pressures of expanding student numbers and a rapidly growing subject he may be obliged to deal with them in the near future. There seems to be a case here for extended research, and for increased information as to the results of such research. Although there is, as has been seen, considerable variation between countries as to their systems of higher education, continuing interchange of research experience in these fields would be of great value.

This report has not been the place to investigate many of these problems, even if the information were easily available, which it is not. It has been restricted to those aspects of the difference between the teaching of economics which can be reasonably easily quantified and assessed. One subject which has been excluded, perhaps to the surprise of some, is a discussion of differences in quality of first degrees in economics, and of those completing them. It is extremely difficult to know how this could be measured satisfactorily, and in any case this report is not intended to be a *Guide Michelin* of faculties of economics. Moreover, it can be questioned whether such a comparison of differences has very great value.

Presumably each country's system of higher education—and within it that sector dealing with economics—should be set up in such a way as to produce a range of outputs appropriate to the needs of that country. Among those outputs, one of a number of joint products will be graduates with first degrees. Whether that output is satisfactory can be judged only in terms of the country in question, and it can probably be judged together with the output of the other possible joint products—post-graduates with higher degrees, theoretical and applied economic research, part-time economic consultants, and partially trained students who do not complete their degrees.

This report has tried to outline the different systems, showing the differences with respect to some of the outputs only in quantitative terms. In order to assess the value of different national systems satisfactorily it would be necessary to determine the national demands which each country is making on its system of higher education. These include not only the 'capital good' aspect—the supply of different kinds of educated manpower—but also the highly income-elastic 'consumer good' aspect of higher education.

It is by no means easy to determine the output-mix at which a system of higher education should be aiming. This is particularly true in economics, where in some countries there are other institutions providing part of post-secondary education in economics and kindred subjects. Assuming that satisfactory methods can be discovered for the assessment of ability and potential at the post-secondary level, how wide a range of ability should be admitted to higher education? Once in higher education, should all students study the same course or would it be preferable to provide a range of courses aimed at different ability levels? If such a range of courses is desirable, is it preferable that they are given in different institutions? How far should the university be concerned with professional training as well as academic education? Is it necessarily the case that the length of the first-degree course should be the same for all graduates? What should be the relationship between undergraduate and post-graduate education? Unless one knows the answers to these questions it will be difficult to determine the range of outputs that higher education is trying to produce, and to judge its efficiency in doing so. It is impossible to talk of European norms for higher education in economics until agreement has been reached as to common objectives for our systems of higher education.

In spite of this general problem of differing national objectives for higher education it is probable that in the case of a number of countries at approximately similar levels of economic development the desired outputs from their institutions of higher education will not be too dissimilar, and in analysing a variety of different systems one is tempted to search for signs of convergence. What follows is one possible interpretation of the current situation in the teaching of economics from which one may be able to discern a common pattern developing out of diversity. Such a tendency to convergency must not be exaggerated, but it may facilitate future work on the equivalence of university qualification in economics.

The pattern which can be discerned in a number of countries is for the study of economics to be divided implicitly into three stages, each frequently lasting two years. The first degree would not always take up the whole of these three stages: there appears to be a general acceptance of the desirability of providing courses of different lengths.

The first of these three stages is frequently not a specialized course in economics as such, but is made up of courses in a number of social sciences, often shared by students from other social sciences. Such an introductory period is particularly necessary, as economics and the social sciences are not generally taught in secondary education. In many cases this stage is a selective one, both of students and of courses. A high proportion of those students who are not to complete their course drop out at this stage, and it is also the period during which, when such a choice is possible, the student chooses his specialization. Such choice is normally made by the student, although in most cases his decision requires the approval of the authorities.

The second part of the degree course will be the terminal part of their studies for most students. It is here that the students receive specialist education in economics. There will frequently be a variety of specializations, covering, for example, general economics, business economics, and quantitative economics. It may be further possible to distinguish between those courses which are terminal—and may thus have a vocational bias—and those which are directed towards the preparation of the student for a higher degree.

The third part of the degree course is usually taken by only a small minority of students, and normally consists mainly of supervised research for a doctorate. In some cases there may be additional lectures and classes, but frequently there are not enough students to make this practicable.

Such a tripartite division of courses does not exist in all countries, but it would seem to be explicit or implicit in a growing number of institutions. In Table 11.1 an attempt has been made to show these three parts of economics courses in a number of institutions in different countries. Although they are not all at the same level, or cover the same material, they would seem to represent broadly similar levels of study. In those cases where a country has been omitted from the table it is because its structure of higher education cannot be fitted into this framework.

The French and Swedish degrees do not fit easily into this framework, and the Netherlands and Norwegian degrees probably reach an appreciably higher level at the end of the second stage than those of the other countries. In those cases where no specific period of time is given for the completion of the doctoral dissertation it normally takes a number of years during which the candidate will frequently be only a part-time student.

Table 11

The Three Sections of Higher Education in Economics

Country and, where appropriate, Institution	Part 1	Part 2	Part 3	Comments
Austria	Part 1 Introduction to Economics and Social Sciences. 2 years	Part 2 2 years. *Mag. Rer. Soc. Oec.*	Thesis 1–2 years *Doc. Rer. Soc. Oec.*	
Belgium	*Candidature* 2 years. Introduction to Social Sciences.	*Licence* 2–3 years	Thesis 1–2 years	
Denmark	Part 1 2–2½ years.	Part 2 2 years.	Doctorate	
France	First 3 years of *Licence*	Fourth year of *Licence* and *Diplôme d'études supérieures.* 2 years	Doctorate 1–2 years	
Germany	First 2 years of Diploma studies	Final 2 years of Diploma	Doctorate 1–2 years	This distinction is clearer at the universities with a *Vorprüfung*

Country and, where appropriate, Institution	Part 1	Part 2	Part 3	Comments
Holy See	*Baccalaureatus* 1 year	*Licentiatus* 2 years	*Laurea* 1–2 years	The Licentiate covers a wider range of subjects than most other degrees considered
Iceland	Part 1 of *Candidatus* 2 years	Part 2 2 years	Doctorate	
Netherlands	*Candidatus* 2–3 years	*Doctorandus* 2–3 years	Doctorate	
Norway	Part 1 3 years	Part 2 2–3 years *Candidatus Oeconomiae*	Doctorate	
Sweden	Two-point course in economics in F.K. or F.P.M.	Three-point course in economics in F.P.M.	*Fil. Lic.* in economics	
Switzerland (German language institutions)	*Vorprüfung* 2 years	*Licentiatus* 2 years	Doctorate 1–2 years	

Table 11—continued
The Three Sections of Higher Education in Economics

Country and, where appropriate, Institution	Part 1	Part 2	Part 3	Comments
Turkey (M.E.T.U.)	First 2 years of B.S. general	3rd and 4th years of B.S. specialized		
United Kingdom	Part 1 of bachelor's degree 1–2 years	Part 2 of bachelor's degree and master's degree or post-graduate Diploma 2–3 years	Doctorate 2 years	The distinction between Part 1 and Part 2 varies between universities

PART II
Country Studies

Austria

From the winter semester 1967–68 a fundamental change is being introduced into the degrees in economics offered in Austria. Previously there were variations[1] among the five institutions of university status (the universities of Vienna, Graz, and Innsbruck, the Hochschule für Welthandel in Vienna, and the Hochschule für Sozial- und Wirtschaftswissenschaften at Linz), but under the new regulations all five will offer standard courses. The courses will lead to a master's degree in social and economic sciences (*Magister der Sozial- und Wirtschaftswissenschaften*) in which there will be seven choices of specialization—sociology, social studies, economic and social statistics, economics, business economics, commercial studies, and commercial education.[2] All five institutions will not—initially, at least—offer all seven courses. The table below shows the range of specialization actually available in 1967–68:

	University of Vienna	Hochschule für Welthandel	University of Graz	University of Innsbruck	Hochschule Linz
Sociology	x				x
Social studies					x
Economic and social statistics	x	x	x	x	x
Economics	x	x	x	x	x
Business economics		x	x	x	x
Commercial studies		x			
Commercial education		x			

[1] A note on these superseded degrees will be found at the end of this section.
[2] This is a course to train students to teach in commercial schools.

Only in some places was the full course available in 1967–68; at the rest it will be established in stages, a year at a time, so that the complete course will first be offered in 1969–70.

Students who have already started on their studies for the degrees now superseded by the new master's degree can either complete them or change to the new degree. These old degrees were the doctorate (*Dr rer pol*) in the law faculties of the Universities of Vienna and Graz, the *Diplom-Volkswirt* at the University of Innsbruck, and the *Diplom-Kaufmann* at the Hochschule für Welthandel. After the new master's degree it will be possible to proceed to a doctorate in social and economic sciences after a minimum of an additional year.

The master's degree is divided into two parts of equal length— each covering two years. The first part is more or less identical for all the specializations, so that students can if they wish change their specialization or their institution during their degree course. In this first part students take six compulsory subjects and one optional. In the economics and business specializations the subjects studied are:

(*a*) Austrian civil and commercial law
(*b*) Austrian constitutional and administrative law
(*c*) General and applied sociology
(*d*) Statistics and mathematics for social scientists
(*e*) Economic theory and policy
(*f*) General business economics
(*g*) An optional subject selected from philosophy, psychology, sociology, political science, ethnology, history, economic and social history, geography, town and country planning, economic geography, econometrics, co-operation, introduction to technology, Austrian labour law, Austrian social law, Austrian financial law, a relevant foreign language.[1]

During the first four semesters each student must register for at least twenty hours a week. This does not necessarily have to be twenty hours a week in each semester—a minimum registration of fifteen hours in a semester can be made up to twenty hours by registering for more than twenty hours in another semester. There are sixty-eight semester hours of basic instruction during the course, supplemented by at least twelve semester hours of additional instruction arranged by the institution. At the end of the fourth semester the student is examined orally in all subjects except economic theory and policy and general business economics. There can be written examinations

---

[1] Instruction may not in fact be available in all these optional subjects.

in Austrian civil and commercial law and in statistics and mathematics. At the Hochschule für Welthandel, for example, students must take and pass a written paper in statistics and mathematics before they are allowed to take the oral examination. The general principle is that students are not examined at the end of the fourth semester in those subjects or subjects they will specialize in during the second part of the course.

The table below shows the percentage distribution of time between subjects for the sixty-eight semester hours of the basic course at the Hochschule für Welthandel. As the course is now standard at all Austrian university institutions it can be taken as of representative pattern. As well as this basic course the student will be attending at least a further twelve semester hours of instruction, including further study of other of the optional subjects on a non-examination basis.

	%
Economics	11·8
Business economics	7·4
Law	35·4–47·1
Other social sciences	13·2–25·0
Accountancy and commercial techniques	5·9
Mathematics and statistics	14·7
Foreign languages	0·0–11·8
Other subjects	0·0–11·8
Total semester hours	68

It is necessary for students who have not obtained equivalent qualifications earlier to study for examinations in accountancy and a foreign language in addition to the basic course.

In the second part of the course there is a distinct course for each specialization. The table below shows the subjects taken in the economics and business economics specialization. The list comes from the detailed regulations of the Hochschule für Welthandel, but the subjects are standard except where there is an optional subject, as here the range offered may vary somewhat from institution to institution.

Before he takes his second set of examinations the student has to prepare a *Diplomarbeit* on a subject related to his main specialization. The second examination is both written and oral, the passing of the written examination being a necessary preliminary to entry to the oral

Economics Specialization	Business Economics Specialization
(a) Economic theory	(a) General business economics
(b) Economic and social policy	(b) A special topic in business economics[2]
(c) Public finance	(c) Another special topic in business economics
(d) General business economics	(d) Economic theory, including the elements of economic policy and public finance
(e) Austrian labour or finance law[1]	(e) One of the optional subjects not taken in Part I

[1] The student may not repeat a subject he has already taken in the first part of the course.
[2] The topics available are industry, commerce, trade, transport, banks and savings banks, foreign trade, auditing and accounting, advertising, and market research and marketing.

examinations. In the second part of the course each student must be registered for at least eighteen semester hours a week. Of the total seventy-two semester hours sixty are taken up by the compulsory subjects.

The table below shows the balance of the second part of the course for the economics and business economics specializations at the Hochschule für Welthandel, which again is quoted as an illustration of one particular example of the standard national regulations.

Throughout the course instruction is by lecture, seminar, and pro-

	Economics Specialization	Business Economics Specialization
Economics	66 ·7	20 ·0–23 ·3
Business economics	16 ·7	55 ·0–56 ·7[(1)]
Law	13 ·3	0 –18 ·3
Other social sciences		0 –18 ·3
Accountancy and commercial techniques	3 ·3	6 ·7
Mathematics and statistics		
Foreign languages		0 –16 ·7
Other subjects		0 –18 ·3
Total semester hours	60	60

[1] For simplicity all the special topics have been treated as business economics, although some might more accurately be credited to other categories.

seminar practical classes. During the first part of the course about 25 per cent of the basic course is in non-lecture instruction, and in the second part at least 46·7 per cent in the economics specialization and 36·7 per cent in the business economics. Active participation in the non-lecture instruction is required throughout the four years of the course.

Before the introduction of the new regulations the master's degree was already being offered at the Hochschule für Sozial und Wirtschaftswissenschaften at Linz, an institution opened in 1966. The other university institutions, however, offered different degree courses, leading at Vienna and Graz to a doctorate (*Dr rer pol*) in the faculty of law, to a *Diplom-Volkswirt* at Innsbruck, and to a *Diplom-Kaufmann* at the Hochschule für Welthandel.

The doctorate at the University of Vienna contained relatively little economics. In the course lasting a minimum of four years students studied economics as only one of three subjects (the others being administrative science and sociology) in the second half of the course. The first half was spent on the study of law, political science, and economic history. As the time available for economics was relatively short, there was a tendency for emphasis to be placed on economic theory rather than applied economics.

The *Diplom-Volkswirt* at Innsbruck was also a four-year course similar to that in German universities. Students were also required to have six months' practical experience in industry or commerce. The degree contained considerably more economics than the Vienna doctorate. About 45 per cent of the instruction was in economics, a further 11 per cent in business economics, 18 per cent in law, and the remainder in other social sciences and mathematics and statistics. All the examinations (except one) were in economics or business economics. Innsbruck has gone straight to the full course for the new master's degree in economics, all four years of instruction being available from the autumn of 1967.

The old *Diplom-Kaufmann* course at the Hochschule für Welthandel lasted three years, although students usually took four years and there were plans to increase the prescribed length to four years. The course was divided into two equal parts. There were three sets of examinations, one at the end of Part I and the other two at the end of Part II, with at least six weeks between them. Students were also required to write a *Diplomarbeit*. The Hochschule will, from the autumn of 1967, offer the full four-year course for the business economics specialization of the new master's degree.

An additional development in Austria which is of interest is the Institut für Höhere Studien und Wissenschaftliche Forschung. This was established in 1962, and aims to give further training in the social sciences to young Austrian graduates. The course lasts for two years, and is attended by a maximum of fifty students. The Institut is able to call on a number of foreign professors, and effectively provides a post-graduate course in economics.

Belgium

In Belgium five universities offer first-degree courses in economics.[1] The table below shows the relative size of the various institutions, and indicates that much the largest is the University of Louvain, which had over half the total number of students of social and commercial science in 1965–66.[2]

University	Number of Students in		Total	
	Social Sciences	Commercial Sciences	Number	%
Louvain	1,896	1,959	3,855	53·2
Brussels	1,275	340	1,615	22·3
Ghent	880	67	947	13·1
Liège	357	379	736	10·1
Namur	94	0	94	1·3
Total	4,502	2,745	7,247	100

There are considerable difficulties with the Belgian statistics, owing to the possibility of students registering for several courses simultaneously. This problem is complicated by the fact that the *Candidature* and the *Licence*—the first and second part of the degree course—are frequently taken in different subjects.

First-degree instruction in economics is available in both French and Flemish in Belgium. At Louvain there are two sections of the faculty, French and Flemish. At Ghent all instruction is in Flemish. The other three universities teach in French, although in Brussels some lectures (but not the complete course) are also given in Flemish.

The main degree is made up of two parts; the first two years comprise the *Candidature*, followed by two or three years for the *Licence*.

---

[1] There are in addition several colleges of commerce, some of whose degrees are of university level, but these have not been covered by this report.

[2] *Fondation Universitaire, Bureau de Statistiques Universitaires, Rapport Annuel*, 1966.

University	Length of Course	Candidature	Licence	Licence Options
Brussels	4	Candidature en Sciences Sociales	Lic. en Sciences Economiques	i. Mathematical
	4	none	Ingénieur Commercial	ii. Non-mathematical
	4	none	Lic. en Sciences Commerciales et Financières	These two differ only in their final year
Ghent	4	Candidature en Sciences Economiques	Lic. en Sciences Economiques	i. General economics ii. Business economics
Liège	5	Candidature en Sciences Economiques	Lic. en Sciences Economiques	i. General economics
	4	Candidature en Economie Commerciale	Lic. en Economie Commerciale	ii. Mathematical economics
	4	Candidature en Economie Commerciale	Lic. en Administration des Entreprises	iii. Economics of development
Louvain	5	Candidature en Sciences Economiques	Lic. en Sciences Economiques	i. Quantitative
	5	Candidature en Sciences Commerciales	Lic. en Administration de l'Entreprise	ii. Non-quantitative
	5	Candidature en Sciences Commerciales	Ingénieur Commercial	
Namur	5	Candidature en Sciences Economiques et Sociales	Lic. ès Sciences Economiques et Sociales	i. Economic theory and analysis ii. The public economy iii. The management of the firm

The length of the second part of the course varies according to the degree and the institution, but the tendency seems to be towards increasing the length to three years. The table on page 152 shows in more detail the various degrees available at each university.

In a number of cases there have been recent changes in the regulations, and some of the degrees described below are only just coming into force, and have not yet been fully introduced. It may well be that there will be further changes towards a general pattern of a five-year degree.

As can be seen from the table, there is normally a choice between specialization in general and business economics either in separate *Licences* or within a common degree. There are also quantitative options in general economics at Brussels, and in general and business economics at Louvain. The table has inevitably had to simplify the position somewhat as far as minor specializations are concerned, but it shows the main possibilities available.

In general in Belgian universities instruction is mainly by lecture, which normally accounts for four-fifths or more of the total instruction time. Group instruction is mainly in practical classes in subjects where these are applicable. There are also some seminars in the later stages of most of the courses. As part of the requirement for the degree, students have to prepare a dissertation (*mémoire d'étude*), which is presented shortly before the final examination is taken.

1. THE UNIVERSITY OF LOUVAIN

At the University of Louvain there are two distinct faculties of economic and social science, the Flemish and the French, both offering almost identical courses. There have recently been substantial reforms in all the courses offered, some of which had not been fully implemented at the time this study was prepared.

It is difficult to be very precise about the balance of the course because of the extent of optional subjects. The tables below, however, show the percentage of instruction time spent in the fields of economics, business economics, accountancy and commercial techniques, and mathematics and statistics. The rest of the student's time is distributed over other subjects in the way indicated in the notes which follow the table. It is impossible to make any attempt in the *Licence en Administration de l'Enterprise* to include the fifth year of the course in which, together with three common courses, students take any one of six specializations. These six are quantitative methods, production, finance, marketing, human resources, and international trade. The common courses are in micro-economic analysis, the policy of the firm, and economic models of the firm.

Percentage of Time in Different Subjects in Economics Courses at the University of Louvain

	Candidature and Licence en Sciences Economiques[1] 5 years			Candidature and Licence en Administration de l'Entreprise[2] First 4 years only
	General Economics	Mathemati- cal Economics	Economics of Development	
Economics	32 ·1–33 ·3	25 ·9	31 ·2–32 ·4	11 ·4
Business Economics	0	0	0	16 ·8
Accountancy and commercial techniques	3 ·1	3 ·1	3 ·1	10 ·8
Mathematics and statistics	8 ·0–21 ·0	14 ·2–27 ·2	8 ·0–21 ·0	16 ·2–19 ·8

(1) In the two years of the *Candidature* optional subjects are divided between the fields of law, other social sciences, foreign languages, and other subjects. In the three years of the *Licence* some time is spent in the study of a complementary discipline—for example, law, mathematics, history, sociology, and in some circumstances business economics or education.
(2) In the *Candidature* some time is spent on other subjects distributed between the fields of law, other social sciences, foreign languages, and other subjects. In the fourth year some time is spent on a further optional subject.

Instruction is both in formal lectures and in groups. The groups do not exceed thirty in the *Candidature*, and are smaller in the *Licence*, a maximum of ten in the first year and twenty-five in the next two. Examinations are mainly oral, though there are preliminary written examinations. The oral examinations last fifteen minutes, and tend to be rather factual in nature.

2. THE UNIVERSITY OF BRUSSELS

The main economics degree at the University of Brussels takes a minimum of four years—two for the *Candidature* and two for the

Licence. The course for the *Candidature* is the same for all students, but in the *Licence* there is a choice between mathematical and non-mathematical options. The table below shows the balance of the course:

	Licence (including Candidature) 4 years	
	Non-maths option	Maths option
	%	%
Economics	34 ·4–38 ·5	34 ·4–38 ·5
Business economics	2 ·1–3 ·4	2 ·1–3 ·4
Law	11 ·7	10 ·3
Other social sciences	17 ·2–20 ·0	15 ·8
Accountancy and commercial techniques	1 ·6	0 ·9
Mathematics and statistics	17 ·2–18 ·6	23 ·4–24 ·5
Foreign languages	0	0
Other subjects	10 ·3	10 ·3

There are also two business economics degrees—the *Ingénieur Commercial* and the *Licence en Sciences Commerciales and Financières*—both having very similar courses differing only in the final year of the course. The next table shows the balance of subjects in the two degrees.

In both these courses most of the 'other subject' courses are in science subjects. There are annual examinations which must be passed in order to continue to the next year. As well as these there are some compulsory tests during the year in certain subjects in the first three years which are taken into account in the results of the annual examinations.

3. THE UNIVERSITY OF GHENT

At the University of Ghent there is a four-year degree course in the second part of which there are two lines of specialization—general economics and business economics. It is possible to follow this course by a special one-year *Licence* in any one of five specializations.

	Ingénieur Commercial	Licence en Sciences Commerciales et Financières
	%	%
Economics	17 ·5–19 ·7	19 ·1–20 ·2
Business economics	14 ·8–16 ·9	14 ·4–16 ·5
Law	7 ·7	9 ·6
Other social sciences	10 ·9–12 ·0	9 ·0–10 ·1
Accountancy and commercial techniques	8 ·2–9 ·3	8 ·0–9 ·0
Mathematics and statistics	15 ·8–16 ·9	15 ·4–16 ·5
Foreign languages	—	—
Other subjects	24 ·0	23 ·4

These are statistics and econometrics, accountancy and finance, international economics, actuarial studies, and marketing and distribution. These courses will be available only to those who have completed a four-year degree.

The table below shows the balance of course for the two specializations in the degree:

	General Economics	Business Economics
	%	%
Economics	36 ·0–39 ·6	17 ·8–21 ·2
Business economics	11 ·5	26 ·8
Law	8 ·4–12 ·0	10 ·9–14 ·3
Other social sciences	8 ·7–12 ·3	9 ·5–12 ·9
Accountancy and commercial techniques	1 ·8	4 ·0
Mathematics and statistics	10 ·8	9 ·2
Foreign languages	9 ·6	9 ·2
Other subjects	9 ·6	9 ·2

Instruction is largely—in both options about 86 per cent—by formal lecture. There are exercise classes in some subjects—for example, languages, book-keeping, and business organization. There are also some purely voluntary courses in languages and mathematics which have not been included in the analysis. In the *Licence* part of the course all students have, in addition to the basic course, to take two further optional subjects chosen from a wide selection.

4. THE UNIVERSITY OF LIÈGE

At Liège there is a five-year economics degree in the Ecole Supérieure de Sciences Commerciales et Economiques, and two four-year degrees in business economics in the Ecole d'Administration des Affaires. All these three degrees were introduced in 1965–66; previously students took a *Licence* in political and social sciences.

The table below shows the balance of course in the economics *Licence* (*Licence en Sciences Economiques*):

	%
Economics	43 ·7–48 ·0
Business economics	4 ·3–8 ·6
Law	9 ·3
Other social sciences	10 ·4
Accountancy and commercial techniques	2 ·9
Mathematics and statistics	18 ·6–22 ·9
Foreign languages	0
Other subjects	6 ·5

Although foreign languages are not a formal part of the course, students are expected during the *Candidature* to show working knowledge of English and another foreign language. Students are also expected during the course to do five individual pieces of written work in addition to the dissertation. They do two of these in the *Candidature*—one in political economy and one in sociology—and the other three, all in aspects of general economics, in the *Licence*.

The next table shows the balance of course for the two other *Licences*. Again, although there is no instruction in foreign languages, students must show a working knowledge of two foreign languages.

	Licence en Economie Commerciale	Licence en Administration des Entreprises
	%	%
Economics	19 ·1–22 ·0	10 ·4–13 ·4
Business economics	27 ·4–29 ·5	33 ·1
Law	9 ·8–14 ·4	12 ·9–15 ·8
Other social sciences	7 ·7	10 ·9
Accountancy and commercial techniques	12 ·0	10 ·9
Mathematics and statistics	9 ·8	14 ·9
Foreign languages	—	—
Other subjects	4 ·4	4 ·0

Both *Licences* require some individual work in addition to the dissertation, and involve factory and other field visits. In the *Licence* in business economics students do nearly a tenth of their course, at the *Licence* stage, in optional subjects. These are generally in economics, business economics, and law (and the maxima attainable in these fields is the second of the two figures shown in the table). It is, however, possible to choose from a wide variety of other subjects.

5. FACULTÉS UNIVERSITAIRES, NAMUR

At Namur there is a common two-year *Candidature* followed by a *Licence* lasting three years. In the *Licence* stage the first three semesters are common, and students then specialize in economic theory or the public economy or the management of the firm. Students usually spend the fourth or fifth semester of the *Licence* at another university, either in Belgium or abroad.

The table shows the distribution of instruction over the various

subject fields for the three variants of the *Licence*. The differences
are not very great because of the length of the common part of the
course. There are further differences in the first two specializations
which do not appear in the table as they are within the courses in
the economics field.

| | *Licence* **Specializations (includes *Candidature*)** | | |
	Economic Theory	**The Public Economy**	**Management of the Firm**
	%	%	%
Economics	28 ·2	30 ·4	19 ·3
Business economics	4 ·4	4 ·4	13 ·2
Law	17 ·1	19 ·3	17 ·6
Other social sciences	12 ·1	11 ·1	12 ·1
Accountancy and commercial techniques	1 ·7	1 ·7	3 ·8
Mathematics and statistics	15 ·5	12 ·1	13 ·2
Foreign languages	6 ·1	6 ·1	6 ·0
Other subjects	14 ·9	14 ·9	14 ·8

Denmark

In Denmark there are four institutions offering first-degree courses in economics—the Universities of Copenhagen and Aarhus and the two Schools of Business Economics (Handelshøjskolen), also at Copenhagen and Aarhus. The universities, as the table below shows, have nearly two-thirds of all the students.

Distribution of Economics Students in Denmark, Autumn 1966

	No.	%
Copenhagen University	885	41 ·0
Aarhus University	480	22 ·2
Total university	1,365	63 ·2
Handelshøjskolen, Copenhagen	547	25 ·3
Handelshøjskolen, Aarhus	249	11 ·5
Total Handelshøjskolen	796	36 ·8
Overall total	2,161	100 ·0

Source: Figures supplied by the Danish Ministry of Education.

It can also be seen that the institutions at Copenhagen are in both cases larger than their counterparts at Aarhus. The universities are growing more rapidly than the schools, and so increasing their proportionate share. At the University of Copenhagen the number of students admitted to study economics grew from thirty in 1954 to 155 in 1964, while at Aarhus there has been an increase in first-year students from twenty-four in 1960 to 109 in 1966.

As the course is shorter at the schools—three years as compared with a minimum of four or five at the universities—their annual output as a proportion of student numbers is considerably greater than that of the universities.

The courses differ considerably between the schools and the universities. The degree course for the *Candidatus Politices* at the

University of Copenhagen is a course lasting a minimum of about five years, divided into two parts. Part I is planned to take two years, and Part II two to two and a half. In fact, the average length of time taken to get the degree in 1964 was 7·3 years. In Part I the course is common and there is no opportunity of selecting special topics. Teaching is concentrated to a large extent into the first of the two years—hours per week being twenty-eight in the first semester, twenty-six in the second, eighteen in the third, and twelve in the fourth. The distribution of instruction is shown below.

Distribution of Course Instruction at the University of Copenhagen

	Part I	Part II	Overall
	%	%	%
Economics	41 ·7	31 ·1	36 ·2
Business economics	9 ·5	—	4 ·6
Law	11 ·9	13 ·3	12 ·6
Other social sciences	9 ·5	—	4 ·6
Accountancy and commercial techniques	4 ·8	—	2 ·3
Mathematics and statistics	13 ·1	28 ·9	21 ·3
Foreign languages	—	—	—
Other subjects	9 ·5	—	4 ·6
Optional	—	26 ·7	13 ·8
Total semester hours	84	90	174
Type of instruction	%	%	%
Lecture	95 ·2	not available	not available
Group	4 ·8	not available	not available

The majority of instruction is in lectures, but there is some group instruction (in groups of fifteen to twenty) devoted to discussing students' written work. In the examination at the end of Part I, students take five subjects as listed below:

1. National economy
2. Danish statistics

3. Danish public law
4. American and European economic history
   (emphasizing Danish and nineteenth- and twentieth-century economic history)
5. General business economics
   (including accountancy).

In the first and the last subjects students take a four-hour written examination, and in all five they have an oral examination. Candidates need additionally to have shown ability in mathematics and accountancy, and their accountancy marks count for a third of their total marks in business economics. The statistics subject is not only descriptive, but also covers statistical methods. In this first part, as is clear from the table, the main emphasis is on economics.

In Part II students have more choice. All study political economy, statistics, and law, and in addition select a number of subjects from a list of optional topics. Each of these further subjects has a point value of one or a half, and students must acquire three points. The subjects with their point values are as follows:

Public finance (1)
Social policy[1] (1)
Industrial and trade policy (1)
Advanced statistical theory (1) or ($\frac{1}{2}$)
History of economic thought ($\frac{1}{2}$)
Money and banking ($\frac{1}{2}$)
International trade ($\frac{1}{2}$)
Agricultural economics ($\frac{1}{2}$)
Public utilities ($\frac{1}{2}$)
Econometrics ($\frac{1}{2}$)
Comparative economic systems ($\frac{1}{2}$)
Sociology ($\frac{1}{2}$).

As can be seen, the majority of these topics fall in the economics field. In the table no attempt has been made to distribute the time taken by the optional subjects, but it can be seen that they take up in all just over a quarter of the course.

The statistics and law courses are taken in the fifth to seventh semesters (statistics in the fifth and sixth and law in the seventh), leaving the students free to concentrate on economics in the latter part of the course. In economics during one semester students must

---

[1] Mainly industrial relations.

attend a small seminar (of twelve students), and each read a paper. Students also have to participate in statistics exercises. Otherwise instruction is by lecture—but groups are at the moment still small, as total student numbers have grown rapidly only in the recent past.

Students must before their final examination prepare a dissertation on some aspect of economics, statistics, or sociology. This is usually of 70–100 pages and takes some three months. The final examination covers all four groups of subjects—economics, statistics, law, and optional topics. There are four written examinations—one in economics, one in law, one in an optional topic, and one in statistics—and five oral examinations in economics, statistics, law, and two on the optional topics. Apart from the law examination, which may be taken earlier, all examinations are taken together at the end of the course.

The overall balance of the complete course is shown on p. 161. It should be stressed, however, that the optional topics have not been distributed between subject fields, and that normally these are in economics, giving a larger proportion of instruction to economics.

The degree course (for the *Candidatus Oeconomices*) at the University of Aarhus is rather different from that at Copenhagen. It is somewhat shorter—students normally take five or six years. It again consists of two parts—Part I can be taken at the end of the second year, and Part II four semesters later. Part I is again a common course, but in Part II there are two options—general and business economics. Of these business economics attracts more students. In 1965–66 there were ninety-eight students taking the business economics specialization and only nineteen (or 16 per cent) the general economics (or political economy) specialization. Again there is a tendency for instruction to be somewhat concentrated on the early semesters of Part I, and to a greater extent in Part II. The table below shows the estimated weekly hours of instruction by semester.

Semester	1	2	3	4	5	6	7	8
Weekly hours of instruction	22	25	19	19	25	25	8–9	8–9

The Part I course covers economics, including monetary theory, the economic structure of society, law, general business administration, sociology, and economic history. Again examinations are written in some subjects (four papers), and oral in all subjects.

Students must also attend a course in accountancy in which there is an examination, and have written six essays in economics before they sit for the Part I examination.

The table shows the balance for Part I, and also for both the specializations in Part II.

Balance of Course Instruction at the University of Aarhus

	Part I	Part II Economics	Part II Business Economics	Overall Economics	Overall Business Economics
	%	%	%	%	%
Economics	30 ·5	54 ·3	26 ·1	41 ·3	28 ·6
Business economics	15 ·3	17 ·1	29 ·0	16 ·1	21 ·4
Law	11 ·8	8 ·6	8 ·7	10 ·3	10 ·4
Other social sciences	7 ·1	8 ·6	8 ·7	7 ·7	7 ·8
Accountancy and commercial techniques	7 ·1	—	5 ·8	3 ·9	6 ·5
Mathematics and statistics	18 ·8	11 ·4	21 ·7	15 ·5	20 ·1
Foreign languages	—	—	—	—	—
Other subjects	9 ·4	—	—	5 ·2	5 ·2
Total semester hours (=100%)	85	70	69	155	154
	%	%	%	%	%
Lectures	78 ·8	94 ·3	94 ·2	85 ·8	85 ·7
Group instruction	21 ·2	5 ·7	5 ·8	14 ·2	14 ·3

In both specializations the basic arrangement of the course is similar; students study statistics, sociology, law (the emphasis differing in the two specializations) special subjects in either general[1] or business economics, and a selected subject in business or general economics (*i.e.*, in the subject of non-specialization). As well as these subjects, primarily taught by lecture, students have also to attend seminars. In the general economics option students have to prepare two seminar papers, and also write the 'three months' paper which in fact usually takes nearer six months; these together account for a third of the marks in the final examinations. One of these three papers must use statistical methods. There are similar requirements in the business economics specialization. In the final examination there are two oral and six written examinations.

If one compares the overall balance of the degree at Copenhagen and the general economics specialization at Aarhus (see tables) the overall effect, taking into account the probable distribution of the optional subjects at Copenhagen, is not very different. Business economics does, however, play a considerably greater part at Aarhus, and mathematics and statistics a somewhat lesser one. The difference is naturally more striking if one compares the Copenhagen degree with the Aarhus business economics specialization.

The difference between the courses at the two universities is far less marked than that between the university and the business school course. The account that follows covers only the Copenhagen School. The first difference is the much shorter length of the course—three years. There is also less retardation. Students normally complete the course in three or three and a half years. As in the universities, there is a tendency for the amount of teaching to decline through the course, as the table below shows.

Semester	1	2	3	4	5	6
Number of weekly hours of lecture instruction	25	26	22	20	18	12

The table relates only to lecture instruction, and to some extent this is counterbalanced by seminar work, which is concentrated in the third to sixth semesters, during which each student has to write four papers, each of twelve to fourteen pages.

---

[1] These are public finance and social policy.

The table shows the balance of the course—the figures are based only on lectures, and exclude the seminars in business economics in the later part of the course.

Distribution of Lecture Instruction at the Handelshøjskolen, Copenhagen

	%
Economics	22 ·8
Business economics	39 ·0
Law	8 ·1
Other social sciences	—
Accountancy and commercial techniques	5 ·7
Mathematics and statistics	14 ·6 or 21 ·1
Foreign languages	0 or 6 ·5
Other subjects	3 ·2
Total semester hours (= 100%)	123

Students take either mathematics or foreign languages, depending on which they did not specialize in at school.

There are some preliminary examinations, partly written and partly oral, which students normally take at the end of their first year. These are in book-keeping, mathematics, descriptive economics, cultural history, or psychology, and English or German. Before their final examination students have to write the four papers mentioned above, which account for a fifth of the total marks, and attend exercises in statistics and data processing. The final examination itself consists of three written papers (one eight-hour and two four-hour) and two oral examinations in business economics, a written paper (four-hour) and an oral in both economics and law, and an oral examination in statistics.

It is possible for students to continue at the School to take the *Cand. Merc.* degree, which normally involves another three semesters. In this they have further training in general economics, and specialize in one out of banking, insurance, business accountancy, marketing, or international trade. Students have to write a paper and take a final examination. Instruction is by lecture and seminar, and there is also some tutorial group work.

It is also possible to take a part-time four-year evening course at the School leading to the H.D. degree. This degree really falls outside the scope of this study, but it is a general two-year course in business subjects followed by two years' specialization on some particular aspect, the choice being similar to that in the *Cand. Merc.* This degree is taken by considerably more students than is the full-time H.A.—in 1966, 1989 were studying for the H.D., as against 580 for the H.A.

Finland

The information for Finland is less complete than that for other countries, as it was not initially intended to include Finland, and it was not possible to visit it. The information comes, therefore, solely from correspondence.[1]

There are in Finland five universities where economics is taught —Helsinki, Turku, Åbo Academy, Tampere, and Oulu—and four schools—two in Helsinki (one Swedish language and the other Finnish) and two in Turku—of which one is attached to Åbo Academy. Of these nine institutions three teach in Swedish—Åbo Academy and its School and the Swedish School at Helsinki (Svenska Handelshögskolan).

Entrance to all the institutions is selective on the basis of a combination of matriculation results and admission examinations. Students with the best matriculation results may be admitted with no further test, but those with less good results undergo further selection; for the schools students also need a period of practical experience, its length varying for the different schools, but not normally being less than three months.

Courses at the universities are longer than at the schools—four or five as compared with three years. There are far fewer economics students and staff in the universities—700 as compared with 3500 or more in the schools and 47 staff (some of them part-time) as compared with nearly 250. In 1965–66 about 65 students graduated from the universities with economics as their main subject, compared with 365 obtaining the *Ekonomi* degree from the schools.

The schools offer specialized degree courses in business economics and related subjects. At Kauppakorkeakoulu, the Helsinki school of economics, for example, there are two first-degree courses—the *Ekonomi*, designed for those intending to enter business and public administration, and the degree of Academic Secretary, which provides secretaries for the business world with a command of several foreign languages and some background in economics and commerce. The subjects taught at Kauppakorkeakoulu are divided into four groups,

---

[1] I am particularly grateful for the help of Professor J. J. Paunio.

and courses of varying lengths in different subjects are combined for the degrees, the student having some choice of subject within the regulations. The first group of subjects is business economics, economics, and closely related subjects;[1] the second, other social sciences; the third, major foreign languages; and the last, Finnish and Swedish.

In the *Ekonomi* degree the student combines the study of various subjects to the *cum laude approbatur*, the *approbatur*, the long-course, the short-course, or the introductory-course level. There are two different ways of combining subjects—the concentrated approach, which entails studying at least six subjects, and the broadly based approach, which involves at least eight subjects. In the concentrated combination each student must take one subject in the first group to the *cum laude approbatur* level, and also two subjects to the *approbatur* or long-course level. Two of these three subjects must be selected from business economics I and II and economics. Each student must also study at least one major language to the long-course level. In the broadly based combination the student takes three subjects in the first group to the long-course level, one of which must be business economics I or II. He also has to do one language to the long-course level. Three short courses and one introductory course are chosen from the first and second group of subjects. Whatever his long courses, each student must, as a minimum, do short courses in both parts of business economics, in economics, and in commercial law. Whichever approach he follows for the *Ekonomi* degree, every student must take two seminar courses (in subjects he is studying for the *cum laude approbatur* or long-course level), which both involve writing and defending a seminar paper of some twenty-five to thirty pages.

The Academic Secretary's degree is similar to the *Ekonomi*, but in it the subject studied to the *cum laude approbatur* level (if one is taken) can be a language or sociology. Again there are two ways of combining subjects—six being required if one is taken to the *cum laude approbatur* level and seven if not. Whatever combination is chosen, the student must take long courses in two major foreign languages, one of which must include a seminar course.

---

[1] The subjects are business economics, which is broadly divided into two parts, the first dealing with problems relating to the field of accountancy with the firm and the second to the organization of the firm; economics; commercial law; economic geography; business mathematics; and commodity study and technology.

For both degrees the course lasts three years. Kauppakorkea-koulu also offers post-graduate degrees. There is a master's degree, a licentiate, and a doctorate. In the master's degree students study four subjects, in one of which, taken to the *laudatur* level, they write a fairly extensive scientific paper, and in the licentiate two subjects, in one of which students do a research paper. The doctorate involves a published thesis, and is very rarely attained.

In the universities the system is similar to the Swedish points system—there are courses for the *approbatur, cum laude approbatur*, and *laudatur* levels. Examinations are mainly written, but supplemented by orals. All economics students have to do a certain minimum amount of work in statistics, and are recommended to take an examination in mathematics as well. The main course also includes various aspects of mathematical economics. Written work is necessary for the final degree—students write seminar papers, essays, and also a dissertation (the *laudatur* thesis). This thesis is 100–200 typewritten pages. Quite a high proportion of students—estimated at 20–25 per cent—start to work towards higher degrees in economics, but relatively few actually complete their studies. Although the number of first degrees with economics as a main subject is small, it has grown rapidly in recent years—in 1962–63 there were thirty (all but three from the University of Helsinki), but in 1965–66 this had risen to sixty-five. Throughout the course students are expected to read books in foreign languages, principally in English, but also in German and Swedish.

France[1]

In French universities a *Licence* in economics is one of the two main degrees given by the faculties of law and economics. The course is generally the same throughout the country, and the syllabus of individual courses is stipulated centrally in some detail. In the fourth year students take three or four courses in an optional subject, and while these do vary from university to university, certain options are frequently found.

It is possible to take some economics at twenty French universities, but a full course is available at only seventeen. Forty per cent, however, of all students of economics are studying at Paris, and no other university has anything like Paris's numbers—the next largest group of economics students (7·2 per cent in June 1965) was at Aix-Marseilles,[2] but here there were just under 1000 students compared with over 5000 in Paris. Apart from these two, few faculties have more than 600 economics students. In 1964 five faculties had over 600 students of economics, five between 400 and 600, six between 200 and 399, and four under 200.

The degree—the *Licence ès Sciences Economiques*—consists of four years of study. Students who successfully complete the course (and many do not) tend to do so in the four years, or slightly longer; for example, at the University of Nancy 80 per cent of the successful students complete their degree in the four years. In Paris successful students, of whom there tend to be fewer proportionally than in provincial universities, tend to take longer over their degrees—less than 10 per cent appear to complete in the four years.

Written examinations made up of a number of three-hour papers take place in June of each year, and cover certain of the subjects studied during the year. Students who fail can retake the examinations in October, and if necessary again the following year, but they may not sit the first-year examination more than four times. These

---

[1] There have been considerable changes in French higher education since the preparation of this report in 1966.
[2] Including Nice.

written examinations are eliminatory, and only those who pass go on to take the oral examinations, which are each of fifteen-minutes and cover subjects studied during the year. Thus in some subjects there may be both oral and written examinations; in others only oral. If students pass the second-year examination they can obtain the *Diplôme d'études économiques générales*, but there is no evidence that this is considered as a satisfactory final qualification. At the successful completion of the fourth-year examinations they obtain their *Licence*.

Teaching is largely by formal lecture—a lecture course normally consists of three hours per semester per subject. Total lecture instruction for a student in a week amounts to about eighteen hours. In addition, there are compulsory *travaux pratiques* (T.P.). During each semester every student has to attend two T.P. sessions of one and a half hours each. In Paris the strain of numbers puts great stress on the teaching, and in the first year the students are divided into three groups—two in Paris, one attending lectures in the morning and the other attending lectures in the afternoon, and one at Nanterre (Hauts-de-Seine). Nevertheless, even if all students wished to attend lectures they could not, as there is simply not enough physical accommodation for them. This, coupled with the fact that lectures are formal, leads to a great deal of use of duplicated or printed sets of lecture notes—*polycopiés*, as they are called. Private instruction is also available, especially for the first-year course. Such instruction is advertised in the newspapers. In the provinces the situation is easier, as the numbers of students are far more manageable; however, *polycopiés* are used almost universally.

The first-year course is largely in common with those students in the faculty proceeding to the law degree. All students take courses for two semesters on introduction to the study of law and civil law, constitutional law and political institutions, general political economy and the history of public institutions, and French social history to the Revolution. The economics students take in addition two one-semester courses, one in statistics and the other in preparatory mathematics for economists. There are two written examinations at the end of the year—one covering the two subjects in which T.P. have been taken and the second covering the other subjects—followed by orals.

In the second year there is one two-semester course on general political economy in which there are also T.P. There are one-semester courses—in public finance, administrative institutions, contemporary economic history, demography, international institutions, mathematics, and statistics. There are T.P. in mathematics and statistics, and also in another subject designated by the faculty. There is also a course on the principles of private accountancy. The examinations consist of three written papers (on general political economy, mathematics or statistics, and one out of demography, international institutions or public finance[1]) and eight oral examinations which cover the other subjects. It is possible for students who already have a degree to take a special course which compresses the normal first- and second-year course into one year, thus enabling them to gain the *Licence* in three instead of the normal four years.

The third-year course consists of four two-semester courses. These are in political economy—fluctuations and growth (in which there are also T.P. in both semesters), international economics, history of economic thought, and commercial law. There are one-semester courses in labour law, mathematics, and statistics. There are three written examinations in political economy, history of economic thought, or either international economics or commercial law, as chosen by the candidate. As well there are five oral examinations.

In the fourth year rather over half the time is taken up by the common-core courses, and the rest by the student's chosen optional field. The core courses consist of a two-semester course in political economy (economic systems, structures, and development) and three semester courses—in financial economics, national income accounts, and economic history. The optional field available varies from university to university, but makes up the equivalent of four one-semester courses. There are three written examinations—in political economy, public finance, and one of the subjects in the optional field—and five or six orals in the other subjects.

The optional field contains three or four subjects, more usually four. Table F.1 gives an idea of the range of options available at the various universities.[2] Most universities offer at least two optional fields. Paris has five—of which by far the most popular is the one concerning the economics of the firm (taken by 40 per cent of all economics students in the fourth-year examinations in June 1964).

---

[1] The choice of subject is made by the dean of the faculty, and is not known to the candidates before they see their actual examination papers.

[2] All this part of the report relates to the options for the academic year 1965–66, a list of which was kindly provided by the French Ministry of National Education

Table F.1

Fourth-year options Available at the Various Universities in 1965–66

University		No. of Optional fields available	Economics of the Firm[1]	Economic Develop- ment	Political Economy	Regional or European Economics	Other
Aix	(51)[2]	3	1	1			Economics of industrial countries
Bordeaux	(52)	3	1	1	1		
Caen	(13)	1			1		
Clermont-Ferrand	(13)	1	1				
Dijon	(17)	2	1	1			
Grenoble	(41)	3	1		1	1	
Lille	(30)	3	2[3]			1	
Lyons	(53)	2				1	Economics of transport
Montpellier	(36)	2	1	1			
Nancy	(24)	1				1	

University	No. of Optional fields available	Economics of the Firm [1]	Economic Development	Political Economy	Regional or European Economics	Other
Nice (11)	1	1				
Paris (418)	5	1	1			Economics of labour; International economic relations; Econometrics
Poitiers (36)	3	2[4]				General economics
Rennes (19)	2	1				Analysis of decisions
Strasbourg (30)	2					Economics and public enterprise; Economics and private enterprise
Toulouse (18)	2					National and regional economics and mathematical economics; Mathematical and rural economics

(1) In each case a general description has been given for the group of fields involved; the exact title varies from university to university.
(2) The figures in brackets refer to the total number of fourth-year economics students in June 1965.
(3) One of these is entitled "Problems of the Firm and of Labour" and the other "Economics and Management of Firms".
(4) One of these is called "The Economics of the Firm" and the other "The Organization of the Firm"

At the same examinations 18·6 per cent of the students took economic development, 17·3 per cent econometrics, 16·6 per cent international economic relations, and 7·3 per cent the economics of labour.

Although fields may have the same or very similar names, the content may vary considerably from one university to another. Four examples in the field of economics of the firm are given in Table F.2.

Table F.2

Fourth-year subjects in the Economics of the Firm

Clermont-Ferrand	Grenoble
Management of the firm and accountancy	The firm and the economic environment
Regional economics and planning	Economic analysis and management forecasting
Theory of the firm	Financial analysis and ways of financing the firm
Economic geography	Statistical analysis applied to the problems of the firm

Paris	Rennes
General problems of company administration.	Organization and economic management of the firm
Financial management	Industrial relations and labour economics
Management control	Macro-economic planning and micro-economic decisions
Commercial management	

There is similar variation in the other options. There seems some tendency for options to be more homogeneous and their different subjects more closely related in larger universities where more options are offered. Particularly where there is only one option, it tends to embrace a number of fairly distinct subjects, though this is not always the case. Quantitative economics rarely appears among the options[1]—except for the Paris option in econometrics.

---

[1] There are courses in econometrics in both the options at Strasbourg and Toulouse, in mathematics applied to political economy at Dijon, and in econometrics and operations research in the general economics option at Rennes.

The most serious problem in French faculties, apart from those caused in Paris by the sheer pressure of numbers, is that of student wastage. Success rates are very low (even allowing for 'ghost' students who are registered but not seriously attending). The wastage is most serious in the first year, but often continues in subsequent years (this was demonstrated for the Paris faculty in a private study by Professor Lecaillon).

OTHER INSTITUTIONS

The courses at the specialized institutions of comparable status to the universities are much more organized. Entry is by competitive examination, usually after a special preparatory year at school after the *Baccalauréat*. This in effect adds another year to the three-year course in the special institution. The Ecole des Hautes Etudes Commerciales (H.E.C.), for example, has recently reformed its entrance examination so that the work done in this preparatory year is more closely related to the work the successful candidates subsequently do at H.E.C. Competition for entry is severe—at H.E.C. in 1965, 1830 men entered the examinations, 535 of them passed the eliminatory written examinations, and finally, after rigorous oral examinations, 260 were admitted.

There are in France altogether sixteen institutions of this type, four of them in or near Paris[1] and twelve in the provinces. It is possible for their students to be registered also in the universities, where they pursue their studies for the *Licence*. In 1962–63, 17·5 per cent of the first-year students in the Paris faculty were registered at one of these other institutions.

These institutions offer three-year courses leading to their own diplomas; the courses of two of them, H.E.C. and the Institut Commercial de Nancy (which is attached to the university faculty there), will be described below.

H.E.C. is probably the most highly rated of these institutions. Unlike all the others, it is wholly residential. Its course is in practice more intensive than that at the other specialized institutions. The course has four main elements—first, lectures and study groups (the latter consist of from fifteen to twenty students and account for just

---

[1] H.E.C., the Ecole Superieure des Sciences Economiques et Commerciales (E.S.S.E.C.), the Ecole de Haut Enseignement Commercial pour les Jeunes Filles (H.E.C.J.F.), and the Ecole Superieure de Commerce de Paris (E.S.C.P.).

over half—53·2 per cent—of the total instruction time); secondly, examinations and written work; thirdly, visits to industrial and commercial establishments, upon which students write reports; and fourthly and lastly, practical work. To take the last element first, students have to do three periods of practical work—one month (industrial work) by the end of the first year, another (abroad) by the end of the second year, and the last during the third year. These periods of practical work are done under the School's control. Students whose results are unsatisfactory may be sent away to do an additional period of practical work, after which they may be allowed to return. The success rate is, however, very high—about 95 per cent.

The formal instruction has a succession of themes around which the semester's work is grouped. In the first semester this theme is the basic techniques of business administration; in the second, the introduction to business administration; in the third, economic, administrative, and legal problems; and in the fourth, financial and social problems. In the last year there is a synthesis of the work that has been done around the theme of the function of the firm in its environment, and the student also takes an optional subject (finance, marketing, international commerce, or human sciences). Throughout the course students study English and other foreign languages.

The overall balance of the course and the amount of instruction is shown in Table F.3. To it should be added the non-academic instruction of factory visits and practical work.

There are examinations at the end of each year as well as tests during the year whose results count towards the student's average. This is considered by a committee of professors at the end of the year, which decides whether the student can continue to the next year or not. Work done in each semester counts, with different weights, towards the student's final result. The few students who are not finally judged worthy of the H.E.C. Diploma may be granted a certificate.

Although students can also register at the university, the H.E.C. official attitude is that successful combinations of two courses is not easy for the student.

The Institut Commercial de Nancy offers a three-year course leading to its *Diplôme d'Ingénieur Commercial*. Here again, students have to do periods of practical work—optional in the first summer vacation and compulsory for two months in the second year, on which a report must be written—and have industrial and commercial visits in which reports are also written. The number of students is considerably smaller than at H.E.C.—a total of less than 150, as compared with over 900.

Table F.3 shows the overall balance of the course. It can be seen that there is quite a difference between it and the H.E.C. course. There is rather more instruction in total—at Nancy students average 21·4 hours of instruction a week over this course as a whole, whereas at H.E.C. the comparable figure is 18·8 hours.

Teaching is partly by ordinary members of the university staff and partly by part-time staff otherwise active in industry and commerce. The *Diplôme* course can be combined with the *Licence* (the Institut is attached to the University of Nancy), but this is not easy.

Table F.3

A Comparison of Courses at H.E.C. and the Institut Commercial de Nancy[1]

	H.E.C.	Institut Commercial de Nancy
	% of course	% of course
Economics	7·1	15·0
Business economics	34·5–36·3	11·8
Law	14·2–15·9	19·7
Other social sciences	6·2–8·0	3·1
Accountancy and commercial techniques	12·4	15·7
Mathematics and statistics	7·1	7·1
Foreign languages	10·6	21·3
Other subjects	6·2	6·3
Total hours of instruction	1,469	1,670

[1] Where a range is shown, the first figure indicates the amount all students do and the second the maximum amount if all possible options are taken in the subject group.

Germany (Federal Republic)

In Germany there are three main first degrees in which a substantial proportion of economics is taught—the *Diplom-Volkswirt* (D.V.), the *Diplom-Handelslehrer* (D.H.), and the *Diplom-Kaufmann* (D.K.). As well as these three it is also possible to combine economics with applied science subjects for the degree of *Diplom-Wirtschafts-ingenieur* (W.Ing.). In addition, at the new University of Bochum and at the University of Giessen there is a degree called the *Diplom-Wirtschaftler* (D.W.) which integrates business and general economics.

The D.K. is the most popular of the three main degrees—in the winter semester 1964–65, 16,340 students were reading for it. It is basically a degree in business economics, while the D.V. is a degree in general economics and the D.H. is a specialized degree intended for those who wish to teach commercial subjects. In the winter semester of 1964–65, 9880 students were reading for the D.V., and only 2942 for the D.H. Comparatively few students take the W.Ing., for which courses are available at only a few institutions, and at some of them on a post-graduate basis only—in 1964–65 there were 809 W.Ing. students. As the D.W. is offered only by two universities there are few students reading for it—in the summer semester of 1966 there were 906, the majority of them at Bochum.

Not all universities offer all three of the main degrees. If one examines nineteen German universities,[1] at eighteen of them is it possible to take a D.V., at twelve the D.K., and at eight the D.H. The W.Ing. degree is available only at the Berlin Technical University and the Technical Universities of Darmstadt, Aachen, and Munich, at the last two only as a second degree. The D.W., as already mentioned, is offered only at Bochum and Giessen.

Among these same nineteen institutions, without doubt the biggest faculty in terms of student numbers is at the University of Cologne, which has just over 20 per cent of the total number of students of economics. The two next largest groups are at Munich

---

[1] This includes the Berlin Technical University and the Mannheim School of Economics, but excludes Bochum, Giessen, and the four Technical Universities of Aachen, Darmstadt, Karlsruhe, and Munich.

and Hamburg, at both of which there are about 10 per cent of the total number of students. Of the other sixteen institutions, four have over 5 per cent of the students (Frankfurt, Erlangen-Nürnberg, Mannheim, and the Berlin Free University). There is thus considerable concentration in the first three universities mentioned, which together account for just over 40 per cent of the total. However, none of the faculties is very small; the four smallest (Heidelberg, Marburg, Mainz, and Kiel) each have about 600 students, which in many countries would be quite a large faculty.

The three main courses (D.K., D.V., and D.H.) all have a prescribed minimum length of four years,[1] but in practice all usually take longer. A recent study[2] showed that in 1961 most students took from nine to eleven semesters to get their degree. Students obtaining the D.V. tended to take rather longer than students obtaining the D.K.

Traditionally in Germany students have been left very free to plan their own courses, but now at nearly all universities there are study plans published either by the faculty or by a student body. These are, however, seldom compulsory. In four of the faculties the first two years are now, officially programmed, and the student is obliged to follow them. These four are Bochum, Giessen, Mannheim (here only for the D.K.), and Saarbrücken. Other faculties may have partial programmes whereby students have to attend certain classes in their early semesters or before they can go on to other instruction —for example, before they can participate in a seminar. At the University of Munich, for instance, there are compulsory lecture classes (Pflichtübungen), each of not more than fifty students for the first two semesters in general and business economics.

As well as freedom to plan their own courses, German students were also traditionally free to move between universities during their course—a survival of medieval university tradition. Precise statistics on the extent of this movement do not seem to be easily obtainable, but it seems to have increased over the last decade. The majority of students who move do so once only. The greater formalization of courses, particularly the introduction of intermediate examinations (a Vorprüfung or Zwischenprüfung), may well tend to discourage movement between universities.

---

[1] The D.K. can theoretically be done in seven semesters if the student has already passed the Kaufmannsgehilfenprüfung.

[2] Gerhard Kath, Christoph Oehler, and Roland Reichwein, Studienweg und Studienerfolg, Berlin, 1966.

There are at the moment considerable differences between German universities in the stage to which they have evolved the traditional course. It seems best, therefore, to describe in more detail the courses at a number of institutions representative of both the more and the less traditional type of courses. The institutions chosen are Marburg, Cologne, and Göttingen to represent the traditional course, slightly modified in the case of Göttingen and under very severe pressures from student numbers in Cologne. The less traditional courses described are those at Saarbrücken, the Free University, Berlin, and Mannheim. The very interesting course at the new University of Bochum was not in existence at the time of my visit to Germany, and so is not fully described, but a brief note on it concludes the discussion of individual institutions.

1. THE UNIVERSITY OF MARBURG

The University of Marburg has a relatively small faculty. It consisted of 594 students in the spring of 1965. Only one first degree —the *Diplom-Volkswirt*—is offered. Of the eight semesters which are the course's minimum length at least two must be spent at Marburg. The final examination consists of six subjects, in each of which students must possess a certificate of attendance at a seminar (*Seminarschein*). Five of the subjects are compulsory—economic theory, economic policy, public finance, business economics, and law. The sixth subject is optional, and students have a choice of statistics, economic history, or sociology.[1] As well as these subjects all students must also pass an examination early in the course in book-keeping and the elements of statistics. The final examination is both written and oral. The written examinations last five hours. All students have to write a dissertation in economics or public finance. This is supposed to take about eight weeks, and is not done before the end of the sixth semester.

Teaching is by lectures, exercise classes (*Übungen*), and seminars. *Übungen* tend to be large, but seminars are usually small, about twenty students. Each student at a seminar must be prepared at some stage to read a paper himself. The *Übungen* are closely geared to examination preparation. In addition to these normal forms of instruction there are also optional *Arbeitsgemeinschaften*; these are

---

[1] From 1968 only five subjects have had to be taken in the final examination, of which four—economic theory, economic policy, public finance, and business economics—are compulsory.

both lecture-related where the lecture is elaborated and specific questions posed for students to answer, and revision classes for examinations. The groups here are small—ten to twenty students—and each group is usually led by a fourth-year or doctoral student. These *Arbeitsgemeinschaften* are one of the departures from the traditional pattern at Marburg. *Arbeitsgemeinschaften* seem now to be fairly general, though by no means universal, in German universities in the early part of the course.

2. THE UNIVERSITY OF COLOGNE

At Cologne there is a serious problem of overcrowding. The faculty is extremely large—it contained in all 8575 students in the summer semester 1965. There is a severe strain on teaching and other resources, extremely limited staff–student contact, and a high drop-out rate (about 50 per cent). A symptom of the pressure is the success of private teachers outside the university, some of whom even hire cinemas to lecture in during the mornings.

The faculty offers the three main degrees—the D.V., the D.K., and the D.H. In the *Diplom-Volkswirt* the compulsory subjects are the same as at Marburg, but there is a far greater selection for the optional subject. Students have a choice of sixteen subjects. Few of these are general economics topics; most are either aspects of business economics or other social sciences.

In the *Diplom-Kaufmann* students take four compulsory subjects and two optional ones. The compulsory subjects are general business economics, economics, a special topic in business economics, and law. The optional subjects are arranged in two groups: students can take both their subjects from Group I (and must, if they choose the second special topic in business economics, see below), but may not take both from Group II. The two groups are constituted as follows:

I. Public finance, a second special topic in business economics, insurance, political science, social policy, economic and social policy, economic and social history, economic and social geography, economic and social education, economic and social psychology, commodity knowledge.

II. Commerce, business tax law, trade, co-operation, the economics of energy, physics, chemistry. (In the latter two subjects particular emphasis is put on their business applications.)

The *Diplom-Handelslehrer* is similar in structure to the D.K., but economic and social education replaces the special topic in business economics as a compulsory subject. The two optional subjects are chosen from three groups, though if one is taken from Group III only one is necessary. Again two subjects can be taken from Group I, but only one from Group II. The groups are as follows:

I. A special topic in business economics, political science.
II. Public finance, commerce, business tax law, insurance, trade, sociology, social policy, economic and social statistics.
III. Economic and social history, economic and social geography, economic and social psychology, commodity knowledge, physics, chemistry, German, English, French, Spanish.

In view of the very large numbers of students, seminars are very large—150 to 300 students. The only instruction for small groups is in *Arbeitsgemeinschaften*. Twenty tutors help with these, but there is considerable difficulty in finding rooms for them to meet in. Some help is also available for students when they are preparing their *Diplomarbeit*, but this is necessarily limited because of the student numbers and the relative shortage of staff.

3. THE UNIVERSITY OF GÖTTINGEN

The University of Göttingen offers the three degree courses. The subjects involved in the courses are identical to those described earlier with the exception of the optional subjects. In the *Diplom-Volkswirt* there is more choice of optional subjects than at Marburg (Göttingen has a larger faculty—1640 students in all in the winter semester 1964–65), but less than at Cologne. In the *Diplom-Kaufmann* one of the optional subjects has to be another special topic in business economics, but the other can be chosen more widely from a list containing other economic and social science subjects outside the business field. The *Diplom-Handelslehrer* is very similar to the *Diplom-Kaufmann*, with the inclusion of education as a special subject. The optional subjects are almost identical, but languages are not included as they are at Cologne.

Göttingen differs from Cologne and Marburg in that the University publishes study plans (*Studienpläne*) for the degrees which provide guidance for students as to the order in which lectures should be attended and subjects studied. They also give some very general guidance on the nature of the degree, and on desirable working methods.

Another difference is that in the *Diplom-Kaufmann* and the *Diplom-Handelslehrer* the preliminary requirements are rather more formalized. Students have to pass examinations in book-keeping, financial mathematics, economic arithmetic, and the elements of statistics by the end of the third semester. This is not as great a formalization of these requirements as at some German universities, where there is a formal *Vorprüfung* or *Zwischenprüfung*, but it is a move in this direction.

Göttingen does not use tutorial or small-group instruction. There is, however, because of the growth of numbers, considerable pressure on the seminars. These often consist of as many as sixty students, and it is impossible in a semester for all students who have prepared papers to read them. Twenty-five may prepare papers, but only twelve will be able to read them, and have them fully discussed.

4. THE UNIVERSITY OF SAARBRÜCKEN

The University of Saarbrücken was the first German university to institute a formal and compulsory *Vorprüfung*. This must be taken at the latest at the end of the third semester, and can normally be retaken once only, although in special circumstances a third attempt may be permitted. This examination covers the usual preliminary subjects (book-keeping and mathematics and statistics), and also the elements of general and business economics. It is identical for students reading for each of the three degrees. There is also a *Vorprüfung* in law, but this is taken later in the course, in or after the fifth semester.

At the moment the basic subject structure of the courses is like that at the other German universities, though in the *Diplom-Kaufmann* one of the two optional subjects is another special topic in business economics. It is planned, however, in the *Diplom-Volkswirt* to offer a choice of law or statistics and econometrics, and in the *Diplom-Kaufmann* of law or operations research. This would mean that law was no longer obligatory, but only an optional subject.[1] In the *Diplom-Handelslehrer* the possibility exists, as at Cologne, of taking only one optional subject if it is chosen from a certain group, which includes languages.

In the first three semesters while students are working for the *Vorprüfung* there are *Arbeitsgemeinschaften*, groups led by selected older students. Each group consists of some fifteen students who

---

[1] *cf.* footnote on page 182.

devote about half the meetings to discussing general problems and half to discussing problems arising from the lecture.

In the more specialized work after the *Vorprüfung* seminars are used, and every effort is made to restrict these to twenty in order that every student may have a chance to participate fully.

The structure of the course now being introduced will be far more planned than at most German universities—first, the two semesters, or sometimes three, of preparatory work for the *Vorprüfung* (*Unterstufe*), followed by a period working on the main subjects of the degree (*Mittelstufe*), and lastly by a period of at least three semesters (*Oberstufe*), working on the last subject for the degree (law or the mathematical alternative), the *Diplomarbeit*, and attending the examination seminar. At the end of the second stage oral examinations are held to regulate progress to the final stage. Students have a course limited to general and business economics and closely related subjects. The amount of choice is relatively limited—between a small number of special topics in the main subject of specialization, general economics in the *Diplom-Volkswirt*, and business economics in the *Diplom-Kaufmann*, and between law and the mathematical alternative. The programme is controlled by the study plan, so the total course allows far less choice and freedom than has been the tradition in German universities.

5. THE FREE UNIVERSITY, BERLIN

The Free University, Berlin, has quite a large economics faculty (2560 students in the winter semester 1964–65), and offers the three main degrees.

In the *Diplom-Kaufmann* there is a *Vorprüfung* covering seven subjects, in each of which there is a four-hour written examination. It is normally taken at the end of the third semester, and can be retaken up to two times, but only after a semester has elapsed. The *Vorprüfung* for the *Diplom-Volkswirt* is far less organized.

The most interesting development in the instruction at the Free University is the use of optional tutorial groups (*Tutoren-Gruppen*) in the first to fourth semesters. These tutorial groups cover the basic groundwork of general and business economics as appropriate for the degree being taken. They are in addition to normal lecture, seminar, and exercise class instruction. Each group consists of ten to fifteen students, and meets weekly for at least two hours under the leadership of post-graduate students. The groups are organized by a special committee representing the teachers of general economics, business economics, and sociology.[1] This committee appoints the group leaders, each appointment being made for a semester but being renewable. Each tutor is paid for a maximum of twenty hours a week: this covers three group meetings plus the appropriate preparation and an hour when he is available for individual consultation by the students in his groups. The small size of the group and the availability of the tutor ensure close contact with the students in the vitally important first years of their university course. It is a modern equivalent of the traditional pro-seminar when these were of a manageable size. It also has the merit of drawing post-graduate students and junior members of the teaching staff into the full work of the faculty.

6. WIRTSCHAFTSCHOCHSCHULE, MANNHEIM

The Mannheim Hochschule is technically a specialized institution, although it is applying for university status. In the winter semester of 1965–66 it had in all nearly 2400 students, 1740 of them reading for the *Diplom-Kaufmann*, 313 for the *Diplom-Handelslehrer*, and 255 for the *Diplom-Volkswirt*. The *Diplom-Volkswirt* course was begun only fairly recently (1963), and is part of the widening of the School's curriculum, first into more general economics, and later to law and other social sciences. Like many specialized institutions in other countries, it is developing from its early purely commercial character.

The School has a compulsory study plan for its main degree—the *Diplom-Kaufmann*. The students take general business economics, a special topic in business economics (either the economics of a particular type of industry or commerce or the study of a functional aspect of business administration), economics, law, and two optional subjects chosen from economics, social sciences, technology, and languages. All students have to have at least six certificates of participation in seminars or exercise classes—two in business economics, one each in general economics and law, and two in subjects which are *not* being taken for examination purposes (*studium generale*). There are *Arbeitsgemeinschaften*, and in the later terms seminars.

There is an advisory study plan for the *Diplom-Volkswirt* students listing subjects and the appropriate semesters in which to take them.

---

[1] There are also tutorial groups in sociology, but these, although in the same faculty, do not concern students reading for economics degrees.

All students take general economics and business economics, with considerably more emphasis on general economics. In the first part of the course (roughly the first four semesters) all do some work in statistics, law, and sociology, and in the second half of the course they continue with one of these three subjects. Sociology so far is much the most popular of the three, being chosen by about two-thirds of the students, while a sixth do each of the others. Students are expected to attend about twenty hours of instruction a week. The exercise classes (*Übungen*) do not run parallel with the lectures, but are lagged by one semester. In the past they consisted of some hundred or more students, but are now entrusted to assistants and limited to forty. Seminars are not compulsory, as no certificates of participation are required. They are small—some fifteen to twenty students—which enables all to participate. In general there is consultation between the teaching staff to ensure that there is no unnecessary overlap in instruction—something which is by no means always the case in the traditional German system.

7. THE UNIVERSITY OF BOCHUM

This new university has a new degree course—the *Diplom-Wirtschaftler*—which is available at only one other German university, Giessen. The course started with some 280 students in the autumn of 1965, and by the summer semester 1965–66 had built up to nearly 800 students. The course integrates, to a greater extent than is usual in traditional German courses, the study of general and business economics. The study plan divides the course into two periods—the first, the *Grundstudium*, ending in the *Zwischenprüfung*, followed by the second period, the *Hauptstudium*. The *Grundstudium* is planned in detail, and students have to follow the prescribed pattern. Great attention is given to the orientation of students by the proper introduction of economics and the right way of studying it. The *Grundstudium* takes four or five semesters, but is strictly limited to five as a maximum. The *Zwischenprüfung* is a written and oral examination in four subjects—general economics, business economics, law, and statistics. The usual preliminary examinations in mathematics for economists and commercial arithmetic are not studied as part of the course, but taken in special, concentrated courses outside the normal lecture term.[1] *Arbeitsgemeinschaften* classes are used in the

---

[1] This is also the case (or proposed) at Giessen, Erlangen-Nürnberg, and Munich.

first two semesters of the course, and are compulsory. They are taken by teaching assistants, of whom the faculty has twenty-four.

In the *Hauptstudium* the student has more freedom to arrange his own course. The final examination deals with four subjects—economic policy, theoretical business economics, applied business economics, and one optional subject chosen from a wide range.

Greece

There are two universities—Athens and Salonika—and one specialized institution—the Athens Graduate School of Economics and Business Science—offering first-degree courses in economics in Greece. In both the universities economics is very closely connected with law. This is particularly true at the University of Athens, where economics is studied only as a specialization within the law degree. All the degree courses have a prescribed length of four years, though at the School it is not possible to take the final examination until the October of the fifth year. Successful students normally take more than four years—five or six are common. For some of this period students may be studying only part-time while they are doing their military service or working. At the School students are not normally allowed to register for the same year of studies more than three times.

At the University of Athens little economics is taught until the fourth year, when the students have the option of specializing in the subject. Until then they follow the law degree course. The majority of students in the faculty continue in law—in 1965, 419 graduated in law and only 20 in political and economic science. Until recently students could register in both specialist sections—law, and political and economic science—but now they are allowed to register in only one. This will have the effect of limiting the political and economic science section to serious students of economics, and will reduce the student numbers. Before this restriction it was estimated that, of 700 students following the fourth-year course, 100 were registered in economics.

In the first year of the course there is economics instruction covering elements of theoretical analysis in micro- and macro-economics and national accounting, and in the second year all students study the theory of public finance and economic and financial policy. The third year of the course contains no economics.

Students come to their fourth year, therefore, having spent rather over a quarter of their time in the first two years on economics and none in the third. Even in the fourth year law still accounts for about a third of the student's time. In economics in the fourth year students have lectures in economic analysis, applied economics, with special reference to Greece, economic history, international economic relations, and the problems and policies of public finance, again with special reference to Greece. There are in addition seminars where other subjects which cannot be included in the course—for example, economic development and statistics—are discussed. Students also prepare and present papers. They are expected to write one paper for each of the three professors of economics. There is also a voluntary course in linear programming which students may attend if they wish.

Examinations take place at the end of each year, and may be oral or written at the discretion of the professor concerned. There are four at the end of the first year, seven at the end of the second, six at the end of the third, and seven in the economics section at the end of the fourth. The final examinations are both written and oral. Students must pass the written examination in all subjects before they can present themselves for the oral.

Instruction is by both lecture and seminars, but until the fourth year seminars tend to be very large—up to 200 students. There are also some purely optional courses, 'free lessons', where special aspects of the main subjects are developed. There is severe pressure on library resources, and first-year students are not in fact permitted to use the library. Some American and English books are used (and more in translation), mainly in the fourth year. It is estimated that half the economics specialists in the final year have a reading knowledge of English, but the short time available does not permit much use to be made of foreign literature.

There have been since 1950 proposals for reform in the system at the University of Athens, as it is generally felt that the present system does not allow economics to be taught properly. It is considered that far too much has to be crammed into the last year, and many aspects of the subject can find no place in the official timetable, but must be fitted into seminars where possible. The chief proposal is for the division of the law faculty into two distinct sections, and the establishment of a separate economics degree.

At the University of Salonika the faculty is one of law and economics, and there is a separate economics degree, though law still takes up a large share of the students' instruction time. Its position is, however, far less dominating than at Athens, as the table below shows.

Economics and law are both taught in all the years of the course. A far wider range of other subjects is included than at Athens, as can be seen from the table. The economics section of the faculty

Balance of Course Instruction (%)

	University of Athens	University of Salonika
Economics	26 ·2†	25 ·4
Business economics	—	3 ·9
Law	72 ·8	39 ·0
Other social sciences	1 ·0	11 ·9
Accountancy and commercial techniques	—	3 ·9
Mathematics and statistics	—†	8 ·5
Foreign languages	—	7 ·6
Other subjects	—	0 ·8
Total (year hours) = 100%	103*	118

† Some statistics are in fact included in the economics seminar, but the exact proportion is not known. It has all been credited to the economics field.

* Includes the voluntary courses ("free lessons") in economics, but not in other subjects.

admits some 500 or more students a year, and awards about eighty licences.

The Athens Graduate[1] School of Economics and Business Science offers degree courses specializing in economic or business sciences. The majority of the students choose to specialize in business sciences, only about 10 per cent specializing in economics.[2] The first two years of the course are common, and then students choose their specialization. The economics specialists are to some extent selected by the academic staff, who insist on a knowledge of English. The table below shows the balance of course instruction for the two specializations, distinguishing the different years of the course. It is not possible

[1] The degrees are in fact first degrees, and students enter the Graduate School direct from high school. University students can register in the third year, but must first take examinations in subjects they have not previously passed at the University.

[2] In 1964–65 in the third year there were 42 students registered in the economics section and 505 in the business section, and in the fourth year 34 and 399 respectively.

	Economics				Business Sciences		Overall	
	Year 1 %	Year 2 %	Year 3 %	Year 4 %	Year 3 %	Year 4 %	Economics %	Business Sciences %
Economics	25·0	20·0	29·0	50·0	17·9	7·4	29·9	17·4
Business economics	8·3	6·6	6·5	—	10·7	11·1	5·6	9·2
Law	20·1	20·0	32·2	—	28·6	29·7	19·6	24·8
Other social sciences	—	—	9·7	18·2	10·7	—	6·5	2·8
Accountancy and commercial techniques	12·5	16·7	—	—	14·3	14·8	7·5	14·7
Mathematics and statistics	12·5	16·7	12·9	18·2	7·1	14·8	15·0	12·8
Foreign languages	12·5	10·0	9·7	13·6	10·7	11·1	11·2	11·0
Other subjects	8·3	10·0	—	—	—	11·1	4·7	7·3
Total hours per week (= 100%)	24	30	31	22	28	27		

to distinguish lecture and group instruction, but teaching is primarily by lectures, with classes in some of the more practical subjects.

Attendance at lectures is not high—only about a third of the students attend in the first year. Later among the business-science specialists it tends to be 35–40 per cent, but for the economics specialists attendance is higher. Students are examined annually on the subjects studied during the year, and must pass these before they can go on to the next year. One subject can be carried from the first to the second year, and from the second to the third. This allowance is increased to two from the third to the fourth. There is also a final examination on the whole course which is held three times a year. Examinations are mainly written, with oral examinations in border-line cases. In the foreign language studied examinations are always both written and oral. Students are also expected to write two term papers of ten to twenty pages each.

The School is larger than either of the universities. In 1964–65 it had 1789 students registered in the first year, as compared with 970 at the University of Athens Law Faculty in 1965 and 500 or more at the University of Salonika. The School output is also considerably larger—335 in 1963–64, compared with 20 from the University of Athens in 1965 (from the economics section), and an annual output of about 80 at Salonika.

As has been mentioned in Chapter 3, there is outside the formal educational structure post-graduate teaching organized by the "Center of Economic Research", the director of which is Professor George Coutsoumaris of the Athens Graduate School. This institution, which is supported by the Greek Government and the Ford and Rockefeller Foundations, makes use of foreign economists for both teaching and research, and its training courses may in time be recognized as an official qualification. It also sends abroad many of its young research workers to complete higher degrees.

Holy See

In the Holy See there are specialist institutes in both the Gregorian and Angelican Universities where economics can be studied. This account is, however, restricted to the Gregorian University.

At the Gregorian University, which is under the direction of the Society of Jesus, there is a three-year licentiate course in social science. Most of the students (about 80 per cent) are priests who come on the recommendation of their bishops, the rest being laymen. The majority of the students are from outside Italy. Teaching was until recently (1964) in Latin, but is now largely in Italian. The *Licence* is usually taken here as a second undergraduate degree, and it is possible for students to go on from it to take a doctorate, either at the Gregorian or at a secular university.

The Gregorian University admits some twenty-five students a year to this *Licence* course, of whom about fifteen are normally from outside Italy, mainly from Latin America. The different educational backgrounds of the students present some problems, but most of them complete the course in the prescribed three years (on average, twenty out of the twenty-five).

The first year of study is common to all students and leads, if all examinations are passed, to the *Baccalauréat*. In the next two years it is possible to specialize in either economics or sociology while doing a number of common courses. About half the students take the economics option.

In the first year students divide their time between economics, sociology, statistics, law, economic history and social Catholic doctrine. In the next two years there are a number of common courses on religious, philosophical, and other subjects relevant to the Church and modern society. As well as this, the student pursues courses in his chosen speciality. The economics specialists study monetary theory, public finance, international economics, economic development, and history of economic thought, and also take courses on urban sociology and social policy. As well as these compulsory subjects students also choose optional subjects centred on one of three themes—either the social doctrine of the Church, or work and industrial life, or the problems of under-developed countries. Two optional courses on research techniques are also available, one on statistical techniques in social investigations and the other on computer-programming (the University has access to a computer). Apart from these, and courses on the problems of the modern firm and on the collectivist economy, options are at the moment largely of a sociological rather than an economic nature, although there are plans to put rather more emphasis on economics. Examinations, both written and oral, are taken at the end of each semester in the subjects studied during that semester.

First- and second-year students all take part in a practical research project, either during the semester in Rome or outside Rome in the Easter vacation. Students are prepared for the project by seminars, and the results are subsequently discussed in a weekly two-hour seminar held throughout the year.

Students are expected by the end of the first year to have a working knowledge of English and French or German, which means most of them have three foreign languages if one includes Italian as well.

Teaching is by lecture and seminar, and there is a staff of eleven, of whom five are economists. Most of the students go on to teach in seminaries, undertake social research, or undertake or direct socio-pastoral work.

Iceland[1]

At the University of Iceland in Reykjavik there is a degree course in economics. At the moment the emphasis of the course tends to be on business economics, but an alternative course specializing in economics is being developed. These will probably share a common first part of two years, followed by two years of greater specialization.

The faculty, as is only to be expected, is a small one. In 1965–66 there were 128 students, thirty-five of whom were admitted in that academic year. In the same year thirteen students graduated. Quite a high proportion of the graduating students—15–20 per cent—go on to higher degrees or specialized training, many of them abroad.

The degree—*Candidatus Economicus*—normally takes four and a half years, though some of the best students do it in four. There is a maximum time-limit of six years. The course is divided into two parts, each of approximately equal length. In the early part of the course students have also to take five preliminary examinations—office practice and mathematics at the end of the first semester and English, accountancy, and philosophy at the end of the second. The main subjects studied are examined at the end of the first and the end of the second year. These subjects are business economics, English, accountancy, economics (which comprises five topics), commercial mathematics, statistics, law, and the economy of Iceland. Examinations are mainly written, and usually last six hours. There are some oral examinations—in some subjects in addition to the written papers and in others as the only form of examination.

In Part II students all study advanced business economics, special topics in business economics, economics, and accountancy. In addition they take a number of optional subjects. The total time spent on these must amount to $7\frac{1}{2}$ semester hours. The list below shows the subjects and the number of semester hours each takes:

Research methods in economics (3)
Public administration (3)
Economic geography ($1\frac{1}{2}$)

---

[1] It was not possible to visit the University of Reykjavik, and this account is based on correspondence.

Economic history (1½)
History of economic thought (1½)
The firm and society (1½)
Market research (1½)

Again examinations may be written or oral or both. Oral examinations take from twenty to fifty minutes each. The Part II examinations must all be taken and passed as a group within six semesters of the completion of Part I. Students who fail may retake the whole examination once only. Students have also to prepare a thesis which can vary in length from twenty-five to eighty pages.

During the course instruction is both by lecture and, where appropriate, practical classes. There are also seminars at which each student must read two papers. As well as this written work students are often required to do written analyses of case-studies in business economics.

The table below shows the balance of the course in subject-group terms.

	Part I	Part II	Total
	%	%	%
Economics	16 ·9	20 ·8–36 ·4	18 ·9–27 ·1
Business economics	8 ·5	39 ·0–42 ·8	24 ·3–26 ·4
Law	8 ·5	—	4 ·1
Other social sciences	—	0 ·0–15 ·6	0·0–8 ·1
Accountancy and commercial Techniques	24 ·0	20 ·8	22 ·3
Mathematics and statistics	14 ·1		6 ·8
Foreign languages	16 ·9	—	8 ·1
Other subjects	11 ·3	—	5 ·4
Total semester hours (= 100%)	35½	38½	74

The faculty has access to a computer—an I.B.M. 1620—and a course exists to teach students to programme in FORTRAN. It is planned to use the computer for business games.

Ireland[1]

In Ireland economics can be studied both at the constituent colleges of the National University of Ireland (Dublin, Cork, and Galway) and at Trinity College, Dublin. It is most commonly studied as part of an arts degree, but to a more limited extent it is also part of degrees in commerce in the Colleges of the National University, and of the degree in business studies at Trinity College.

At University College, Dublin, the arts degree course currently lasts three years, but a Government Commission has recently recommended that the honours degree course should be extended to four years. At present it is possible, in certain circumstances, to take a four-year course combining the B.A. and B.Comm., and to emerge with both qualifications. Economics may also be taken as one of three subjects for the B.A. General degree. An honours degree in commerce of the same standing as the full-time degree can also be attained by four years of part-time evening study.

For both the B.A. Honours and the B.Comm. degrees, students take four subjects for the first year, which ends in the First University Examination. For the B.Comm. they take political economy, together with accountancy, mathematics, and one further subject—English, history, geography, Irish, or a modern Continental language. For the B.A. Honours, political economy is combined with Latin or Greek and two other subjects, one of which can be mathematics. If the student wishes to take his final degree in political economy and mathematics, as opposed to political economy and national economics, he must select the mathematics option in the first year. In fact, few take their final degree in political economy and mathematics; in 1964 two students graduated in it as compared with twenty-four in political economy and national economics. In May 1967 there were 154 students studying economics for the honours degree in arts, 399 for a general arts degree, and 316 day and 125 evening students in the first year of their B.Comm. studies.

In the second year the students taking the B.Comm. (of whom

---

[1] I am most grateful to Professor O'Mahony of University College, Cork, and to Professor P. Lynch of University College, Dublin, for considerable assistance in preparing this study.

there were 167 full-time and 77 part-time in May 1967) prepare for the Second University Examination, in which they take political economy, accountancy, statistical mathematics, commercial law, and economic history. In the third year, which leads to the final degree examination, they study accountancy, political economy, national economics, statistics, public and business administration. In the third year, in connection with the business administration course, students write reports on factory visits and case-studies. In May 1967 there were 139 full-time and 66 evening students taking the B.Comm. third-year course. Although not normally an Honours degree, the B.Comm. can be awarded with honours to students who do particularly well. Most students, however, achieve a simple pass—in autumn 1964, 166 students took the Final Examination; of these 126 passed, only 21 of them with honours.

In the B.A. Honours course there is no formal university examination at the end of the second year, although there is a college examination. Students specializing in political economy and national economics study these subjects in both their second and third years, together with politics as minor subject in both years. Additionally in their second year they take another minor subject course in either jurisprudence and Roman law or economic statistics. The students specializing in political economy and mathematics take honours courses for two years in both these subjects, and in national economics. In May 1967 there were fifty-three students in their second year taking honours courses in economics, and seventy in their third.

At University College, Cork, there is a similar, but four-year, B.Comm. degree, which in its earlier three-year form was obtained by thirty-seven students in 1964. The course for the First University Examination consists of introductory accounting, introductory law, mathematics, modern history, and a language which can be English or Irish. The second-year course, which leads to the Second University Examination, consists of either accounting, law, statistics, and applied psychology (Course I) or economics, social philosophy, statistics, and applied psychology (Course II). In the third year, Course I students take accounting, law, economics, sociology, and public administration, and Course II students the same subjects, omitting accounting. In the fourth and final year, Course I students take accounting, law, economics, and sociology, and Course II students economics, sociology, and public administration. The introduction of the four-year course is relatively recent, the new regulations being first applied in 1966–67. In the course economics accounts for a maximum of five hours a week in the last three years, and in 1967 there were twenty-four students taking it in the second year and thirty-nine in the third, as well as twenty-seven students taking the degree part-time in the evening.

Economics can also be studied by students in other faculties, mainly in the early part of the course (in the first year in the faculties of science and law, and the second year in that of agricultural science). It is also possible to study economics throughout an arts degree, although it must always be combined with other subjects—in the first year with three others, and in the next two for the B.A. General with two others. There is also a B.A. Honours degree where economics may be taken with geography, history, or sociology, or with statistics and mathematics as a minor subject. However, few students appear to take these honours degrees—in 1964 two students obtained them, both combining economics with a social science. In 1966–67 a total of sixty-four students from the faculty of arts were taking economics, of whom forty-four were in the first year, fifteen in the second, and five in the third.

The University College of Galway differs importantly from the other Irish university colleges, as the Professor of Commerce lectures only in Irish. The B.Comm. can therefore be taken only by students working primarily in the Irish language, although most books are necessarily read in English. For the first year examination students take economics, including a course in economic history, accounting, and business administration, two languages or one language and a science subject, and commercial mathematics. Students seeking honours are recommended to take mathematics as a science subject rather than commercial mathematics. In the second year students study economics, one of the languages they studied in the first year, a course on the organization of industry and commerce, economic geography, and a course on Irish history. In the third year there are courses in economics (the history of economic theory, the economics of transport, and methods and applications of statistics), the organization of industry and commerce (comprising industrial relations, banking and currency, and accounting), and in industrial and commercial law. The final B.Comm. can be taken with or without honours, but those candidates seeking honours take a slightly different course, so that in their third year they study only economics and industrial and commercial organization, and do all the minor subjects as subsidiary subjects only in their second year.

At Galway, too, economics can be studied as part of an arts

degree, though here, as at Cork, it can be taken only in an honours degree with another subject, and few students appear to do it. (In 1964 there were four honours graduates with economics as one of their main subjects.) In the B.A. General degree it can be one of three subjects.

At Trinity College, Dublin, courses are all four-year.[1] Economics can be studied for a B.A. Honours degree in economics and political science or for the bachelor's degree in business studies (B.B.S.) in the School of Business and Social Studies. In 1964 twenty-eight students obtained their B.A. Honours (Moderatorship)[2] in economics and political science, and a further one got a supplemental moderatorship, while twenty-five students obtained the B.Comm. (the forerunner of the B.B.S., which was introduced only for those entering in or after 1961).

In the B.A. Honours degree students have written examinations at the end of each year in the subjects studied during that year. In the first year students take courses in economics, political institutions, elementary statistics, social and economic history, and mathematics for economists. In the second year the courses deal with theories of value and distribution, the economy of Ireland, political institutions, statistical methods and sources, and either economic history or mathematics. From the second year on students may specialize in statistics,[3] mathematical economics,[3] politics, or business administration. In both their third and fourth years all students appear to take two courses in economics, together with two in their speciality.

The B.B.S. course also has examinations every year. In the first year students study introductory economics, economic geography, social and economic history, and scientific method and elementary statistics. In the second year there are courses in accountancy, economics, psychology, organization and management, and public finance, together with compulsory seminars on current economic affairs and classes in the elements of science and technology. Students also have to have one month's practical business experience, preferably in the long vacation. In the third year examinations take place in April instead of at the end of the academic year, so the third-year

---

[1] The Irish Government have decided that Trinity College and University College, Dublin, shall be associated under one university authority, but the full implementation of this decision will take time.

[2] This is the name given to the B.A. at Trinity College, and is unique to this institution.

[3] These students must do mathematics in their second year.

course is only two terms, while the 'fourth-year' course is four terms. The third-year course consists of further courses in accountancy and economics, together with courses in political institutions, the law relating to business, and employment relations. There are seminars in both current economic affairs and business administration, as well as classes in the elements of science and technology. In the fourth and final year, courses in accountancy and economics are continued, together with courses in administration and government in the economy. The two compulsory seminars continue, as does the class in the elements of technology.

In addition to the course described above, B.B.S. students can if they wish also study an arts subject chosen from English, French, history, or history and fine arts, pure mathematics, applied mathematics, or philosophy. It appears from the university calendar that most students do in fact register for one arts subject.

Italy

Economics is taught in three different faculties in Italian universities—the faculties of law, political science, and economics and commerce. This division, linked as it is with the fact that admission to the faculties of economics and commerce demands lower qualifications than admission to other faculties, makes it difficult to give a clear overall picture of the teaching of economics in Italy. This study will begin with a discussion of the faculties of economics and commerce, and will also include some reference to the teaching in other faculties.

The degree course in economics for the *Laurea* in economics and commerce is more or less standard at all universities. The compulsory subjects studied are laid down centrally, and the optional subjects, two of which are included in each student's course, are centrally approved. There are in all nineteen Italian universities with a faculty of economics and commerce which, together with the University Institute of Economics and Commerce at Venice and the faculty of political science at the University of Perugia, all offer the economics and commerce *Laurea* course. The table below gives some idea of the distribution of students between these twenty-one universities. It can be seen from this that three of these universities each contain 10 per cent or more of the students—the University of Rome, the University of Bari, and the Sacro Cuore University at Milan—making up together one-third of all students.

The *Laurea* course in economics and commerce has a prescribed length of four years, although students normally take longer over the course than this. The course consists of nineteen compulsory subjects, listed below, and at least two additional subjects; in the compulsory subjects all courses last for one year, except for those marked with an asterisk, which last for two years, and for the languages (marked with a dagger), which last for three.

1. Institutions of private law
2. Institutions of public law
3. Commercial law*
4. General mathematics

Numbers of Economics and Commerce Students[1]

University	Number	%
Rome	7,626	12·1
Bari	7,006	11·1
Sacro Cuore, Milan	6,302	10·0
Naples	5,195	8·2
Bocconi, Milan	4,550	7·2
Venice	3,798	6·0
Pisa	3,550	5·6
Turin	2,929	4·7
Messina	2,914	4·6
Catania	2,224	3·5
Bologna	2,165	3·4
Palermo	2,148	3·4
Florence	1,997	3·2
Parma	1,739	2·8
Genoa	1,669	2·6
Perugia	1,591	2·5
Cagliari	1,521	2·4
Padua (Verona)	1,500	2·4
Urbino (Ancona)	1,490	2·4
Trieste	743	1·2
Pavia	433	0·7
Total	63,090	100

[1]Source: *Annuario Statistico Italiana*, 1966.

5. Financial mathematics*
6. Statistics*
7. Political economy*
8. Labour law
9. Science of finance and financial law
10. Agricultural economics and policy
11. Economic and financial policy
12. Economic history
13. Economic geography*
14. General and applied accountancy*
15. Professional and banking techniques
16. Industrial and commercial techniques
17. Science of merchandise
18. French or Spanish†
19. English or German†

The range of additional subjects varies from university to university, and the students' choice may in fact be rather narrow. At Rome, the largest university, there are twenty-two additional subjects —eight of them in law, six languages, four in business economics, three in economics, and one social-science subject. At Genoa there is a choice from eight subjects—five of them in law, one specialized aspect of business administration (economics and techniques of the Army and Navy), one in specialized accountancy (accountancy of a maritime firm), and one language (Romanian). At Florence the timetable is so organized that there is a choice between demography and tax law in the third year and between civil trial law and administrative techniques in agricultural and mining enterprises in the fourth.

The order in which subjects are studied varies somewhat from university to university. This is illustrated for a number of universities in the table below.

Examinations are primarily oral, and there is an oral examination at the end of each year in each of the subjects studied during the year, except for those subjects with a two- or three-year course, which are not examined until completed. On average there are some six oral examinations at the end of each year.

For the final examination, which cannot be taken until all the course examinations have been passed, the student must submit and then defend a dissertation. This can vary very much in quality, and may often contain relatively little original work. The dissertation theme is approved some time before the examination—at Florence at least three months before, at the Bocconi University by the February of the third year, and at the Sacro Cuore University at least six months before the examination. As well as defending this thesis, the student must also develop a number of propositions. The number of these varies from university to university—at Rome and Florence it is one, at Genoa two, and at Sacro Cuore three. The student does not appear to be given very much notice of the proposition, but may have some choice. In some universities the subjects studied are divided into groups, and the propositions relate to different groups. At Genoa, for example, there are three groups of subjects, in two of which propositions have to be defended and discussed. The groups are firstly techniques—for example, accountancy and mathematics; secondly, law; and thirdly, economics, including statistics and economic history and geography.

The amount of oral examination puts a considerable strain on

Years in which Subjects are studied at a Sample of Italian Universities

Subject	Florence	Genoa	Messina	Milan—Bocconi	Milan—Sacro Cuore	Parma	Perugia	Turin	Urbino
Institutions of private law	1	1	1	1	1	1	1	1	1
Institutions of public law	1	1	1	1	2	1	1	1	1
Commercial law	2–3	2–3	3–4	2–3	2–3	2–3	2–3	2–3	2–3
General mathematics	1	1	1	1	1	1	1	1	1
Financial mathematics*	2–3	2–3	2–3	2–3	2–3	2–3	2–3	2–3	2–3
Statistics*	2–3	2–3	1–2	2–3	2–3	2–3	2–3	2–3	2–3
Political economy*	1–2	1–2	1–2	1–2	1–2	1–2	1–2	1–2	1–2
Labour law	2	2	2	4	4	2	4	3	4
Science of finance and financial law	3	3	3	3	4	4	4	4	3
Agricultural economics and policy	3	4	3	4	4	4	3	3	4
Economic and financial policy	4	4	4	3	3	3	4	4	4
Economic history	4	4	2	4	3	3	3	3	3
Economic geography*	1–2	1–2	3–4	1–2	1–2	1–2	1–2	1–2	1–2
General and applied accountancy*	1–2	1–2	2–3	1–2	1–2	1–2	1–2	1–2	1–2
Professional and banking techniques	4	4	4	4	4	3	4	4	2
Industrial and commercial techniques	3	3	4	3	4	4	3	4	3
Science of merchandise	1	3	4	1	1 or 3	1	2	4	4
French or Spanish†	1–3	1–3	1–3	1–3	1–3	1–3	1–3	1–3	1–3
English or German†	1–3	1–3	1–3	1–3	1–3	1–3	1–3	1–3	1–3
First additional subject	3	2 or 3	3	2	3	3	4	2	1‡
Second additional subject	4	2, 3 or 4	4	4	4	4	4	4	2‡

* 2-year course.   † 3-year course.   ‡ Can be done in years 3 and 4, if necessary.

university teachers. Partly as a result of this, the lecture year is short in Italy—only twenty to twenty-two weeks. In a few universities preliminary written examinations are being used as a filter. This is, for example, the case at the University of Urbino (whose economics and commerce faculty is in fact at Ancona), where there are three written tests during the year, and only if students do well in these (as about half do) are they permitted to take the oral examination. At Florence there is a preliminary written paper in the two languages, and until this is passed students cannot take the oral examination. Some screening examinations are also used at the University of Rome, and at the Sacro Cuore University at Milan.

Wastage is a very serious problem in Italian universities. Success rates are very low, and retardation is general. Many students do not attend lectures, and quite substantial numbers have full- or part-time jobs. An extremely interesting sample survey[1] of first-year students in the faculty of economics and commerce in Rome found that 39 per cent had full-time jobs, 18 per cent part-time jobs, and 13 per cent irregular jobs. Even among those with no jobs, 38 per cent attended no lectures.

The economics and commerce faculties admit students with lower qualifications than do other faculties—for example, law and political science. They take students with commercial leaving certificates (*Maturita*), as well as the normally accepted classical leaving certificates. They also admit students from various specialist schools —for example, maritime and agrarian technical institutes. In the sample survey in Rome previously cited most of the respondents gave as a reason for choosing the faculty of economics and commerce the fact that they did not possess the qualifications to enter another faculty. Only 16 per cent had qualifications which would have permitted them to do so.

This tends to reinforce the importance of the law and political science faculties in the training of economists. In the past many academic economists have received their own training in the faculties. As some economics is taught in them, it is still possible for students in these faculties to select their dissertation topic in economics and go on to make themselves into professional economists by further study, often abroad. It is possible to take rather more economics in the faculty of political science than in the faculty of law, but in both students can—and some do—write their dissertation on economic topics.

---

[1] *Bollettino della Doxa*, Anno XVI, Nos. 17–18, October 27th, 1962.

There are, however, only five faculties of political science, and in them and the faculties of law only a relatively small proportion of students will be specializing in economics. There is still, however, a certain prestige attached to the faculty of law, and professors may consider a move from a Chair in economics in a faculty of economics and commerce to a Chair in the faculty of law as a promotion. It may be that this question of relative prestige also affects assistants, who may prefer a post in a faculty of law, if it can be obtained, to one in a faculty of economics and commerce.

It is very difficult to change the pattern of Italian higher education as the framework of the course is centrally determined by law. Changes are thus more easily made in the content of subjects while retaining the prescribed titles. The faculty at Ancona (of the University of Urbino) shows, however, the changes that can be made. The faculty has introduced two specializations in the second and third years, where the set subjects are taught separately to those specializing in social economics and those specializing in business economics. The following table compares the balance of the course with that at a more traditional faculty—that of the University of Parma.

Ancona have also introduced a very interesting teaching pattern based on a two-week cycle. This enables teaching by any particular professor to be concentrated into one week, leaving the other free for him to pursue his own work, either at Ancona or more probably in Rome or Milan. The extent of outside work and the difficulty of attracting professional staff to universities outside Rome and Milan are grave problems in Italy, and this scheme helps to overcome the problem.

At Ancona there is general use of filter examinations, and students are also expected to do two shorter pieces of written work in addition to their dissertation. The faculty also organizes discussions in which all students are invited to participate. Ancona suffers from the general problem of low attendance—some 70 per cent of the students have jobs. It does, however, indicate the possibilities of development even in the fairly rigidly defined course.

Apart from the problems of the quality of the students entering the faculties of economics and commerce and those arising from a centrally determined curriculum, the other major problem of Italian universities is that the *Laurea,* or doctorate, is the only degree. This means that generally there is no post-graduate teaching, and as economics makes up only a relatively small share of the degree course the level of economics knowledge of a graduate with the title of

Doctor in Economics and Commerce is lower than that of holders of doctorates, and in many cases lower qualifications, in economics from other European universities.

Balance of Course at Ancona and Parma (in %)

	Ancona[1] Social Economics	Ancona[1] Business Economics	Parma[1]
	%	%	%
Economics	30 ·1	23 ·6	12 ·4
Business economics	1 ·8	8 ·4	4 ·1
Law	12 ·8	12 ·9	14 ·0
Other social sciences	7 ·3	7 ·1	9 ·9
Accountancy and commercial techniques	5 ·5	5 ·3	19 ·0
Mathematics and statistics	21 ·9	22 ·7	18 ·2
Foreign languages	11 ·0	10 ·7	14 ·9
Other subjects	4 ·1	4 ·0	2 ·5
Total Year–Hours = 100%	109½	112½	121
Type of instruction	%	%	%
Lecture	59 ·4	58 ·7	62 ·0
Group	40 ·6	41 ·3	38 ·0

[1] In all cases the two additional subjects have been omitted. They account for 5·5, 5·3, and 5·0 per cent of the time respectively, and can be in most of the subject fields.

An attempt has recently been made to organize post-graduate teaching in economics at the University of Rome, where professors of economics from the three faculties of law, political science, and economics and commerce give courses at the Istituto per gli studi e le ricerche economiche. These courses, which are limited to thirty students—normally assistants of professors at the University of Rome—last for two years. In the first year there is some sixteen hours a week of instruction, covering eight subjects, seven in economics and one in statistics, and in the second year considerably more seminar work and a choice between courses specializing in comparative economic systems and the history of economic thought or in econometrics and models for economic forecasting and planning. This institute, which began teaching in 1964–65, could provide the basis for a higher degree in economics in Italy in the event of a substantial reform in the Italian university system.

Malta

Higher education in economics in Malta is given at the Royal University of Malta at Valletta. Economics was taught until recently as part of the B.A. General degree, where it could (and still can) be taken as one of three subjects, and in the first part of the law degree. In October 1966 the first students were admitted for the B.A. Honours course in economics. About fifteen students comprise the first-year group, and three or four were admitted to the second year of the course.

The degree takes three years—four terms being spent on Part 1 and five on Part 2. In Part 1 the students do five subjects, of which three—economics, statistics, and social structure—are compulsory and two optional. These two are chosen from public administration, political philosophy, mathematics, history, history of Mediterranean civilization, and a modern foreign language. In Part 2 six compulsory subjects and two optional subjects are to be taken. The compulsory subjects are economics, economics of industry, social structure, public finance, economic planning and econometrics, and management economics. The two options are chosen from modern economic history, commercial law, international trade, business finance, philosophy, history, and mathematics.

The general teaching pattern is modelled on that of British universities, and teaching is in English. Each honours student attends eleven hours of lectures and has two one-hour tutorials a week. Examinations are written, although an oral examination may be given in marginal cases. As in the United Kingdom, students need to have passed the school-leaving examination at the Advanced Level for admission to the University, and in economics three Advanced Level passes are required.

Netherlands

Five institutions in the Netherlands confer first degrees in economics. Three of them are universities—the Municipal University of Amsterdam, the Free University of Amsterdam, and the State University of Groningen—and two are specialized institutions—the Netherlands School of Economics at Rotterdam and the Catholic School of Economics at Tilburg. In the Netherlands there is no essential difference between the degree courses offered by the universities and those offered by the specialized institutions. Though the schools had a vocational bias at their inception, this has now largely disappeared, and they are far more comparable to, say, the London School of Economics than they are to specialized institutions such as the Danish Handelshøjskolen or the H.E.C. in France. By far the largest of the individual institutions is the Netherlands School of Economics, as the table below shows.

Institution	No. of Students (1967*)	%	No. of Students (1956–57)	%
Netherlands School of Economics	2,966	40 ·2	1,389	43 ·7
Municipal University of Amsterdam	1,599	21 ·6	689	21 ·7
Catholic School of Economics	1,282	17 ·3	483	15 ·2
Free University of Amsterdam	820	11 ·1	430	13 ·5
State University of Groningen	727	9 ·8	189	5 ·9
Total	7,394	100	3,180	100

* The figures relate to April 1st, 1967.

As in many other countries, there has been a great increase in student numbers over the last few years. In 1956–57 there were 3180 students of economics, as compared with the 7394 in 1966–67. The table above gives some idea of the relative growth of institutions.

At present the courses consist of two main parts, the first leading to the *Candidaats* examination and the second to the *Doctoraal* examination. It is possible after the *Candidaats* examination to go on not to the *Doctoraal* but to a shorter, one-year course leading to the *Baccalaureaat* examination, but this possibility has been rarely taken. In the academic year 1964–65 only seventeen bachelors' degrees were awarded, as compared with 327 *Doctorandus* degrees. In the same year 611 students passed the *Candidaats* examination.

It is, however, proposed to introduce a fundamental change in the degree system by replacing the present *Candidaats* examination with a *Baccalaureaat* examination which will then be the first degree. It is anticipated that the majority of students—say 80 per cent—will terminate their studies with this new examination, while the minority will continue with post-graduate work. The new course leading to this *Baccalaureaat* examination will provide a general education in economics, and will not involve specialization. It is, however, likely that in the new examination the time taken by ancillary subjects may be somewhat diminished. It is proposed that instead of studying economic geography, economic history, and law, as students now do in the *Candidaats* course, they shall have a choice of just one of these three subjects.

At the Municipal University of Amsterdam and both the Netherlands and the Catholic Schools of Economics there is also a propaedeutic examination which is taken at the end of the first year of study. At the Free University of Amsterdam and the University of Groningen there is no one formal set of propaedeutic examinations, but a number of preliminary examinations have to be taken during the first year.

In general the *Candidaats* part of the course is more or less common to all economics students, and specialization does not normally start until the *Doctoraal* course is begun. The exceptions to this are that there is prior specialization in one or two years in the *Candidaats* course at both the schools and at the University of Groningen for those who plan subsequently to take one of the quantitative specializations in the *Doctoraal*.

At each institution there are a number of different possible specializations in the *Doctoraal*. There are basically two different ways in which specialization is achieved—either by choice from a number of different lines (as at the Netherlands School, the Catholic School, and the University of Groningen) or by emphasis within a common framework (as at the two universities in Amsterdam). At the three institutions where there is a choice of lines the possibilities are as summarized below:

	University of Groningen	Netherlands School of Economics	Catholic School of Economics
General economics		x	x
Business economics		x	x
Economics*	x		
Quantitative-general economics	x	x	x
Quantitative-business economics	x	x	x
Fiscal economics	x	x	x
Free	x		

* With the possibility within this of emphasis on general or business economics.

There are also more lines in which other social sciences—for example, sociology—play a major part, but these are not shown. In the free *Doctoraal* at Groningen a student takes as his specialization any subject that is taught in the faculty; it is thus possible to choose subjects such as economic history.

At the Amsterdam universities all students take some general and some business economics, though they can put the emphasis on one or the other (at the Free University by their choice of seminar and at the Municipal University by the way in which they choose the five examinations, three to a higher level and two to a lower level, that are compulsory). In addition to this, students take two optional subjects chosen at both universities from an extensive list. This choice enables students to give their course, for instance, a quantitative or public-finance emphasis.

All students must prepare a number of essay papers, or in some cases a short dissertation, as part of their work for the final examination. In general teaching is so arranged that most of the lectures for the *Doctoraal* take place in the earlier part of the course, leaving the student time to work mainly in seminars in the final semesters. In theory the whole course can take as little as five years, but in practice students tend to take about six and a half years.

At the three institutions where specialization is achieved by following a particular line it is possible to show in tabular form the composition of the whole course. For the Amsterdam universities this is not feasible because of the degree of choice within the common framework. In the tables that follow, therefore, the balance of the course for some of the options at the two Schools of Economics and the University of Groningen will be shown. The tables cover both the general and business economics options and the alternative quantitative options. The business economics option is by far the most popular one at the Catholic School of Economics, where about 80 per cent of the students follow it. At the Netherlands School at Rotterdam about 40 per cent of the students take the general economics line and about 40 per cent the business economics.

At the two Amsterdam universities the *Candidaats* course is standard, and the table on page 219 shows its composition. At the Municipal University students can take additional mathematics if their school background makes this necessary, or they can take fiscal law in place of economic history or geography if they intend later to specialize in fiscal economics. Otherwise there are no variations, unlike the other three institutions, where there is a specialized *Candidaats* course for students intending to follow one of the quantitative lines. For comparison the two *Candidaats* courses at the Catholic School are shown in the table on page 219.

For the *Doctoraal* examination at the Municipal University there are nine subjects, five in political economy and four in business economics. For these nine economics subjects each student takes five examinations, three of them "great tentamena" (or examinations) and two shorter ones. He must also take two optional subjects. The subjects in which he chooses to take the higher-level examinations and his choice of optional subjects determine the emphasis of his specialization.

At the Free University the system is similar: all students take both general and business economics and can specialize in either, depending on which seminar they choose to attend. In addition they study two optional subjects chosen from a long list.

The lists of optional subjects at both the Amsterdam universities are very similar, and that of the Free University is given below as an illustration. It consists of: general and descriptive sociology, business sociology, economic and social history, economic geography, civil and commercial law, constitutional and administrative law, labour law, public finance, statistical analysis, econometrics, economic problems of developing countries, agricultural economics, administrative organization, business psychology.

In addition to the list, students can also choose any other subject taught in the university.

217

General and Business Economics Lines (percentage of instruction in each subject)

	General Economics	Economics	Business Economics	
	Netherlands School	University of Groningen	Netherlands School	Catholic School
Economics	39·5	25·0–35·4	22·5	19·7–22·7
Business economics	20·3	32·2	36·7	24·2–27·2
Law	7·2	3·5–13·9	5·9	10·6–13·6
Other social sciences	12·0	6·1–16·5	11·8	9·1–12·1
Accountancy and commercial techniques	9·0	2·6	11·3	16·7
Mathematics and statistics	12·0	20·2–30·6	11·8	6·1
Foreign languages	0·0	0·0	0·0	0·0
Other subjects	0·0	0·0	0·0	7·6

Quantitative Lines (percentage of instruction in each subject)

	Quantitative General Economics			Quantitative Business Economics	
	University of Groningen	Netherlands School	Catholic School	University of Groningen	Netherlands School
	%	%	%	%	%
Economics	24·0	26·8	22·1	12·0	18·8
Business economics	18·4	15·6	16·9	30·7	24·3
Law	1·7	0·0–5·6	6·5	1·7	0·0–5·5
Other social sciences	5·8	6·7–11·2	5·2	5·8	6·6–11·1
Accountancy and commercial techniques	2·5	8·4	1·3	2·5	8·3
Mathematics and statistics	47·6	35·8	42·8	47·3	35·4
Foreign languages	0·0	0·0	0·0	0·0	0·0
Other subjects	0·0	0·0	5·2	0·0	0·0

Candidaats Course

	Free University of Amsterdam	Municipal University of Amsterdam	Catholic School of Economics Tilburg	
			Economics	Quantitative
	%	%	%	%
Economics	26·3	22·5	24·3	18·7
Business economics	21·1	22·5	21·6	16·7
Law	10·5	15·0	13·5	10·4
Other social sciences	15·8	15·0	16·2	8·3
Accountancy and commercial techniques	7·9	5·0	2·7	2·1
Mathematics and statistics	10·5	20·0	10·8	35·5
Foreign languages	0·0	0·0	0·0	0·0
Other subjects	7·9	0·0	10·8	8·3

Norway

In Norway there are two institutions where a first degree in economics can be taken—the University of Oslo and the Norwegian School of Economics and Business Administration (Norges Handelshøyskole) at Bergen. In 1966–67 there were 511 students reading economics at the University and 645 studying at the School. There is some compulsory economics in the course for the *Tekniskekandidat* at the Norwegian Technical High School (Norges Tekniskehøyskole), but the economics in this course is a subsidiary subject.

At the University of Oslo students can take the five-year course for the *Candidatus Oeconomiae* degree. The course is divided into two parts—Part I starts at the beginning of the second semester and lasts till the end of the sixth, followed by Part II. The first semester is spent on courses in philosophy, in which there is a preliminary examination at the end of the semester; in mathematics, with a preliminary examination at the end of the second semester and various other introductory courses. The Part I examination is divided into two sections—economic and statistical. The economic section, in which there are four six-hour papers—two in economic theory, one in social studies, and one in industrial economics—is normally taken at the end of the fifth semester. There are two papers in the statistical section—one in theoretical and one in applied statistics—and these are usually taken at the end of the sixth semester. The bulk of Part I is thus in economics and statistics. Teaching is partly by lecture and partly by seminar and classes. Students are also expected to participate in *kollokvier*, informal, small instruction classes taught by senior and post-graduate students. Attendance at lectures is not compulsory, but attendance at seminars is required.

In the Part II examination there are three compulsory subjects—advanced theoretical economics, advanced industrial economics, and monetary economics and public finance—and one optional subject. This can be in econometrics, mathematical business economics, international economics, economic systems, history of economic thought, or law. Students have also to write a paper on a subject chosen by themselves, but which must not be purely descriptive, and must show use of economic theory. This usually takes two to four months to write. Most of the instruction is by lecture, though there are some seminars, including one immediately prior to the examination for Part II candidates.

In general the course is an academic as opposed to a vocational one, and offers a very good training in economics with a strong quantitative bias. The output of the faculty is at present relatively small—thirty-two students passed their Part II examination in 1966–67. The faculty is growing, and it is possible that a *numerus clausus* may be imposed, as it is in many other faculties of the University. It is thought that business economics may be further developed, with an emphasis on those aspects of it related to economic theory and mathematical statistics. The main stress, however, is likely to remain on general economics as at present. About half the graduates go into Government service—to the Central Bank, the Central Bureau of Statistics, and the various Ministries.

The best students in each year—about four of them—are invited to stay on at the University to do research; on average one doctorate is awarded a year.

The Norwegian School of Economics and Business Administration offers a very different course. Students enter rather older—the average age of entry is twenty-two. They have often before admission had some time at a commercial high school, or some months' practical commercial experience. The course is much shorter than at the University, only three to three and a half years as opposed to over five years in practice at the University. Success rates are very high—about 90 per cent. Students go mainly to industry and commerce on graduation—of those who had graduated up to 1964 two-thirds were working in administration, finance (including accounting), and marketing. About 7 per cent go into Governmental service—this is far fewer proportionately, though not necessarily in absolute terms, than from the University.

The School not only offers a first degree, it also has a number of research institutes in various aspects of industrial and business economics, and awards higher degrees. There is a special teachers' degree involving a year's study after the first degree, a *Licence* lasting about three years for which a thesis is required, and a doctorate. In 1967, 225 students were admitted to the first-degree course which gives them the qualification of *Siviløkonom*, but about three times this number applied.

For the first four or five semesters all first-degree students do a common course ending with five examinations, each of equal weight

—these are in statistics, accountancy, economics, the financial and the sociological aspects of business administration. They also take two optional subjects chosen from a list of eight—law, economic geography, economic history, mathematics, English, French, German, and Spanish. Students are recommended to take a language, and about half do, most of them studying English. On the whole, however, languages are not very popular, whereas mathematics is becoming increasingly so. Teaching is a combination of lectures, discussion classes (of about twenty students), and seminars. Students are also encouraged to form their own groups of six to ten (*kollokvier*) for self-instruction.

The last two semesters of the course are occupied by advanced courses in economics and business economics (in this case-studies are much used). Students also specialize in two or three topics in economics or business economics in which they attend seminars. They are allowed to do either two special topics and write two term papers or three topics and write only one paper. Almost all the special topics are in fact in business economics, apart from one in social economics. In this latter part of the course much of the work is in seminars of fifteen students for the main subjects and twelve for the special topics.

The table on page 223 compares the overall balance of the courses at the University and the School.

Where two figures are given, this indicates the range, depending on the options chosen—for example, all students at the University do 52·8 per cent of their course in economics, but it is possible to do as much as 60·2 if economic, not mathematical, options are taken in Part II. Within the mathematics and statistics category there is a number of courses in econometrics. There is a law option at the University, but it is so seldom taken that it has not been shown. The distribution of course for the School assumes a student takes three special topics in Part II; if only two were taken the maximum figures for the economics or business economics ranges would be somewhat reduced.

The table shows very clearly the concentration in the University on economic and mathematical subjects. The concentration on business economics is far less marked at the School, where the range of the course is wider, to provide contextural background to the students' vocational studies.

As well as the students who study in Norway, substantial numbers of students go abroad for first-degree work. Altogether in 1966–67

	University of Oslo	Norwegian School of Economics and Business Administration
	%	%
Economics	52 ·8–60 ·2	19 ·2–21 ·2
Business economics	8 ·3	26 ·9–30 ·8
Law	—	0 ·0–15 ·4
Other social sciences	7 ·4	0 ·0–30 ·8
Accountancy and commercial techniques	—	11 ·5
Mathematics and statistics	24 ·1–31 ·5	7 ·7–23 ·1
Foreign languages	—	0 ·0–30 ·8
Other subjects	—	—
Total semester hours (= 100%)	108	104
Type of instruction	%	%
Lecture	77 ·8	73 ·1
Group	22 ·2	26 ·9

some 15 per cent of all Norwegian students were abroad, and there is no particular reason to think the proportion of economics students was significantly lower. The Ministry of Education has very elaborate regulations recognizing the equivalence of courses in foreign universities. This covers European countries and the U.S.A., and where there are differences within countries, as in the United Kingdom, stipulates particular courses at particular universities. In 1966–67 there were 468 Norwegian students abroad reading for degrees similar to the *Siviløkonom*. At the Hochschule at St Gallen there were, it is known, 109 Norwegian students, and others were studying at many other European universities, though probably in no other one institution was there as large a concentration as at St Gallen. The Norwegian Government is anxious to see that all qualified young people have a chance to study, and so supports financially the majority of its students abroad.

There are plans for university expansion in Norway—new universities are projected at Trondheim and Tromsø. The University of

Bergen, which was established in 1948, does not offer an economics degree, but it is planned to develop its faculty of social sciences in close co-operation with the Norwegian School of Economics and Business Administration, which is also situated in Bergen. Links between these two institutions are likely to become closer in the future, though the University faculty will start only modestly, with an annual intake of about fifty.

Spain

In the universities in Spain the main teaching of economics is confined to the faculties of political, economic, and commercial sciences at the universities of Madrid, Barcelona, and Valladolid (the latter located at Bilbao). There is some teaching of economics in the faculty of law in eleven Spanish universities, including the three mentioned above, but it plays only a minor part in the law degree, and with the development of separate social-science faculties is increasingly taught from a legal point of view, frequently by professors with a primarily legal training. A new faculty of economics has recently been established at Malaga, in the University of Granada, and it now offers first- and second-year courses. First-year courses under the inspection of this faculty are also available in a private institution in Valencia. Another faculty is planned for Santiago.

As well as the State universities there are private institutions with religious sponsorship, where economics is taught largely as a preparation for careers in business and commerce. There are four of these, all run by the Jesuits[1]—the Escuela Superior de Direccion de Empresas (I.C.A.D.E.) in Madrid, the Escuela Superior de Administracion y Direccion de Empresas (E.S.A.D.E.) in Barcelona, the Instituto de Economia de la Empresa of the private University of Deusto at Bilbao, and the Escuela Superior de Tecnica Empresaria (E.S.T.E.) at San Sebastian. All these offer a five-year *Licence* course in business administration, which at the University of Deusto is taken concurrently with the five-year *Licence* in law.

The greater number of economics students are found in the universities. In 1965–66 there were nearly 6000 in Madrid, over 2000 at both Bilbao and Barcelona, and nearly 500 in the new faculty at Malaga. In the private institutions there were probably nearly 2000 students in all—about half of them in Madrid at I.C.A.D.E., a

---

[1] There is also a post-graduate course for a master's degree in business administration at the Instituto de Estudios Superiores de la Empresa (I.E.S.E) in the private Opus Dei University of Navarra in Barcelona, but no first degrees in economics are given.

quarter at E.S.T.E., and the remaining quarter split between Deusto and E.S.A.D.E., with fewer at E.S.A.D.E.

At the universities the course is standard, there being only minor variations in the subjects taught. There is no specialization until the students come to the final year, when they can specialize in general economics, business economics, or insurance. At Barcelona about half the students choose each of the first two specializations, and very few take the insurance option. Hours of instruction offered do not vary very much from year to year of the course; total instruction offered in the first year amounts to twenty-one hours a week, in the second year to twenty-three, in both the third and fourth years to twenty-two, and in the fifth to twenty or twenty-two, depending on the option taken.[1] (The figures given below are for Barcelona, but those for the other universities are very similar.) Teaching is predominantly by formal lecture, though there is some work in groups, but these tend to be fairly large—anything from thirty to 150, depending on the subject. The tables below show the composition of the course by year and the overall course composition for each of the three options.

The insurance option in the fifth year is largely concerned with the mathematical and actuarial theory of insurance, private insurance law, and social security. In the first year (second year at Bilbao) students have to take an examination in a foreign language (at Barcelona French, English, German, or Italian; at Bilbao French or English; at Madrid French, English, or German), though instruction in this is not formally included in the course.

Examinations are chiefly written, and take place at the end of each year. The wastage rate is high, especially in the early years of the course. Students are of two kinds—the 'official' and the 'free'. Official students attend lectures and practicals, while free students, on the whole, only take the examinations, though they may come to some practical classes or attend evening courses where these are given by younger members of the university teaching staff. The free students are mainly either students who have failed examinations earlier or students who live a considerable distance from the university. Instruction tends to be very theoretical—there is very little empirical work. To some extent, as in many other European countries, there is a difference between the older generation of

---

[1] Both the general and business economics specializations have twenty hours a week, while the insurance option has twenty-two.

Composition of Licence Course at the University of Barcelona (in %)

	Year 1 %	Year 2 %	Year 3 %	Year 4 %	Year 5 General Econ. %	Year 5 Business Econ. %	Year 5 Insurance %	Overall General Econ. %	Overall Business Econ. %	Overall Insurance %
Economics	19·0	30·4	45·4	41·0	60·0	15·0	13·6	38·8	30·6	30·0
Business economics	—	—	—	13·6	15·0	30·0	27·3	5·6	8·3	8·2
Law	14·3	13·0	9·1	13·6	20·0	20·0	27·3	13·9	13·9	15·4
Other social sciences	33·3	30·4	—	—	—	—	—	13·0	13·0	12·7
Accountancy and commercial techniques	—	—	18·2	9·1	—	30·0	—	5·4	11·1	5·5
Mathematics and statistics	23·8	17·4	18·2	13·6	—	—	27·3	14·8	14·8	20·0
Foreign languages	—	—	—	—	—	—	—	—	—	—
Other subjects	9·5	8·7	9·1	5·1	5·0	5·0	4·5	8·3	8·3	8·2
Total hours of instruction per week (=100%)	21	23	22	22	20	20	22	21·6	21·6	22

Subjects studied in the "Licence" Course

Year 1	Year 4
Economic theory	Economic theory
Civil law	Economic policy
World economic history	Theory of public finance
Sociology and methodology	Economics of the firm
Mathematical analysis	Administrative law
Elements of philosophy	Theory of insurance
	Econometrics and statistics
	Religion
	Political education
Year 2	**Year 5—General Economics Option**
Economic theory	Organization, accountancy, and
Economic structures	procedure of State and public firms
Commercial law	Economic policy
Theory of the State	History of economic thought
Spanish economic history	International economic organization
Mathematical analysis	Economics of the firm (accountancy
Religion	and financial)
Political education	Spanish and comparative fiscal
	systems
	Religion
Year 3	**Year 5—Business Economics Option**
Economic theory	Economic policy
Economic structure	Economic policy of the firm
Economic policy	Mathematics of financial operations
Labour law	Spanish and comparative fiscal systems
Accountancy theory	Accountancy and cost statistics
Statistical theory	Auditing, analysis, and consolidation
Religion	of balance sheets
Political education	Religion

university teachers and the younger, many of whom have studied abroad. The latter are more likely to use case-studies and actual examples and have closer contact with students who may be used to assist with research projects.

Outside Madrid there is considerable difficulty in recruiting professors. In 1966 the latest figures show that of the eleven economics Chairs at Barcelona seven were vacant, at Bilbao two out of seven, and at Malaga two out of three. About half the teaching is done by professors, and the rest by more junior teachers. A new grade of professor agrege has recently been created to improve the career structure of university teaching, and, so it is hoped, increase the number of assistants. In Madrid there is private supplementary teaching outside the university, particularly for the first year of the course. Assistants are not allowed to do this teaching.

The courses in the private institutions are both more tightly organized and more closely related to the real world. Success rates are higher, and intake is to some extent selective. In I.C.A.D.E., in Madrid, students take the University *Licence* as well as doing specialized vocational studies in one of three options—business administration, law and business administration, or economics and business administration. They carry a heavier work-load (about thirty hours instruction a week), and have a rather longer term (thirty-two weeks as against twenty-eight at the university). Groups tend to be smaller, and students are given experience in preparing independent written work, of which very little is done at the university. In the sixth year students work in firms in the morning, but return to I.C.A.D.E. in the afternoon to discuss their experience.

At E.S.A.D.E., in Barcelona, students prepare only for the School's own *Licence*. Over the whole course students have on average nearly twenty-six hours' instruction a week, but over the course the amount falls—in the first year it is nearly thirty hours, in the second and third twenty-eight, and in the last two years about twenty-one. As the total group in each year is small, all instruction can be relatively informal. In 1965–66 the largest year—the first— contained fifty-four students, while in the second year there were only twenty, in the third thirty-six, and in both the fourth and fifth years twenty-four. The table below shows the overall distribution of the course. It can be seen that it starts more generally and becomes more specialized towards the end; in the fifth year business economics and economics between them account for just over three-quarters of the student's instruction time.

The foreign language taught is English. The School is well equipped, and has a language laboratory. Students also have to pass an examination in French in their second year. Term papers are expected of the students in the middle three years, and in the fifth they prepare a report laying out the information required to launch a hypothetical new company. In their last year they can attend the advanced management seminar the School runs, and

Balance of Course at E.S.A.D.E. (in %)

Subject	Year 1 %	Year 2 %	Year 3 %	Year 4 %	Year 5 %	Total
Economics	15·1	12·2	16·1	15·0	14·2	14·5
Business economics	—	—	—	35·5	62·2	16·2
Law	—	15·7	11·2	18·7	—	9·0
Other social sciences	7·5	8·6	13·3	7·5	—	7·8
Accountancy and commercial techniques	19·9	15·7	11·9	7·5	4·7	12·6
Mathematics and statistics	19·2	16·4	16·1	—	18·9	14·7
Foreign languages	17·8	15·7	15·3	—	—	10·9
Other subjects	20·5	15·7	16·1	15·9	—	14·3
Total hours (= 100%)	730	700	715	535	530	3,210

also participate in a business game. The School will soon have its own computer.

Altogether E.S.A.D.E. offers a very different course from the universities—a much more vocational course with a great deal more supervision of the students, in a small and selected group (in 1965 there were eighty applicants for the fifty-four places), as opposed to a very large university entry. Naturally, given these differences, success rates are higher, and successful students almost invariably finish their course in the prescribed time, whereas in the universities there is some retardation and high wastage.

Sweden

Far-reaching reforms of university teaching in economics are in preparation in Sweden. Unfortunately, details of them were not fully available to me, so that this account relates to the situation in 1967 only.

In Sweden there are seven institutions where it is possible to take a degree including a substantial proportion of economics. These seven are five universities—Gothenburg, Lund, Stockholm, Umeå, and Uppsala—and two Handelshögskolor—Stockholm and Gothenburg. None of the degrees available is solely in economics, but economics can be taken as part of the course for a number of different degrees. These are the *Civilekonom*, which can be taken at the two Handelshögskolor and at the universities of Lund and Umeå, and the *Filosofisk ämbetsexamen* (F.M.), the *Filosofisk Kandidatexamen* (F.K.), and the *Filosofisk-samhällvetenskapligexamen* (F.P.M.), available at the universities.

Some economics is also studied in the two first degrees in law—the *Juris Kandidatexamen* (J.K.) and the *Juridisk-samhällvetenskapligexamen* (J.P.M.). The J.K. is the traditional first legal degree, and in it all students take a little economics. The J.P.M. is a more recent degree, analogous to the F.P.M., and in it half the time is spent on legal and half on social-science subjects, which can include economics. These two degrees will not be described further, as they are basically law rather than economics degrees.

The degree courses vary considerably in the amount of choice which they leave the student. The least flexible is the *Civilekonom* course, and the most flexible the F.M. and the F.K. courses. At the moment these latter, particularly the F.K., offer the student a great deal of choice of subject. The whole system is, however, being fundamentally revised, and the choice of combinations of subjects is likely to be restricted, although in many cases there will be an extension of the possibilities of specialization within a subject. The courses will also be more programmed, and will have to be taken in a specified order.

There are various important ways in which Swedish degree courses at present differ from those in other Western European universities.

In general subjects (apart from languages) are studied consecutively, not concurrently. Usually a student is required to amass a certain number of points (*betyg*). A subject can normally be taken to the one-, two-, or three-point level. Usually courses for the higher number of points are more detailed and last longer than those for only one point. Normally the lower-point courses are necessary pre-requisites to embarking on the higher-point courses. A one-point course is expected to take the whole of a student's attention for five months—that is, three and a half to four months of teaching and one and a half months of work on his own. A two-point course is expected to last ten months, etc. The points system is also under revision, so it should be stressed that this account applies only to the situation in 1967.

In both the F.K. and the F.M. students need to collect six points in all. In either of these degrees students can take one-sixth, one-third, or one-half of their studies in economics. The remaining courses can come from a wide range of subjects, not only in the social sciences but in the humanities as well. In the case of the F.M. (which is designed primarily for prospective teachers) this choice is restricted, economics being normally combined with political science and history, and taken for either one or two points. In the F.K., however, there is at present an unlimited choice, though at least two subjects must be taken.

The F.P.M. is a more recent and specialist degree in the social sciences for which a student needs seven, not six, academic points. The choice of subject is restricted to the social-science and related fields, which include general economics, business economics, political science, statistics, human geography, and law. Each student must have a minimum of two points in general economics, and one each in statistics and political science. One point is made up of two pre-liminary half-point courses—in law and business administration. One possible combination is two or three points in general economics (the three-point course often being taken after the student has the seven points required for the degree), two in business economics, two in statistics, and one in political science. Students take first the two preliminary courses in law and business administration and then go on to courses in the main subjects. Further courses in business economics cannot be taken until the one-point statistics course has been completed.

The *Civilekonom* degree is more vocational than the main university degrees, and the economics taught in it is integrated with business economics. Students need six points for the degree. At the Handel-shögskolan at Gothenburg new regulations introduced from the autumn of 1967 stipulate that students take one point in economics and business law and two points in business economics, with a choice of one point in either economic geography, statistics, or international economics and the further point from one of the main subjects—economics, business economics, or business law. Courses are offered consecutively (apart from language courses, not included in the six-point requirement, which run concurrently). Students are not obliged to attend the courses—there are no attendance controls—but they are recommended to take courses in the order in which they are offered.

At the Stockholm Handelshögskolan courses are available in economics, business economics, economic geography, and law. Language instruction is also available, and students must study at least one foreign language, though not for points. Common combinations of courses for the six points are: (*a*) Economics (1),[1] business economics (3), economic geography and/or law (2). (*b*) Economics (2), business economics (2), economic geography and/or law (2). Other combinations are, however, possible.

At the University of Lund at least two of the six points required must be in business economics, one in economics, and one in commercial and tax law. Another point is to be taken in any of these three subjects, and the last in a wider list of subjects,[2] which includes economics but not business economics. A foreign language and a certain standard of mathematical knowledge are also demanded.

In general the degree courses take four to five years, with the exception of the *Civilekonom*, which takes only three and a half. Theoretically, the six-point degrees could take only three years to complete, but this is in fact almost never achieved. Examinations (*Tentamena*) are related to each course, but there is no overall final examination.

It is difficult to be exact about student numbers because of the degree of choice in the F.M. and the F.K. degrees. However, in the autumn of 1964 there were some 2763 students studying economics

---

[1] The figures in brackets refer to the number of points for which the subject is taken.

[2] There are in all thirteen of these—economics, commercial and tax law, economic geography, international economics, economic history, education, psychology, sociology, statistics, political science, mathematics, mathematical statistics, and numerical analysis.

for the *Civilekonom*—1468 at the Stockholm School, 818 at Gothenburg, and 477 at the University of Lund. For the universities the figure is far more difficult to ascertain, but there were probably in 1964 approximately the same number in all the universities. The largest group was at Stockholm—probably about a third, or at a rough estimate 900 students.[1] Uppsala came next, with some 750 students, then Gothenburg and Lund, with probably about 500 each, and lastly Umeå, with perhaps 100 students.

Given the degree of variation in the courses individual students may take at the universities, it seems most useful to describe briefly the one- and two-point courses in economics at the universities of Stockholm, Uppsala, and Lund, indicating the topics covered and the form of instruction.

1. THE UNIVERSITY OF STOCKHOLM

The first part of the one-point course is taught primarily in lecture classes of forty students each, and covers the basic elements of economics, roughly the contents of Samuelson's first textbook. These classes cover fifty-six hours of instruction in all—eight hours a week for seven weeks. At the same time students spend two hours a week in small discussion groups of ten to fifteen students which cover the same ground, and in which the students do practical exercises. At the end of this preliminary course there is a five-hour written examination. The second part of the one-point course deals with economic policy, including monetary policy, public finance, and current problems of the Swedish economy, and lasts for six weeks. Again lecture classes of forty students are the principal means of instruction and account for five hours a week. There is also a one-hour lecture each week for all the students together. The discussion groups continue for two hours a week. The total amount of instruction in the whole course therefore amounts to eighty-two hours of lecture classes, eight hours of lecture, and twenty-four hours of discussion and exercise groups.

The two-point course[2] is also basically taught by lecture classes. The course consists of lecture classes in micro-economics (six hours

---

[1] These figures are, it must be stressed, highly tentative. They do, however, serve as a very rough guide to the order of magnitude of the groups at the various universities.

[2] It should perhaps be repeated that, as has been mentioned earlier, the one-point course is a prerequisite for the two-point course.

a week for five weeks), macro-economics (six hours a week for six weeks), and international trade (six hours a week for three weeks). In the second two topics there are also two hours a week of group discussion. In addition there are seminars of eighteen students which meet for eighteen hours over three weeks to discuss the essays which the students have written. At the end of the course there is another written examination, again lasting five hours. The total instruction for the two-point course consists of eighty-four hours of lecture classes, twenty-four hours of discussion and exercise groups, and eighteen of seminars.

2. THE UNIVERSITY OF UPPSALA

At Uppsala lecture classes are not used as they are at Stockholm, but instead instruction is by a combination of formal lectures and small discussion and exercise groups for about fifteen students. There are two different courses—one (the A course) intended for students taking the F.K. and the F.P.M., and the other (the B course) intended for the rest of the students. It is possible for students reading for an F.K. to take the B course. This distinction continues at the two-point level. Those F.K. students who take the A course in the one-point level go on to the A two-point course, and those who have done the B course to the two-point B course. The F.M. students may take either the A or the B two-point course. The courses described below are in both cases the A course.

In the one-point course there are lectures on economic theory and policy (fifty-six hours), elements of economic method (twelve hours), and micro-economic theory (fifty-six hours).[1] Throughout the fourteen weeks of the course there are also six hours a week of small-group work. Total instruction, therefore, amounts to 124 hours of lectures and 84 of discussion and exercise group.

In the two-point course the same basic pattern of instruction continues with the addition of seminars for the discussion of students' essays. There are lectures on macro-economics (fifty-six hours), economic systems (twelve hours), international economics (twelve hours), and the economic theory of public finance (fifty-six hours). There continues to be six hours a week of small-group work. The seminars occupy two hours a week. The total amount of instruction

---

[1] In the B course this is replaced by a course on economic systems and economic development.

is therefore 136 hours of lectures, 84 hours of discussion groups, and 32 hours in seminars, making an overall total of 252 hours.

3. THE UNIVERSITY OF LUND

In the one-point course at the University of Lund instruction is partly in lecture classes for twenty-five to thirty students and partly in discussion and exercise groups each of about ten students. There are lecture classes in statistics (six hours), micro-economics (twenty-eight hours), and macro-economics (thirty-two hours), together with thirty hours of discussion and exercise groups, making ninety-six hours in all. In addition to this there are occasional lectures on economic policy by visiting lecturers.

In the two-point course there are lecture classes in applied mathematics (twenty hours), economic theory (forty hours), and economic policy and international economics (forty hours). In addition there is a two-hourly discussion and exercise class and eighteen hours of seminars for the discussion of essays which students have written. The total instruction amounts to 138 hours—100 hours of lecture classes, 20 hours of discussion and exercise groups, and 18 hours of seminars.

Switzerland

There are in Switzerland three different patterns of first degrees in economics—the three-year *Lizenzen* offered by the French-language universities, the fairly recently instituted four-year *Licences* at the German-language universities,[1] and the specialist degree offered by the Hochschule at St Gallen. There are three French-language universities—Geneva, Lausanne, and Neuchâtel—and three German —Basle, Berne, and Zürich. The University of Fribourg offers instruction for a three-year *Licence* in both French and German. At St Gallen all instruction is in German.

Swiss universities have a particularly high proportion of foreign students. Of the 513 students gaining the *Licence* in economics from the seven universities in 1965, 176, or 34·3 per cent, were foreign. At St Gallen too there are a substantial number of foreign students— in 1965 of the total student body of 1202, 363, or 30·2 per cent, were foreign.[2]

FRENCH-LANGUAGE UNIVERSITIES

In all the three-year *Licences* offered in the French-language universities (including Fribourg) there are different specializations or different degrees, as the table below shows.

It can be seen that there is everywhere a choice between specialization in general and business economics, with mathematical economics also available at Geneva. At Lausanne economics is taught in the University's Ecole des Hautes Etudes Commerciales (H.E.C.), which is attached to the faculty of law.

The following tables compare the balance of the courses at three of the four universities (comparable data were not available for Fribourg). They are grouped by specialization to facilitate comparison.

Group instruction is used more at Geneva than at the other two

---

[1] Previously students in these universities took a doctor's degree, as in Austria.
[2] The largest two groups were from Germany (132 students) and from Norway (109). In all, 320 of these 363 foreign students were from European countries covered by this survey.

University of Fribourg	University of Geneva	University of Lausanne	University of Neuchâtel
Licence in economic and social sciences specializing in	*Licences* in	*Licence* in commerce and economics specializing in	*Licence* in economics specializing in
1. Economics	1. Economics	1. Economics	1. Economics
2. Economics of the firm	2. Economics, specializing in mathematics	2. Business economics	2. Business economics
	3. Economics and actuarial science	There is also a *Licence* in commerce and actuarial science.	
	4. Economics and commerce There are four other *licences* which contain some economics, but those above are the ones in which economics plays a major part.	It is also possible to specialize in economics in the law degree, but few do	

universities. Seminars play an important part of the Geneva course, and students have to write a paper or attend a practical class in each subject they study.

The number of students in each year of this economics degree in Geneva is small—about thirty in the first year, declining somewhat as the course proceeds.

In the business economics specialization there are also quite a number of differences between the three courses, as shown in the table. Group instruction is more used at Geneva, but to a less marked extent than in the economics degree. In all the courses law plays an important part (as it did in the economics degree in all but Geneva). At both Lausanne and Neuchâtel the business economics and the economics specializations are rather similar—the only variations being in the proportion of the course in economics and business economics—whereas in Geneva the two degrees differ more markedly.

Degrees with Economics Specialization

	Geneva %	Lausanne %	Neuchâtel %
Economics	22 ·4	41 ·2	25 ·4
Business economics	13 ·8	21 ·2	31 ·0
Law	3 ·4	21 ·2	23 ·9
Other social sciences	27 ·6	4 ·7	11 ·3
Accountancy and commercial techniques	—	5 ·9	2 ·8
Mathematics and statistics	25 ·9–32 ·8	5 ·9	2 ·8
Foreign languages	—	—	2 ·8
Other subjects	0 ·0– 3 ·4	—	—
Total semester hours (= 100%)	116	170	142
	%	%	%
Lectures	58 ·6	87 ·0	85 ·9
Group instruction	41 ·4	13 ·0	14 ·1

Degree with Business Economics Specialization

	Geneva %	Lausanne %	Neuchâtel %
Economics	15 ·0	34 ·1	22 ·6
Business economics	18 ·0	28 ·2	33 ·8
Law	20 ·3–22 ·6	21 ·2	23 ·9
Other social sciences	15 ·0	4 ·7	11 ·3
Accountancy and commercial techniques	18 ·0–19 ·5	5 ·9	2 ·8
Mathematics and statistics	10 ·5–13 ·5	5 ·9	2 ·8
Foreign languages	—	—	2 ·8
Other subjects	0 – 3 ·0	—	—
Total semester hours (= 100%)	133	170	142
	%	%	%
Lectures	71 ·4	87 ·0	85 ·9
Group instruction	28 ·6	13 ·0	14 ·1

At Lausanne and Neuchâtel the courses for the two specializations are basically common, with a few variations towards the end, whereas in Geneva only the first year is more or less common.

The next table shows the composition of course for the two remaining Geneva degrees:

	Geneva	
	Economics, Mathematics Specialization %	Economics and Actuarial Science %
Economics	19·6	11·8
Business economics	8·2	11·8
Law	4·1	6·8
Other social sciences	20·6	6·8
Accountancy and commercial techniques	2·1	11·8
Mathematics and statistics	45·4	51·0
Foreign languages	—	—
Other subjects	—	—
Total semester hours (= 100%)	97	102
	%	%
Lectures	79·4	71·6
Group instruction	20·6	28·4

In both degrees mathematical and statistical subjects play a predominant part; group instruction is at much the same level as in the economics and commerce degree, but for both these degrees the total number of students per year will be very much smaller than it is for the economics and commerce degree.

All these French-language universities have three main sets of examinations, normally at the end of each year.

Examinations

	Fribourg	Geneva	Lausanne	Neuchâtel
Written	5 (3 hr)	11	2 (4 hr)	5 (4 hr)
Oral	13	13	13*	18

* This is an estimate, and there may be more, possibly as many as eighteen.

The table above shows the number of written and oral examinations at each university—it can be seen that written examinations are more used at Geneva than at the other three universities. Examinations tend to occur at the end of each year, although students may have some choice in when they offer the various subjects. Most successful students complete the course in three years. There are problems of wastage in the course; these have in the past tended to be more severe with foreign than with Swiss students, and it is now necessary for students from abroad to take an admission examination.

GERMAN-LANGUAGE UNIVERSITIES

The three German universities—Basle, Berne, and Zürich—have fairly recently initiated four-year *Lizenze* courses. At Basle and Berne the courses are for the *Licentiatus rerum politicarum* (*Lic.Rer.Pol.*), and at Zürich for the *Licentiatus Oeconomiae Publicae* (*Lic.Oec.Pub.*). At all three there are various specializations which students may follow. At Basle students can specialize in applied economic research (basically econometrics and operations research). At Berne there is a choice, after a common course of two semesters, between specialization in general economics, business economics, or social science. In Zürich a great deal of the course is common, but students have the choice of three specializations—general or business economics or administration. About half the students take each of the economics options, and very few in fact follow the administration specialization.

The table below compares the balance of course for the general and business economics options at Berne and Zürich. Composition of course information has not been obtained for Basle).

	Business Economics		General Economics	
	Berne	Zürich	Berne	Zürich
	%	%	%	%
Economics	30·3–35·5	35·1–52·0	43·1	38·8–48·1
Business economics	27·0	18·2–31·2	23·5	9·2–22·4
Law	25·0	17·5–29·6	14·4–20·9	16·4–30·5
Other social sciences	1·3– 7·9	2·6–23·1	1·3– 7·8	9·9–15·6
Accountancy and commercial techniques	2·6	7·1	2·6	4·6
Mathematics and statistics	6·6	6·5	6·5	7·9
Foreign languages	—	—	—	—
Other subjects	0·7	—	0·7	—
Total semester hours (= 100%)	152	152	153	154
	%	%	%	%
Lectures	78·9	84·2	79·7	81·8
Group instruction	21·1	15·8	20·3	18·2

At Zürich all students take at least twenty hours of lectures[1] chosen from the fields of economics, business administration, law, and social sciences. This has been shown by the higher figure of the ranges in the table; it is, however, not necessary for all these twenty hours to be in the same group of subjects. Thus it is quite possible that a student's instruction time would fall between the lower and upper points of the range shown in all four groups in the table.

It can be seen from the table that at the two universities the balance of the course is not very dissimilar.

At all three universities there are certain preliminary examinations which have to be taken early in the course. At Berne and Basle these are rather less formalized than at Zürich, where there is a *Vorprüfung* at the end of the third semester. At all three written work is required in addition to the *Diplom-Arbeit*—at Zürich and Basle three seminar papers and at Berne one paper.[2] The final examination consists of written and oral examinations. The written papers are four or five hours in length, and the orals fifteen to twenty minutes.

Seminars and classes are used in all the universities. At Zürich, for two semesters following the *Vorprüfung*, the Economics Pro-seminar meets weekly for two hours; the full seminar consists of thirty-five to forty students, but in addition groups of four or five students prepare written answers to a series of questions which are handed out every fortnight at the seminar. In the winter semester the seminars cover macro-economic topics, and in the summer micro-economic.

All these courses can be completed in eight semesters, but there is a tendency for students to take rather longer. At Zürich, for example, a normal time is five years.

HOCHSCHULE ST GALLEN

At the Hochschule there is a common course for four semesters, followed by four semesters of more specialized study. In this latter period the student can choose from a large number of detailed options, twenty-one in all. In the table on page 245 the balance of the common course and that for two of the options, banking and econo-

---

[1] For statistical purposes this has been treated as twenty hours exactly.

[2] This one paper is done in the fifth semester at the earliest and must be in some subject other than that from which the topic for the *Diplom-Arbeit* will be selected.

mic policy, are shown. As well as these options there are also specializations in:

Industrial production	Tourist traffic
Distribution and trade	The economics of transport
Organization	Auditing and trusteeship
Personnel	Financial policy
Finance and book-keeping	International economics and
Operations research	development policy
Private and social insurance	Economic law
	Economic education

In addition there are five specializations giving a less economic orientation.

The common course has at its end a *Vorprüfung* which is taken at the end of the fourth semester. The final examination is not taken all at the end of the eighth semester, but instead some subjects are taken at the end of the sixth, seventh, and eighth semesters. Examinations are both written and oral. All students have to prepare a *Diplom-Arbeit* of fifty to sixty pages, normally taking six weeks. Students are also expected to do other written work during the course.

All students at the Hochschule are expected to have six months' practical experience in industry or commerce, and this can be fitted in between the fourth and fifth semesters, or done before the course starts. Most of the students do their practical work in private industry, but a few do it in the public sector.

The course as it now stands at the Hochschule was introduced only in the academic year 1966–67. Before its introduction the course was shorter (only seven semesters) and there was no *Vorprüfung*. The reform gives students a longer common period of study before they decide on their specialization, and somewhat reduces the pressure of the course.

The Hochschule is growing rapidly—the total number of students has risen from 968 in 1962–63 to 1409 in 1965–66. The number of graduates is also rising—113 in 1962–63 and 147 in 1965–66. It is expected that the Hochschule will have as many as 2000 students in the fairly near future. Restrictions on entry of foreign students are imposed, and their numbers should not exceed 25 per cent. Quite a high proportion of students continue their studies at the Hochschule for the doctorate. To obtain the higher degree takes at least three semesters after the *Lizenz* examination. In 1965–66 twenty doctorates were awarded.

The Degree Course at the Hochschule, St Gallen

	1st–4th Semesters	5th–8th Semesters		Overall Course	
	Common Course	Banking Option	Economic Policy Option	Banking Option	Economic Policy Option
	%	%	%	%	%
Economics	18·9	31·8	34·1	24·6	25·7
Business economics	18·9	31·8	18·8	24·6	18·8
Law	18·9	20·0	18·8	19·4	18·8
Other social sciences	7·5	—	16·5	4·2	11·5
Accountancy and commercial techniques	—	3·5	—	1·6	—
Mathematics and statistics	9·4	4·7	2·4	7·3	6·3
Foreign languages	11·3	7·0	8·2	9·4	9·9
Other subjects	15·1	1·2	1·2	8·9	8·9
Total semester hours (= 100%)	106	85	85	191	191
	%	%	%	%	%
Lectures	75·5	65·9	63·6	71·2	70·2
Group instruction	24·5	34·1	36·4	28·8	29·8

STATISTICS

The following statistics give some idea of the relative size of the various institutions. The table on page 247 shows the output of graduates in 1965 from the different universities, and from the Hochschule. For the universities the number of foreign graduates included in the total is also shown.

The next table shows the total number of students at the various institutions in 1965.

Although the student numbers and the graduate output is larger in the French-language universities, at the doctoral level this is no longer so marked, as the table shows on page 249.

This may in large part be due to the fact that until recently the doctorate was the first degree in the German-language universities. It is indeed still possible at Zürich for students to proceed direct to the doctorate without taking the *Lizenz*, though the course still lasts much the same length of time as if the *Lizenz* were taken as a preliminary degree.

Economics Graduates 1965

	French-language Universities				German-language Universities			St Gallen
	Fribourg	Geneva	Lausanne	Neuchâtel	Basle	Bern	Zürich	
Total	72	112	168	35	24	40	62	114
of whom foreign	40	45	57	6	9	10	9	n/a
Group total	387 (148*)				126 (28*)			114

n/a = not available   * foreign

Economics Students 1965

	French-language Universities				German-language Universities			St Gallen
	Fribourg	Geneva	Lausanne	Neuchâtel	Basle	Berne	Zürich	
Number	465	839	492	346	346	346	523	1,202
Group total	2142				1544			1,202

Overall total = 4888

Economics Doctorates Awarded 1965

	French-language Universities				German-language Universities			St Gallen
	Fribourg	Geneva	Lausanne	Neuchâtel	Basle	Berne	Zürich	
Total	27	9	5	11	23	16	6	20
Foreign	20	8	3	3	11	3	1	n/a
Overall totals	52 (34*)				45 (15*)			20

n/a = not available   ( ) * foreign

Turkey

In Turkey there are three universities awarding first degree in economics—the University of Ankara (faculty of political science), the University of Istanbul (faculty of economics), and the Middle East Technical University, M.E.T.U. (faculty of administrative sciences). M.E.T.U. is based on the American university structure, and all teaching is in English; it thus differs considerably from the State universities of Ankara and Istanbul. Entry to Ankara and Istanbul universities is by a national university entrance examination, while M.E.T.U. has its own special admission examination. As well as these three, there are also four public academies of commercial science and five private ones which provide some training in commercial economics. These academies and Roberts College, a private institution in Istanbul giving a B.A., which includes some courses in economics, have not been included in this survey.

One of the chief problems for the teaching of economics in Turkey is the lack of textbooks in Turkish, which necessitates a great reliance on the lecture and the use of books in foreign languages. As has been mentioned, M.E.T.U. solves the problem in a drastic fashion by doing virtually all its teaching in English. At Ankara and Istanbul readings in English, German, and French are recommended. At Istanbul all students have to take a language test within four semesters, and unless they pass in that period they cannot go on to the second part of the course, but there are still considerable difficulties in persuading students to use foreign textbooks.

Another problem for the two State universities is the difficulty of getting staff. At M.E.T.U., although outside work is not allowed, salaries are about three times those in the State universities, so the staff situation is easier. In general M.E.T.U. is an institution drawing largely from the private schools, where instruction is in English, and its students, compared with those of the State universities, would appear to have many advantages.

At the University of Ankara a little economics is taught in the faculty of law,[1] but the main economics degree is the *Licence* in

---

[1] All students taking a law degree have four hours a week instruction in economics (micro- and macro-economics) in their first two years and do

political science. This has a prescribed course of four years, but most students take five or six. There is a maximum time-limit of eight years on the course, as the annual examinations cannot be repeated more than four times. The first two years of the course are common for all students in the faculty, and comparatively little economics is done—in the first year three hours out of twenty-eight, and in the second six hours are in economics. In the third and fourth years it is possible for students to specialize in public administration, economics and public finance, international relations, or business administration (this last option is still being developed). In the economics and public finance option in the third year students take history of economic thought, economic systems, economic analysis, and Government finance, together with some accountancy and statistics, the two latter taking up about a third of their time. In the fourth year they follow a course almost wholly devoted to economics, but with a little business economics, and accountancy.

At the University of Istanbul there is a *Licence* awarded by the faculty of economics, the course for which nominally lasts four years, but on which students normally spend six or seven years. The first two years of the course are common to all students in the faculty, but in the last two each student takes two of the five fields of specialization—public finance and policy, business administration, political science, statistics, and social policy. Most students (about 90 per cent) choose public finance and policy and business administration. Instruction is mainly by formal lecture, and the group instruction is in large groups. In the first year groups would be of 150 or 300, depending on the subject, if all students were to attend.

There are three sets of examinations—Part I covering the first year's work, which must be passed before a student starts on the second year's work, Part II at the end of the third year of the course, and the final, Part III, which cannot be taken before the end of the eighth semester. A student can begin the fourth-year classes even if he has not passed the Part II examination, but must pass it before he can take Part III. Examinations consist of written and of oral papers. As well as these three sets of examinations, students also have to pass a language test before they start on third-year work.

In the first year just under a quarter of the instruction is in economics. Students also have courses in economic history and

some business economics and history of economic thought in their third year.

geography, law, business administration, accountancy, and commercial and ordinary mathematics. In the second year the largest single share of instruction time is devoted to economics—students study price theory, the theory of income and employment, agricultural economics, and applied economics. They also continue to study law, business administration, and accountancy, and take courses in statistics and sociology. Some foreign-language instruction is also available.

Assuming that in the next two years the student specializes in public finance and policy and business administration—as most do—his course is more or less confined to these two subjects, although some law and accountancy courses are also taken.

The Middle East Technical University is different from the two State universities, being more comparable to an American university. M.E.T.U. has very close links with the U.S.A., where most of the staff have studied, and where many of the graduates go to do postgraduate work. M.E.T.U. has its own preparatory school, where a year's intensive course in English is provided to enable students otherwise qualified to enter M.E.T.U. to acquire the necessary mastery of English.

Entry to M.E.T.U. is by a competitive examination, and this, coupled with the language requirement, ensures a relatively high-quality intake. Economics is taught in the faculty of administrative sciences. After a common first two years students can specialize in economics and statistics, management or public administration for their Bachelor of Science (B.S.) degree. The course is a four-year one. In the first year students study economics, English, mathematics (including calculus), and take an introductory course in the social and political sciences, with an optional subject in law or one of a number of social-science subjects. In the second year students study accounting, economic theory, statistical analysis, and administration, with—for Turkish students—courses in Turkish government and administration (one semester) and an introduction to international politics in the next semester and—for non-Turkish students—a two-semester course in Turkish. (M.E.T.U. admits students from the countries of the Middle East as well as from Turkey itself, although the bulk of the students are Turkish.)

In the third year the common course ends and students specializing in economics embark on a course in which they can concentrate on either economics or statistics. They all take courses in the first semester of the third year in economic analysis, monetary theory and policy, and applied economics, together with two other courses (depending on the aspect of the subject they are concentrating on). For the economics concentration, these are history of economic analysis and an optional subject in mathematics, statistics, or the social aspects of development and for the statistics concentration, an introduction to probability and calculus. In the second semester of the third year the course follows a similar pattern—the three common courses are economic analysis, the structure of the Turkish economy, and applied statistics, together with, for the economics concentration, the history of economic analysis and an optional subject in statistical inference or political sociology or calculus, and for the statistics concentration statistical inference and calculus.

In the fourth year there are only two courses common to both concentrations—the economics of growth and a seminar in economics for which each student prepares one paper a semester. As well as this students taking the economics concentration do eight more courses—compulsory in international economics (2 semesters), public finance and fiscal policy (1 semester), and applied economics (1 semester) and two optional subjects in each semester. In the first semester of the year these are chosen from introduction to mathematical economics, national income and input-output analysis, research methods in social sciences, economic decision-making, and business economics, and in the second from linear programming, introduction to econometrics, administration of Government economic institutions and public corporations, budgeting and financial administration, and business economics. Those concentrating on statistics combine a compulsory two-semester course in statistical inference with two optional subjects in each semester. The choice in the first semester is from courses on sampling, introduction to mathematical economics and national income, and input-output analysis, and in the second from courses entitled experimental designs,[1] linear programming, and introduction to econometrics.

Students who take the B.S. (Management) degree do a substantial amount of business economics. These students also take a number of common-core courses, with further courses in one of these concentrations—industrial management, marketing, or finance and accounting. For the B.S. (Administration) degree students can do some economics, but mainly in optional rather than core courses.

At M.E.T.U. classes are small and the university is well-staffed

---

[1] This deals with mathematical models for experimental problems.

and has a good library. A considerable amount of written work is expected from students. The course has, as shown above, a mathematical and statistical basis. Fewer students take the economics and statistics degree than the management one—roughly fifty students take the economics and statistics degree (thirty concentrating on economics and twenty on statistics), as compared with two hundred taking the management degree. Ninety per cent of the graduates in economics and statistics go abroad for further study.

There is quite a high failure rate for the first year—about 50 per cent of the students have to repeat, and when they do so more than half succeed at their second attempt. In the second year about 20 per cent of the students fail and repeat, but in the third and fourth years there is virtually no failure and drop-out. Examinations are chiefly written, and are supplemented by tests during the semester ('quizzes'). For the next five years the faculty is limited to 1000 students.

The output of M.E.T.U. goes largely into the Civil Service, with some to university teaching after further study abroad, and a very few into the private sector.

From all this it is clear M.E.T.U. is a very different type of institution from the other Turkish universities. It might in a sense be compared with a French *grande école*, as contrasted with an ordinary French university. Facilities are far better, and teaching more intensive and individual.

United Kingdom

This more detailed study of the teaching of economics in United Kingdom universities is divided into a number of sections:

(1) A general description of the situation.
(2) Description of courses at a number of individual universities—Bristol, Cambridge, the London School of Economics, Manchester, St Andrews, and some of the new universities (Keele, Sussex, York, and Warwick).
(3) A note on external-degree students.
(4) A note on post-graduate course degrees in the U.K.

Section 1—General Description

In the United Kingdom there are a large number of universities offering what may broadly be described as economics degree courses. In England in 1967 there were thirty-four (counting the four colleges of London University where an economics degree can be taken as separate institutions), in Wales five (counting each of the four university colleges of the national University of Wales offering economics degrees separately), in Northern Ireland one, and in Scotland five (which increased to six when the Dundee part of the University of St Andrews became an independent institution). This made in all forty-five institutions. The vast majority, being autonomous, are able to determine their own pattern of study, and there is thus an extremely wide range, both as regards the pattern of teaching and the balance and content of courses. Some examples to illustrate this diversity are included in Section 2 of this study.

In addition to these it is also possible to take a degree course in economics for a London University external degree, either by private study, or by correspondence course, or in a non-university college of further education. Some of these colleges now offer their own degrees, authorized by the Council for National Academic Awards instead of their students taking the London degree.

In the universities of the United Kingdom there are two distinct patterns of degree. In Scotland the first degree is the M.A., which can be taken as an ordinary degree after three years or as an honours degree after four. The Scottish educational system is less specialized than the English, and the students tend to go to the university younger, at seventeen or eighteen, rather than at eighteen or nineteen. The first two years' study is of a fairly general nature, especially the first year, and many students go on to take the ordinary degree. At the Queen's University, Belfast, the system is similar to the Scottish—an ordinary degree (B.Comm.) in three years or an honours degree in four. It is also possible there to take the degree on a part-time basis, which means five years for the ordinary B.Comm. and five years' part-time and one year full-time for the honours degree.

In general in English and Welsh universities courses take only three years (the only normal exceptions to this being the course at the University of Keele, where a compulsory foundation year makes the course four, and in combined honours degrees in a foreign language and economics at Reading, where the course is similarly lengthened to four, but in this case by a year abroad.) Ordinary (pass) degrees tend to exist only as less demanding alternatives to the honours course to which students may be steered during their course, or simply as a grade in the final examination given to those who, although studying for an honours degree, are not judged worthy of honours. There are still, however, some pass degrees in their own right with direct entry (for example, at Liverpool, Newcastle, and in the University of Wales), but the trend in recent years has been for these degrees to disappear.

Although there are single honours degrees in economics at most universities in England and Wales, there are also a great number of ways in which economics can be combined with other subjects in a joint or combined honours degree. The best known of these is probably the Philosophy, Politics, and Economics (P.P.E.) degree at Oxford, where there is in fact no single honours degree in economics. The subjects with which economics can be combined are largely other social sciences—for example, economic history, politics, sociology, and philosophy—but economics can also be combined with statistics and/or mathematics and with languages. There are some fairly recent established courses where economics is combined with engineering, but in these economics is normally a subsidiary element.

In the final years, and in general at the smaller universities, student numbers tend to be small, so what is in principle formal teaching can in practice be fairly informal. Lectures, tutorials, discussion classes, and seminars are used in varying proportions. The Robbins Committee found that the average British full-time student in the social sciences received the following amounts of instruction per week:

	Hours
Lectures	7·0
Discussion periods	2·6
Practical and other teaching	0·3

(*Source:* Robbins Report, H.M.S.O., Cmnd. 2154, October 1963, p. 186, Table 86.)

At Oxford, on the other hand, the Franks Committee found that the average P.P.E. undergraduate went in a week to:

	Numbers
Lectures	3·5
Classes/Seminars	0·9
Tutorials	1·7

(*Source:* University of Oxford, Report of Commission of Inquiry, II, Statistical Appendix, Oxford, 1966, Tables 100 (p. 18), 120 (p. 138), and 137 (p. 155).)

British students normally prepare at least one piece of written work a fortnight, and many one a week.

The pattern of university examinations varies, but basically there are two patterns. Either (and this is most common) there are two sets of university examinations which may be supplemented by internal departmental examinations, or there are three sets of university examinations, one at the end of every year. In the first pattern the examinations are commonly at the end of the first and third years, though there are variations on this. Examinations are predominantly written, though an oral may be included in the final examination. Where there is an oral it tends increasingly to be only for candidates on the borderline between two classes.

The emphasis in courses varies very much from university to university. It is common, however, for the first year to include a good deal of work in other social sciences. The amount and extent of emphasis on the quantitative aspects of the subject also varies, although in single honours courses some mathematical knowledge is essential. There are still, however, certain combinations in which mathematics and statistics can be avoided.

In the accounts of individual universities that follow, an attempt has been made to select some representative examples of the various types of courses and trends in the U.K.

Section 2—Courses at a Number of Individual Universities

(*a*) THE UNIVERSITY OF BRISTOL

The courses for the B.Sc. in social sciences in which economics plays a major part can be divided into two groups. Firstly, there are two courses for which mathematics at Advanced Level in the school-leaving examination is required; and secondly those joint honours courses for which there is no advanced mathematical requirement. The first group consists of economics and economics with statistics; these share a common entry and have a common first year. In 1963 seven students were admitted to read economics, and nine economics and statistics. The second group is composed of economics and accounting, economics and economic history, economics and politics, economics and sociology, and philosophy and economics. Again in 1963, thirty-eight students were admitted to these courses.

The first group courses are both "intended to provide a thorough grounding in modern techniques of economic analysis with emphasis on quantitative methods".[1] In the common first year the students divide their time between economics, mathematics and statistics, and a third subject (either philosophy, politics, or sociology). In the second year both schools study principles of economics, but while those reading economics alone take history of economic thought, economic statistics and econometrics, economic history of the Great Powers since 1850, together with elements of accounting or political theory or logic and scientific method, those reading economics and statistics take more statistics with the same economic history course, and either accounting or logic and scientific method. In the third year the students have more choice: the economics students choose four optional subjects from a list of twelve topics (see Table UK 1 on p. 260). In addition to these four options they have a course in economic statistics and econometrics. Those studying economics with statistics do much more statistics and choose only two options from what is virtually the same list of topics as that available for economics (see Table UK1).

The second group of courses can perhaps be subdivided into three—firstly, economics and accounting, a course "intended to provide a general education, with business management particularly in view, and with a strong bias towards the use of quantitative

---

[1] University of Bristol, Faculty of Social Sciences Prospectus, Session 1966–67, p. 28.

techniques in general";[1] secondly, economics and economic history; and thirdly, economics and politics, economics and sociology, and philosophy and economics. These last three have separate entries, but have sufficiently similar first years for transfer from one to another to be possible at the end of the first year.

In the economics and accounting course economics, accounting, statistics, and law are all studied in the first two years. In the first year there is also a course in mathematics for accounting. In the third year the study of economics continues, and the students take two options in economics from a shorter form of the list of topics (see Table UK1) available to students of economics. In addition there are courses in accounting and in commercial law, as well as two seminars, one on contemporary economic problems and the other on accounting and business problems. In addition to this programme of studies students may have to do a vacation course in computer programming.

The economics and economic history course "is intended to give students a broad training in economics and in economic history, in such a way that the two illuminate each other".[2] Besides the two main subjects there are courses in British history from 1688 in the first year and in economic statistics in the first and second years. In the third year students do two optional subjects in economics (see Table UK1), a seminar on the principles of economics, a course in comparative economic history, and a special subject in history. At present these history special subjects are on the epoch of the American Civil War, 1850–76, on British social conditions and on social policies, 1880–1914, and on the industrialization of the Soviet Union, 1926–56.

The three other courses where economics is combined with another subject follow similar lines. In the first year all take courses in the principles of economics, an introduction to contemporary economic institutions, in sources and methods of economic statistics, two courses in their other subject, and one in one of the other two subjects. For example, a student reading economics and politics must do a course in either philosophy or sociology. In the second year about half the time is spent in economics and the rest in the other subject. This is also true in the third year, when the students take two economics options and attend two economics seminars, one on principles of economics and the other on contemporary economic problems.

---

[1] *Ibid.*, p. 34.   [2] *Ibid.*, p. 37.

Table UK 1
University of Bristol
Economics Optional Subjects

	Economics	Economics and Statistics	Economics and Accounting	Economics and Economic History	Economics and Politics	Economics and Sociology	Philosophy and Economics
				Available in Degree Schools of:			
Agricultural economics	X	X	X				
Business behaviour	X	X	X				
Financial markets and institutions	X	X		X	X	X	X
Growth, stabilization, and economic planning	X	X		X	X	X	X
International monetary and commercal policies	X			X	X	X	X
Labour economics	X	X	X	X	X	X	X
Models of resource allocation	X	X	X				
Optimal business decision making	X	X	X				
Public enterprise	X	X	X	X	X	X	X
Public finance	X	X	X	X	X	X	X
Topics in the history of economic thought	X						
Trade and economic development	X	X		X	X	X	X
No. of options taken in 3rd year	4	2	2	2	2	2	2

N.B. All options are not necessarily available in all sessions and students' choices are subject to the approval of the Head of Department of Economics.

In all the courses there is a departmental examination at the end of the first year and university examinations at the end of the other two. Part I of the Final, at the end of the second year, is composed of two papers[1] on minor and self-contained subjects—e.g., in the economics school, economic history, and the chosen second-year option. Part II comes at the end of the third year, and consists of from seven to nine papers. An oral examination may be required in addition in some schools.

Throughout the course students are expected to do written work in term-time, and in the first year also in the two short vacations. All essays have a maximum length of 1000 words. Students can, if their performance is poor, be required to repeat sessional examinations at the end of the first and second years, to repeat a year's study, or to leave the University.

(b) THE UNIVERSITY OF CAMBRIDGE

At Cambridge the degree course (tripos) is divided into two parts —Part I is taken at the end of the first year and Part II at the end of the third. It is possible for undergraduates to change from or to economics after the first part of the tripos examination. An undergraduate could, for example, take Part I of his tripos in mathematics or a natural-science subject and then take Part II in economics.

Part I of the tripos includes some economic history (that of England, 1750–1914) and some political science ("A Comparative Study of the Political Institutions and Ideas of Great Britain and the U.S.A."), but economics is the dominant subject in the examinations, accounting for three of the five papers. The economics courses for Part I are "concerned with the outlines of economic theory, emphasizing its uses and its applications, including applications to problems of economic policy, and with the organization and conditions of industry, labour and finance, having particular reference to the United Kingdom and its position in the world economy today".[2]

In Part II the undergraduate has some choice—in the final tripos examination there are six papers, of which half are in optional subjects. The common courses cover economic principles and problems, and economic and social relationships. The options, in each of which there is normally one paper (exceptionally two), are as

---

[1] Except in philosophy and economics, where there are three.

[2] *The New Economics Tripos at Cambridge*, prepared by the Faculty Board of Economics and Politics (Cambridge, 1962).

follows: economic theory and analysis; mathematical economics; international economics; banking, credit, and public finance; economics of under-developed countries; industry and labour; applied economic and social statistics; theory of statistics; social structure of advanced societies; political sociology; comparative economic development of India and Japan, 1858–1938; economic history of Russia. A further subject in sociology or politics may also be available.

An undergraduate could therefore by his choice of options include a substantial amount of mathematical economics and statistics in his course, or he could concentrate on the less mathematical aspects of the subject, or even move away from economics to sociology, politics, or economic history.

(c) LONDON SCHOOL OF ECONOMICS

The L.S.E. is a large and specialist school of social studies. In 1964–65 there were 929 day students reading for the B.Sc. (Econ.), though some of these were not strictly speaking economics students, since of the sixteen special courses available in the last two years only four are in economics. In addition to these day students, there were 156 evening (part-time) students. As well as the B.Sc. (Econ.) course, there is also a joint B.A. honours degree in philosophy and economics which fifteen students were reading in 1964–65.

The first year of the B.Sc. (Econ.) is common, and leads to the Part I examination at the end of the year. In Part I there are three compulsory papers—in economics, British Government, and economic or political history—and two optional papers chosen from a list of fourteen subjects, including mathematics, statistics, languages, law, and social-science subjects. In Part II, the examination for which is not until the end of the third year, the student chooses a specialization, in which he does eight papers. There are sixteen specializations, all of a social-science or kindred nature. The following constitute the different types of economics specializations that may be followed:

> Economics—applied and descriptive
> Economics and econometrics
> Monetary economics
> Industry and trade

The second and fourth demand that a mathematics course has been taken in Part I.

The eight papers for applied and descriptive economics are as follows:

(1) Political thought
(2) A history or a mathematics paper
(3) A paper in law, statistics, accountancy, public finance, economic geography, sociology, or scientific method
(4) Economic principles
(5) Problems of applied economics
(6) Economic statistics
(7) Development of economic analysis
(8) One out of monetary economics, international economics, history of economic thought, economics treated mathematically, and public finance (if not taken under (3) above)

An identical degree, but with a more limited number of specializations in Part II, has recently been started at Queen Mary College, London, with an annual intake of fifty students. University College, London, offers its own degree in economics, which differs from the common London University degree described above.

(d) THE UNIVERSITY OF MANCHESTER

In the first year of the B.A. Honours degree in economics at Manchester students follow courses in economics, government, and sociology, together with a course in mathematics, accountancy, or economic history. In economics the course is taught in lecture-classes consisting of some twenty-five students each, rather than by lectures and tutorial groups. The other subjects are taught in lectures combined with tutorial groups for which written work is done.

At the beginning of the second year students start on more specialized courses while retaining a common-core element. The three relevant lines of specialization are economics, economic and social statistics, and accountancy. The first line is the most popular —there are usually forty-five to fifty economics students, six to ten students of economic and social statistics, and about twelve accountancy specialists. In the second year all three groups take economic statistics, economics, and either sociology or government. The economics course is in two sections, covering macro- and micro-economic theory. In addition those students specializing in economics do two optional courses chosen from elements of economic development, industrial economics, agricultural economics, accountancy for economists, and certain other social-science subjects. The students taking the economic and social statistics line take mathematical statistics together with one course chosen from those listed above. The accountancy students take an accountancy course and one in commercial law.

The economics students in the third year take courses in macroeconomics, international economics, and public finance and policy, together with two optional subjects. These are chosen from the following list: comparative economic systems, economics of transport, history of economic thought, industrial economics, business organization, economics of labour, comparative industrial relations, money and banking, case studies in economic development, agricultural economics, quantitative economics. Students specializing in economic and social statistics take mathematical economics, introduction to econometrics, national income and social accounting, social survey techniques, and a further relevant subject in economics. The accountancy line consists of accountancy courses of various kinds together with the course on public finance and policy taken by those specializing in economics.

It is possible at Manchester to take an ordinary B.A. degree in economics by part-time and evening study, but the range of choice offered in this case is more limited. Students take this part-time degree primarily in the evening, but also attend some day-time instruction by obtaining day release from their employers.

(*e*) THE UNIVERSITY OF ST ANDREWS

The University of St Andrews was until 1967 divided between St Andrews itself and Dundee. As at a number of British universities, it was possible to take economics either in the faculty of social science (at Dundee) or in the faculty of arts (at St Andrews). The two geographical parts of the univeristy became separate universities in 1967.

In the faculty of social science the degree is the M.A. in social sciences, ordinary (three years) or with honours (four years). As in all Scottish universities, the entry to the honours course is not direct. At St Andrews a student can enter the honours course in his second year. In the first year there is a common course for all social scientists "designed to introduce the students to the methods and content of the social sciences through a study of the political, social, and economic structure of modern Britain and its geographical and historical background".[1] Students then go on in the second year to study three subjects—economics, philosophy, and one out of civil law, constitutional law and history, English, French, geography, German, jurisprudence, mathematics, modern history, political science, psychology, or statistics. In the third year the student takes any two of the following subjects—economics, geography, modern social and economic history, philosophy, political science, psychology, statistics or mathematics with economics or psychology. This means a student specializing in economics in the ordinary degree will have taken it as one of three subjects in the second year and one of two in the third.

The honours student goes to classes in at least two Part II subjects, including economics, and then in his last two years attends honours classes in economics either as a single-subject honours course or with statistics, geography, modern social and economic history, philosophy, political science, or psychology. In the final honours examination there are eight papers, either all in economics, or divided equally between economics and another subject, or five in economics and three in the other subject, or vice versa.

Where economics is the single honours subject these eight papers consist of

1 and 2.	Economic principles.
3 and 4.	Applied economics.
5.	Essay.
6.	Economic statistics.
7 and 8.	Two subjects chosen from: economic theory and analysis, industry, labour, international economics, money, industrial applications of statistics, economic history, any other approved subject.

Where economics is one of two combined honours subjects students take papers in principles of economics (only one paper), applied economics (two papers), and, as appropriate, one or two optional subjects chosen, subject to approval of the head of the department, from the list given above.

In the faculty of arts there is also an ordinary and an honours M.A. In the first two years students do five subjects to "the general level", which can include political economy and must include a philosophy subject and mathematics or one classical or two modern

---

[1] *Faculty of Social Science Degree of Master of Arts in Social Science* (University of St Andrews, 1965–66, p. 19).

languages. Normally three of these subjects are taken in the first year and two in the second. In the third year Ordinary M.A. students do two subjects to what is called the special level, and here political economy can be offered with a variety of other subjects—history of various kinds, mathematics, statistics, geography, philosophy, music, or Biblical studies. The subjects to be taken to the special level are normally taken to the general level in the first two years, so a student will have studied political economy in two of his three years.

For the honours degree the students follow the same course as for the ordinary degree for the first three years, but may have additional work in the third year. In the fourth year they go on to do honours work, and here political economy can be taken with history (medieval or modern), mathematics, geography, moral philosophy, or logic and metaphysics.

(f) THE NEW UNIVERSITIES

Since the war a number of completely new universities have been established in England, and to some extent they have pioneered new kinds of courses. This account will look briefly at the degree courses in economics available at three of them, and attempt to show the general educational context into which they are fitted. The distinctive contribution of the new universities has been perhaps primarily a clearer educational philosophy, and especially a greater attempt to relate subjects clearly and explicitly. There have been similar developments in older universities—and some of these were even pre-war, for example, the establishment of the P.P.E. course in Oxford—but they have probably been less far-reaching and less publicized.

(i) KEELE UNIVERSITY

Keele is the oldest of the new universities, and its main distinctive feature is an emphasis on general education. All students do a common foundation year with a basic lecture course supplemented by discussion groups touching on most aspects of modern society. In addition to this, in the first year students take two sessional classes in a subject which they have not studied in the final years of secondary education, and three different terminal classes in subjects which they have. All subjects are divided into the three groups—humanities, social sciences, and natural sciences—and at least one of the four sessional and terminal subjects must be taken from each group.

After the Foundation Year students take four subjects, of which two are normally at the principal level and two at the subsidiary level. Here again, at least one subject must be taken from the natural sciences group. A student taking economics as a principal subject would study it for three years, and could combine it with any one of sixteen other subjects, including political institutions, law, mathematics, and geology. As well as this there would be the two subsidiary subjects, both studied for one year and examined at the end of that year. Here again there is a wide choice, but an economics student could, for example, do computing science as one of them. In it he would learn to programme and take two examination papers—one on computing principles and methods, including the application of information-processing techniques, and one on a computer-programming project requiring the solution of specific problems on the computer.

In the final examination at the end of the fourth year in economics the student would have five papers:

1. Principles of economics
2. Income and employment
3. Industry and finance
4. Two special subjects, one chosen from List *A* and one List *B*.

List A	*List B*
International economics	Economic fluctuations and
Economic development and	government
trade	Public finance
Social economics	Marketing
Operations research	Government and industry
Advanced analysis	

These lists are changed from time to time, and some restrictions of choice may be imposed on students.

(ii) THE UNIVERSITY OF EAST ANGLIA

At this new university there is a broadly based course for the first two terms covering all the social sciences before the student starts on his honours course proper, which lasts seven terms. In the School of Social Studies he takes twelve courses, of which one must be in elementary statistical method. The other eleven are picked from five lists of economics, history, sociology, philosophy, and joint courses. As many as eight could be from the economics list, but in this case they would have to include economic theory and mathematics for economists. The full list of courses in economics, each of which take a term, is at present mathematics for economists, the world economy (structure and problems), economic theory, international economics, economics of public policy, quantitative applied economics, economic statistics, mathematical economics, monetary economics, economic dynamics, problems of developing countries (two courses), econometrics, advanced economic theory, business mathematics. Two courses are taken a term, and then the seventh term is spent on revision for the final examination, in which there are six papers. Marks in course-work during the seven terms are also taken into account in assessing the candidate's class, and there may also be an oral examination.

(iii) THE UNIVERSITY OF SUSSEX

As well as the School of Social Studies, the University of Sussex also has Schools of African and Asian, and of European, Studies where economics can be studied as a major subject. The first two terms are taken up by a preliminary course terminating in an examination. All students take courses in languages and value, and an introduction to history, with one additional course which for economists is economic and social framework. After this preliminary examination students begin their major study, with which they take contextual courses in the broader field to which their specialization belongs. In the School of Social Studies these contextual courses are on concepts, methods, and values in the social sciences, philosophy and international politics or world population and resources or an introduction to social psychology. Students also have to do an elementary course in statistical methods. In the School of African and Asian Studies the contextual courses are on cultures and societies, Westernization and modernization, and two out of world population and resources (which economics majors are expected to do), social microcosms, imperialism and nationalism, the tropical environment, and concepts, methods, and values in the social sciences. In the School of European Studies the contextual courses are on the foundations of European culture, the modern European mind or contemporary Europe, a history subject, and philosophy. Students are also expected to study one European language, in which they will have a proficiency examination.

In the major subject students in all schools take the same two

Table UK 2

University of Sussex
Optional Economics Courses

	School of Social Studies	School of African and Asian Studies
1. Economic and political history of Europe since 1945*	x	
2. European institutions and the economics of integration	x	
3. Mathematical Statistics	x	x
4. Econometrics	x	x
5. Economics of social policy	x	x
6. Labour economics	x	x
7. Development of economic thought	x	x
8. Economic planning	x	x
9. Economics of industry	x	x
10. International economics	x	x
11. Conflict co-operation, and choice†	x	x
12. Recent economic history‡	x	x
13. Development of the British economy 1760–1960‡	x	
14. Economic geography‡	x	
15. Social psychology of industry‡	x	
16. Industrial sociology‡	x	
17. Economics of transport	x	

* If this option is chosen No. 2 must also be done. This combination makes the course very similar to an economics major in the School of European Studies.
† This course covers game and decision theory, etc.
‡ A student can take only one of these courses.

basic economics courses in their final examinations, together with three other courses which vary from school to school. In the School of Social Studies they are on economics and under-developed countries, and two courses chosen from a wide list of economics and social science subjects (see Table UK2 on page 269). In the School of African and Asian Studies students also take the course in development economics, together with the economy of an approved African or Asian country (at present India or Nigeria) and one subject from a list of the economic options (in the widest sense) available to economics majors in the School of Social Studies (see Table UK2). In the School of European studies the other courses are in economics and political history of Europe since 1945, European institutions and the economics of integration, and the economy of an approved country or region. The latter is normally examined by dissertation. Students in this School can spend a year abroad in a continental European country, and in this case the course lasts four years.

Section 3—External Degree Students

In 1966 about twenty-six colleges in the U.K. provided courses for the London external B.Sc.Econ. In addition, as mentioned above, the Council for National Academic Awards was in process of recognizing some non-university college degrees in business studies and economics. On the whole, though, these will be offered by colleges as a substitute for the London external degree, for which they are at present teaching students. It has been estimated that in 1966–67 there were some 1700 students enrolled for first degrees in economics in colleges of further education. In the past the number of students getting external degrees has been relatively small, but this is likely to increase. In 1964–65 University Grants Committee statistics showed that 664 external degrees in social studies were awarded, and one may perhaps estimate that 160 of these were in economics. The Robbins Committee showed that in 1961–62, on a different and narrower definition of social studies, 378 external degrees were granted—perhaps 125 of these would be in economics. The Robbins Committee does, however, additionally show how these graduates had studied:

Colleges of further education	154
Other institutions	83
Private study	141
	——
Total	378
	——

(*Source:* Robbins Report, Appendix Two (A), Cmnd. 2154—ii(a), p. 107.)

The eighty-three at other institutions include forty-three at internal colleges of London University not aided by the University Grants Committee.

The Robbins Committee also show—as one would expect—that the wastage rate is considerably greater for external students. A study of the 1954–55 new registrations in social studies indicated a success rate of about 24 per cent for external students in the U.K. (for those overseas it was even lower at 17 per cent).[1]

Section 4—Post-graduate Course Degrees

In the United Kingdom an increasing number of post-graduate degrees of one or two years with definite courses of instruction are being offered. This is a movement towards the American system, and away from the traditional British view that once a man had a first degree he could go on to do a pure research degree, working entirely on his own except for a little supervision from a more experienced scholar. It is in reality an acceptance of the fact that one cannot produce a professional economist in a three-year undergraduate course. This view as applied to university education in general was stressed by the Committee on Higher Education under the chairmanship of Lord Robbins (*cf.* the discussion in Chapter 8 of the Report).

These advanced degrees with course instruction are mainly for either a Master of Arts (M.A.) degree or a Master of Science (M.Sc.). In 1966,[2] nineteen universities[3] offered between them thirty-five such degrees, of which fifteen were for an M.A., thirteen for an M.Sc., four for a Diploma,[4] and three for a Bachelor of Philosophy (B.Phil.) degree.[5] The majority of these courses always or normally lasts for one year. In some cases where there was a normal one-year course

---

[1] *Source:* Robbins Report, Appendix Two (A), Cmnd. 2154–ii(a), p. 326.

[2] This section is largely based on the information in the Social Science Research Council's publication, *Postgraduate Training in the Social Sciences —Awards and Courses*, 1966.

[3] These totals include as separate units four colleges of London University (the Business School, the London School of Economics, University College, and the School of Oriental and African Studies).

[4] This includes the University of Southampton, where a student may be awarded a Diploma when he presents either no thesis or a poor one. Students with a satisfactory thesis obtain an M.Sc. The other universities offering Diploma courses are Oxford (2 courses) and Glasgow.

[5] Only Oxford, Glasgow, and York Universities award a B.Phil. degree.

graduates in subjects other than economics are, if admitted, required to do an additional year, and in some cases graduates in economics from other universities may have to take a two-year course.

All degrees are primarily taught by formal courses culminating in examinations with usually from three to four papers,[1] but in some cases a dissertation is required. This was so in twelve of the thirty-five degree courses, and in a further one[2] a dissertation is optional.

The thirty-five degrees cover a wide range of aspects of economics —eight of them are simply in economics, five are in economic development, four in econometrics, two in business studies, but the titles of the rest vary from university to university. They include such subjects as regional economics and planning (Lancaster), the economics of public policy (Leicester), and micro-economic decision-making (Birmingham). There is considerable variation in the topics covered by the degrees. The range of choice within the degree naturally tends to be greatest at the larger universities. It will be of interest to give two examples of the degrees simply entitled economics —from the University of East Anglia, one of the newest British universities, and the London School of Economics, the largest single institution for the training of economics students in the U.K. At East Anglia the degree is a one-year one for the M.A. in Economics. There are examination papers in contemporary economic theory, quantitative economic analysis, and one further subject chosen from economic forecasting and macro-economic planning, regional development, project design and evaluation, survey methods, or advanced economic theory. At the London School of Economics the degree is an M.Sc. in Economics, again normally lasting one year.[3] Students have examination papers at the end of the course, in economic theory, methods of economic investigation, and in one of the following fields: advanced economic theory, history of economic thought, international economics, labour economics, monetary economics, economics of public enterprises, economics of transport, public finance, economics of industry, business administration, business finance, economics of poor countries and their development, agricultural economics, economic problems of a particular region,

---

[1] In the two-year Glasgow Diploma B.Phil. course there are thirteen papers, but this is exceptional.

[2] The Oxford B.Phil.

[3] Both at East Anglia and L.S.E. students without sufficient background in economics may require an extra, qualifying year.

economic aspects of accountancy, or any other approved economic field. There is, then, it is clear, far more choice at the London School of Economics than there is at East Anglia, and the same would be true if one compared, say, the Oxford B.Phil. in Economics with the York B.Phil. or the Essex M.A.

Appendix 1

UNIVERSITIES AND OTHER INSTITUTIONS
VISITED IN PREPARATION OF REPORT

Austria

University of Vienna: Faculty of Law	March 1966
Vienna School of Economics and Business Administration (Hochschule für Welthandel)	March 1966

Belgium

University of Liège: Faculty of Law	December 1965
Business School	December 1965
University of Louvain: Faculty of Economic and Social Studies	May 1966

Denmark

University of Copenhagen: Faculty of Law and Economics	May 1965
Copenhagen School of Economics and Business Administration	May 1965

Finland

—

France

University of Grenoble: Faculty of Law and Economics	April 1966
University of Lille: Faculty of Law and Economics	May 1966
University of Lyon: Faculty of Law and Economics	April 1966
University of Nancy: Faculty of Law and Economics	May 1966
University of Paris: Faculty of Law and Economics	May 1966
Ecole des Hautes Etudes Commerciales, Jouy-en-Josas	May 1966

Germany

Free University of Berlin: Faculty of Economic and Social Sciences	July 1965
Technical University of Berlin: Faculty of Economics	July 1965
University of Bonn: Faculty of Law and Political Science	July 1965
University of Cologne: Faculty of Economic and Social Sciences	July 1965
University of Göttingen: Faculty of Law and Political Science	July 1965
Mannheim School of Economics	July 1965
University of Marburg: Faculty of Law and Political Science	July 1965
University of Saarbrücken: Faculty of Law and Economics	July 1965

Greece
University of Athens: Faculty of Law   March 1966
Athens Graduate School of Economics and   March 1966
    Business Administration

Holy See
Gregorian Pontifical University: Institute of Social   March 1966
    Sciences

Iceland
—

Ireland
—

Italy
University of Parma: Faculty of Economics and   April 1966
    Commerce
Luigi Bocconi Commercial University, Milan   April 1966
Sacro Cuore Catholic University, Milan: Faculty of   April 1966
    Economics and Commerce
University of Rome: Faculty of Economics and   March 1966
                        Commerce
                        Faculty of Law   March 1966
                        Faculty of Political Science   March 1966
University of Turin: Faculty of Economics and   April 1966
                        Commerce
                        Faculty of Law   April 1966
University of Urbino (at Ancona): Faculty of   April 1966
    Economics and Commerce

Malta
—

Netherlands
Free University of Amsterdam: Faculty of Economics   May 1966
Municipal University of Amsterdam: Faculty of   May 1966
    Economic Science
Netherlands School of Economics, Rotterdam   May 1966
Catholic School of Economics, Tilburg   May 1966

Norway
University of Oslo: Faculty of Social Sciences   May 1965
Norwegian School of Economics and Business   May 1965
    Administration, Bergen

Spain
University of Barcelona: Faculty of Political, Economic March 1966
    and Commercial Sciences
School of Business Administration and Management   March 1966
    (E.S.A.D.E.), Barcelona

University of Madrid: Faculty of Political, Economic and Commercial Sciences	March 1966
Faculty of Law	March 1966
School of Business Management (I.C.A.D.E.), Madrid	March 1966

Sweden

University of Lund: Economics Institute	May 1965
Business Economics Institute	May 1965
University of Stockholm: Economics Institute	May 1965
Stockholm School of Economics	May 1965
University of Uppsala: Economics Institute	May 1965

Switzerland

University of Geneva: Faculty of Economic and Social Sciences	April 1966
University of Lausanne: Faculty of Law	April 1966
Business School (H.E.C.)	April 1966
St Gallen School of Economics and Business Administration	April 1966
University of Zürich: Faculty of Law and Political Science	April 1966

Turkey

University of Ankara: Faculty of Law	March 1966
Faculty of Political Science	March 1966
Middle East Technical University, Ankara	March 1966
University of Istanbul: Faculty of Economics	March 1966

United Kingdom
—

Appendix 2

LETTER TO CORRESPONDENTS:
STUDY OF THE TEACHING OF ECONOMICS
IN EUROPEAN UNIVERSITIES

The Committee for Higher Education and Research of the Council of Europe has decided to undertake a number of studies on the teaching of individual subjects in European universities. It is hoped that such studies will have value in providing information as to the present state of university teaching, which in a period when in many countries universities are revising and reorganizing their curricula may be particularly useful in suggesting alternative approaches to the teaching of the individual subjects. In the long run, the availability of this sort of information can only further the Committee's aim of promoting a closer drawing together of the universities of Europe, and increasing the free movement of ideas and people between universities.

The studies are intended to cover the nature and content of courses of instruction, the methods of teaching adopted, and the conditions in which higher education takes place. Each study is being undertaken by an individual universitity teacher of the subject concerned.

Economics presents some special problems. Within universities it is frequently taught as part of a degree in law, business administration, or the social sciences, and it is necessary to define its particular place within these degree courses. It is also taught in specialized institutions of higher education outside the universities, and it is not always clear how far these should be included in the study.

In visiting universities and other institutions of higher education, I am trying to find out in some detail the content of courses in economics and the way in which they are taught. In particular I should like to discuss the following:

1. how students are admitted (the question of *numerus clausus*);
2. how students are assessed, both during their course and at the first degree;
3. the proportion of students completing their course, and the average length of time required;
4. the relative importance of lectures and less formal small-group instruction;
5. the particular problems of students in their first year of study as they begin a subject which for the most part they will not have studied at school;
6. the amount of independent written work expected of the student;
7. the teaching responsibilities of the different grades of university teachers;

8. the problems of recruitment of teaching staff;
9. the provision of assistance to university staff—research assistants, secretaries, computers, etc.;
10. library provision and the library needs of first-degree students;
11. plans and proposals for change in the teaching of economics of the degree structure;
12. the subsequent careers of students of economics.

Although a great deal of this information could no doubt be gathered by a questionnaire, the opportunity to discuss these questions with a number of university teachers in each country not only enables me to obtain a more vivid picture of the conditions of higher education in economics in each country but also to discover further topics which other university teachers feel should come within the framework of such a study.

J. F. H. ROPER
University of Manchester

January 1966

Appendix 3

A group of university teachers of economics, whose names are given below, met in Strasbourg on 17th to 19th May, 1967. They were in general agreement with the report, and on the basis of it and of their discussion made the following recommendations:

1. Any degree in economics must contain a significant proportion of economics courses. While it is not easy to lay down a precise percentage, a degree in economics in which less than 30 per cent of the instruction deals with economics, including business economics, cannot be considered satisfactory.
2. Economics is one of the social sciences, and economists need to realize the interrelation between their subject and the other social sciences. An economist's training should therefore include an introduction to the other social sciences, including the institutional framework in which the economy operates. A programme of studies that includes more than 15 per cent of law reflects an outdated approach to the teaching of economics. A good working knowledge of at least one foreign language should be a condition of admission to the study of economics.
3. The increasing use of mathematics in economic theory and of statistics in applied economics make a training in quantitative methods an essential part of an economist's education. It is important that students not only acquire the techniques of mathematics and statistical analysis but that they learn how to apply them to economic problems. When courses in mathematics are given by non-economists these courses must be properly co-ordinated with those in economics.
4. It is difficult to express present staff-student ratios for departments of economics in different European universities in a way which permits meaningful comparisons to be made. It is even more difficult to establish international standard staff-student ratios which permit, in some sense, the most efficient use of teaching resources. It is none the less important that there should be sufficient staff, so that the individual student should have someone to consult about his difficulties. In the early years of his studies small-group instruction and discussion help to ensure that a student grasps the underlying principles of economics, which in most cases will be a completely new subject to him.
5. The methods of higher education in economics should avoid the dangers of both over- and under-teaching. On the one hand a student must be brought to think for himself and not to rely on

the regurgitation of second-hand ideas, and on the other he must have sufficient guidance to ensure that he uses the limited time at his disposal to obtain a proper introduction to a rapidly growing subject. A satisfactory middle path would require relatively less reliance on formal lectures in some countries. Reading-lists for courses in economics should provide a variety of references, and the habit of relying exclusively on the textbook of the professor giving the course should be abandoned.

6. It is important that the student of economics should undertake written work in economic analysis from an early stage in his training. Later in his course seminars in which the written work of a student is discussed are necessary to enable him to develop his critical judgment, and ensure that he can use the tools of economic analysis.

7. As part of any training in statistics and econometrics there must be adequate opportunity for practical exercises. It is far better for a student to learn from his mistakes while he is in a university, where his mistakes can be corrected relatively inexpensively, than after he has started on his career outside.

8. The increasing need for economists with training at an advanced level makes it advisable to develop post-graduate education further. Such education should consist largely of research carried out under supervision and finally submitted for a degree.

9. Whatever the form of examinations, they should be regarded primarily as a test of the student's capacity to think for himself and to use economic analysis, and not as a measure of how many facts he has managed to accumulate.

10. Adequate library facilities are not yet available to all students of economics from the start of their degree course. This should be remedied by making sufficient places in reading-rooms available, and these should be equipped with journals and at least some monographs to help the student develop his general interest in the subject. For research work it is important that libraries should have satisfactory coverage of foreign as well as of national literature in economics.

11. There will be a growing need for additional university teachers of economics to deal satisfactorily with the increased student numbers. In order to ensure that there is an adequate number of recruits to the profession it will be necessary to provide satisfactory career prospects. The insecurity of many junior university posts at the moment may be considered a necessary deterrent to the incompetent, but it will have to be modified if university teaching is to compete successfully with alternative employment for the competent.

12. The salaries of university teachers should be such that it can be a full-time occupation. While experience in the public and private sector of the economy may be valuable to the university teacher of economics, the holding of outside consultancies should not cause teaching and research to suffer.

13. The university should provide full facilities for the university teacher to carry out research. His teaching load should be such as to allow him sufficient time and energy to carry out research in addition to his teaching duties. Appropriate provision for sabbatical leave should be made.

14. There is insufficient information on many aspects of higher education in economics, and for this research is required on such topics as the relative efficiency of different methods of teaching and examining, criteria for selecting students for courses in economics, and appropriate staff–student ratios for different systems of higher education. On many occasions such research is carried out for the internal use of individual institutions. Wider publication and circulation of research results would be of considerable value to other institutions facing similar situations.

In addition to the above recommendations on the teaching of economics, the meeting of experts adopted the following recommendations designed to promote intra-European co-operation in the teaching and studying of economics:

(a) Universities and specialized institutions of higher education in economics should support and encourage the work of the Association Internationale des Etudiants en Sciences Economiques et Commerciales (A.I.E.S.E.C.) in organizing exchanges of students for practical experience and promoting international student seminars in economics. While the bulk of A.I.E.S.E.C.'s traineeships have been in industry and commerce, ways should be sought to extend them into the economic sections of central, regional, and local government.

Teachers of economics in higher education should be ready to co-operate fully with A.I.E.S.E.C. in its programmes of seminars, and consider other ways of developing the educational aspects of A.I.E.S.E.C.'s work.

(b) In order to facilitate movement of post-graduate students of economics between European universities, systematic listings of post-graduate courses and degrees should be prepared. It would be helpful if the Council of Europe could co-ordinate such information. At the moment the European post-graduate student and his teacher of economics are more likely to know of the facilities and financial possibilities for further study and research on the other side of the Atlantic than in neighbouring countries.

(c) As a measure to make the movement of students easier it would be helpful if universities maintained in the languages of the Council of Europe summaries of their undergraduate courses and reading-lists in a prescribed form. This would help in the assessment of applicants. Such assessment would be further aided if universities published information showing the distribution of students between the different classes of degree. At the moment the information available frequently means little or nothing to the applications committee of a foreign faculty, and to those who have to evaluate education obtained abroad.

The question of a common European Graduate Admission Test in Economics should be considered in due course.

(d) The movement of teaching staff between European faculties of economics should be encouraged on a long- or short-term basis.[1] This could often be developed by means of exchanges and links between individual institutions; one of the many means of doing this would be by 'twinning'. Such legal restrictions as prevent the free movement of university teachers between countries should be modified.

Although short visits to deliver single lectures, if well planned, may serve a useful purpose, it seems advisable that the visit should last long enough to allow the visiting professor to give a series of lectures which can form, where appropriate, a part of the students' course, and to have satisfactory contacts with his colleagues and with students.

(e) It might be particularly useful to encourage the movement, for periods of at least a year, of those at the beginning of their career in university teaching. They would have the opportunity to participate in another system of university teaching, and to learn therefrom.

(f) Associations of academic economists, such as the Association des economistes de langue française, the Nordic Business Economics Teachers, the Verein für Sozialpolitik, and the Association of University Teachers of Economics in the United Kingdom should consider publicizing their conferences more widely among university teachers in other European countries. Although there are clearly problems of language, it might be that such conferences could provide useful meeting-grounds for economists from different European countries. Such associations should be encouraged to discuss the problems of the teaching of economics.

(g) The International Economic Association might consider a meeting on a regional basis to discuss the problems of the teaching of economics, and might encourage national associations of economists to discuss the questions raised in this report.

(h) Universities and other institutions publishing journals should be encouraged to increase the practice of exchanging them with the libraries of other European institutions. There is a need for journals to include summaries of articles in the major European languages.

PARTICIPANTS

Austria
MR W. BOUFFIER   Institut für Betriebslehre, Hochschule für Welthandel, Wien

---

[1] 'Long-term' is intended to mean periods of one year or more. 'Short-term' is intended to mean periods of at least six weeks to almost one year.

Belgium
MR F. BEZY   Président de l'Institut des Sciences Eco-
                             nomiques, Université de Louvain
Cyprus
MR P. PHANOPOULOS   Ministry of Education, Nicosia

Denmark
DR J. DICH   Professor of Economics at the University
                             of Aarhus
Federal Republic of Germany
DR K. G. ZINN   Department of Economics, University of
                             Mainz
France
MR P. COULBOIS   Professeur à la Faculté de Droit et des
                             Sciences Economiques et Politiques de
                             l'Université de Strasbourg
Ireland
MR P. LYNCH   Associate Professor of Economics, Uni-
                             versity College, Dublin
Italy
MR C. CIPOLLA   Professor of Economic History, University
                             of Pavia
Malta
MR S. BUSUTTIL   Head of the Department of Economics,
                             Royal University of Malta
Netherlands
DR C. F. SCHEFFER   Professor of Industrial Economics at the
                             Katholieke Hogeschool, Tilburg
Norway
MR J. SERCK-HANSEN   Institute of Social Economy, Oslo

United Kingdom
MR J. F. H. ROPER   Faculty of Economic and Social Studies,
(Rapporteur)   University of Manchester
MR A. BEACHAM   Edward Gonner Professor at the Depart-
                             ment of Applied Economics in the Uni-
                             versity of Liverpool

OBSERVER

Finland
MR J. J. PAUNIO   Professor, Institute of Economics, Helsinki

Appendix 4

SELECTED BIBLIOGRAPHY ON HIGHER EDUCATION IN ECONOMICS IN EUROPEAN COUNTRIES

Austria
Richard Kerschagl: *The Teaching of the Social Sciences in Austria*. Social Science Information, The Hague, December 1964.

Belgium
Paul de Bruyne: *Formation à la Direction des Entreprises*. Librairie Universitaire Uystpruyst, undated.

Denmark
Handelshøjskolen i København: Beretning 1959/60–1961/62, Section V. (Detailed survey of examination successes for the last ten years.) Copenhagen, 1964.

France
Denise Flouzat: *L'Etudiant Economiste: Etudes—Carrières—Documentation*, 1962–63. Editions Cujas, 1962.
Faculté de Droit et des Sciences Economiques de Paris: Reports by Bergasse (February 1965) and Lecaillon (November 1965) on student success in the faculty. (Duplicated for circulation in the faculty.)
Faculté de Droit et des Sciences Economiques de Lyon: *Enquête sur les causes d'echec en 1963* à l'examen de première année dans la Faculté. (Duplicated for circulation in the faculty.)

Germany
Dr Knut Borchardt: *Denkschrift zur Lage der Wirtschaftswissenschaft*. Deutsche Forschungsgemeinschaft, 1960.
E. von Böventer & W. Müller: Der Studienbeginn in den Wirtschaftswissenschaften. *Beiträge zur Hochschulreform Heft* 1. Verlag Anton Hain, Meischheim am Glan, 1967.
Kath, Oehler, & Reichwein: *Studienweg und Studienerfolg*. Institut für Bildungsforschung, Berlin, 1966.
Taschenbuch für Studierende der Wirtschaftswissenschaften. Betriebswirtschaftlicher Verlag Dr. Th. Gabler, 1965. Includes articles by Professors Gutenberg, Sauermann, Münstermann, and Albach, among others.

Greece
Xenophon Zolotas: *Economic Development and Technical Education*. Bank of Greece Papers & Lectures 4, Athens, 1960.

Italy
Francesco Vito: "Gli Studi Economici nelle Facoltà di Scienze Politiche e Sociali". In *Gli Studi Politici e Sociali in Italia—I Divitti dell'Uorno nelle*

Teoria e nella Prassi Politicia. Societa Editrice Vita e Pensiero, Milan, 1965, and earlier articles by the same author in the *Rivista Internazionale di Scienze Sociali*, May–June 1958, and March–April 1957.

F. M. Pacces: *La Formazione dei Quadri Dirigenti Compito Comune dell'Universita e dell'Industria.* Scuola di Amministrazione Industriale dell'Universita di Torino, 1965.

Alberto Valentini: *Formazione e Prospettive del Laureato in Economia.* Societa Editrice il Mulino, 1963.

P. Luzzatto Fegiz: "Un'Indagine Campionaria fra gli Studenti di Economia e Commercio dell'Universita di Roma." *Bollettino Doxa*, No. 17–18, 1962.

Netherlands
F. J. Jong: "The Teaching of Economics at Netherlands Universities." In *Higher Education and Research in the Netherlands*, Vol. II, No. 2, June 1958.

Norway
(*Report of*) *Den IV Nordiske Foretaksøkonomiske Studiekonferanse i Bergen 24–26 August 1964.* Forretningsøkonomisk Institutt, Norges Handelshøyskole, Bergen, 1965.

Sweden
Council of Europe Committee for Higher Education and Research: *Report on Higher Education in Sweden*, Strasbourg, 1966.
Högre Studier. (Annual publication of the Statistiska Centralbyrån, Stockholm.)

Switzerland
Dr W. Bickel: "Das Studium der Nationalökonomie an der Universität Zürich." In *Vereingung Akademischer Volkswirtschafter, Mitteilungsblatt, November 1964.*
Schweizerische Hochschulzeitung: "Sonderheft zur Einweihung der Neubauten der Hochschule St Gallen für Wirtschafts-und Sozialwissenschaften." Zürich, June 1963.

Turkey
Tuncer Bulutay: "Türkiye' de Iktisadin Okutulusu üzerine." In *Ankara Universitesi, Siyasal Bilgiler Fakultesi Dergisi*, December 1965.

United Kingdom
Department of Education and Science: *Report of the Committee on Social Studies* (The Heyworth Report). H.M.S.O., Cmnd. 2660, June 1965.
University Grants Committee: *Report of the Committee on University Teaching Methods* (The Hale Committee). H.M.S.O., 1964.
Committee on Higher Education: *Higher Education, Report & Appendices*, (The Robbins Report). H.M.S.O., Cmnd. 2154, 1963.
University Grants Committee: *Returns from Universities and University Colleges.* (Annual publication.) H.M.S.O., London.

U.N.E.S.C.O.
The University Teaching of Social Sciences–Economics. U.N.E.S.C.O., July 1954.
Roger Gregoire: *The University Teaching of Social Sciences—Business Management*, U.N.E.S.C.O., 1966.

SALES AGENTS FOR PUBLICATIONS
OF THE COUNCIL OF EUROPE

AUSTRIA
Gerold & Co.
Graben 31
Vienna, 1

BELGIUM
Agence et Messageries de la Presse
14-22 rue du Persil
Brussels

CANADA
Queen's Printer
Ottawa

DENMARK
Ejnard Munksgaard
Nörregade 6
Copenhagen

FRANCE
Librairie Générale de Droit et
    de Jurisprudence
R. Pichon et R. Durand-Auzias
20 rue Soufflot
Paris Ve
Armand Colin
103 Boulevard St Michel
Paris Ve

**FEDERAL REPUBLIC
OF GERMANY**
Verlag Dr Hans Heger
Goethestrasse 54, Postfach 821,
D-5320 Bad Godesberg

GREECE
Librairie Kauffmann
21 rue Stadiou
Athens

ICELAND
Snaebjörn Jonsson & Co. A.F.
The English Bookshop
Hafnarstroeti 9
Reykjavik

IRELAND
Stationery Office
Dublin

ITALY
Libreria Commissionaria Sansoni
Via Lamarmora 45
Florence

LUXEMBOURG
Librairie-Papeterie
Galérie d'Art
Paul Bruck
22 Grand-rue
Luxembourg

NETHERLANDS
N. V. Martinus Nijhoff
Lange Voorhout 9
The Hague

NEW ZEALAND
Government Printing Office
20 Molesworth Street
Wellington

NORWAY
A/S Bokhjörnet
Olaf Thommessen
Akersgt. 41
Oslo

PORTUGAL
Livraria Bertrand
73-75 rua Garrett
Lisbon

SPAIN
Aguilar S.A. de Ediciones
Juan Bravo 38
Madrid

SWEDEN
Aktiebolaget C.E. Fritze
Kungl. Hovbokhandel
Fredsgatan 2
Stockholm

288

SWITZERLAND
Buchhandl. Hans Raunhardt
Kirchgasse 17
8000 Zurich, 1

Librairie Payot
6 rue Grenus
1211 Geneva 11

TURKEY
Librairie Hachette
469 Istiklal Caddesi
Beyoglu, Istanbul

UNITED KINGDOM
H.M. Stationery Office
P.O. Box 569
London, S.E.1

George G. Harrap & Co Ltd
182-184 High Holborn
London, W.C.1.

UNITED STATES
Manhattan Publishing Company
225 Lafayette Street
New York, 12—N.Y.

STRASBOURG
Librairie Berger-Levrault
Place Broglie

Education in Europe

Harrap have been appointed the English-language publishers of this series launched by the Council for Cultural Co-operation of the Council of Europe, in order to make known the comparative studies and surveys produced under its twenty-nation programme of educational co-operation.

THE TEACHING OF ECONOMICS AT UNIVERSITY LEVEL

This study of the teaching of Economics at university level was prepared on the basis of information obtained during a series of visits to some fifty European Faculties and specialized institutions in which economics is taught. A list of institutions and the dates of visits is given in an appendix. This was supplemented, and in most cases preceded, by the collection of documentary information from as many as possible of the teaching institutions within the study area.

The author has received valuable help from the teaching staffs of the various institutions visited, and in some cases from national authorities responsible for higher education, in compiling this record. The countries covered are Austria, Belgium, Denmark, Finland, France, Germany (the Federal Republic), Greece, Iceland, Ireland, Italy, Malta, Netherlands, Norway, Spain, Sweden, Switzerland, Turkey, the United Kingdom. There is also a section on the Holy See. The author is Lecturer in Economics at the University of Manchester.

SBN 245 59754 9

55s / £2.75 net in UK

AUSTRIA	ITALY
BELGIUM	LUXEMBOURG
CYPRUS	MALTA
DENMARK	NETHERLANDS
FEDERAL REPUBLIC OF GERMANY	NORWAY
FINLAND	SPAIN
FRANCE	SWEDEN
GREECE	SWITZERLAND
HOLY SEE	TURKEY
ICELAND	UNITED KINGDOM
IRELAND	

HARRAP